LLEWELLYN'S 2019

HERBAL

ALMANAC

© 2018 Llewellyn Publications
Llewellyn Publications is a registered trademark of
Llewellyn Worldwide Ltd.

Cover Designer: Kevin R. Brown
Editor: Lauryn Heineman

Interior Art: © Fiona King
Garden plan illustrations on pages 290–91
by Llewellyn Art Department

You can order annuals and books from *New Worlds,*
Llewellyn's catalog. To request a free copy, call 1-877-
NEW WRLD toll-free or visit www.llewellyn.com.

ISBN: 978-0-7387-4608-1
Llewellyn Worldwide Ltd.
2143 Wooddale Drive
Woodbury, MN 55125-2989

Printed in the United States of America

Contents

Health and Beauty

DIY and Crafts

Plant Profiles

Gardening Resources

Introduction to
Llewellyn's Herbal Almanac

Holistic care for the mind, body, and soul starts in the garden. Gardeners of all skill levels and climates can find common ground in early morning weeding, combating pests, marveling at this year's abundant harvest, and impatiently waiting to plan next year's plot. The work is hard, but the rewards are bountiful. Growing herbs is good for the spirit, and using them in home-cooked meals, remedies, and crafts is clean, healthy, and just plain delicious.

The 2019 edition of the *Herbal Almanac* is a love letter and guidebook to the hands-on application of herbs in our daily lives. With sage advice appealing to novice gardeners and experienced herbalists alike, our experts tap into the practical and historical aspects of herbal knowledge—using herbs to help you connect with the earth, enhance your culinary creations, and heal your body and mind.

In addition to the twenty-seven articles, this book now offers brand new reference materials tailored specifically for successful growing and gathering. Use this book to log important dates, draw your garden plan, practice companion planting, find a helpful herbal remedy, and keep track of goals and chores in the personal logbook pages.

Reclaiming our connection to Mother Earth in our own backyards can bring us harmony and balance—and a delicious, healthy harvest. May your garden grow tall and your dishes taste divine!

Note: The old-fashioned remedies in this book are historical references used for teaching purposes only. The recipes are not for commercial use or profit. The contents are not meant to diagnose, treat, prescribe, or substitute consultation with a licensed health-care professional. Herbs, whether used internally or externally, should be introduced in small amounts to allow the body to adjust and to detect possible allergies. Please consult a standard reference source or an expert herbalist to learn more about the possible effects of certain herbs. You must take care not to replace regular medical treatment with the use of herbs. Herbal treatment is intended primarily to complement modern health care. Always seek professional help if you suffer from illness. Also, take care to read all warning labels before taking any herbs or starting on an extended herbal regimen. Always consult medical and herbal professionals before beginning any sort of medical treatment—this is particularly true for pregnant women. Herbs are powerful things; be sure you are using that power to achieve balance.

Llewellyn Worldwide does not participate in, endorse, or have any authority or responsibility concerning private business transactions between its authors and the public.

Growing
and
Gathering

Getting to "Perennial"

﹥ by JD Hortwort ﹤

When I was a young gardener at my first home, I had the same aspirations as most gardeners. I envisioned my little starter home with a luscious border in front of the windows, billowing with flowers that would inspire envy from passersby. In the backyard my flower beds would produce copious floral harvests to fill each room with bouquets. How hard could it be? There were only five rooms in the house! I would achieve this ambition with perennials, plants that would come back year after year. After all, my gardening magazines assured me, perennials would be cost-effective, durable, and relatively insect and maintenance free. And, they would have been—if I could have gotten them to a "perennial" state.

The gardening community has a long-standing joke (a definition, actually) for perennials. It states a perennial is a plant that, had it survived, would have lived three to five years. The plant tag in the container may say "perennial," but it is up to you to make that dream a reality. You do that by understanding what a perennial is, where and how it likes to grow, and just how much you can realistically expect from it.

Perennial: "Lasting a Long Time"

To be considered a **perennial**, the plant in question has to survive for at least three years. A one-year plant is an **annual**; a two-year plant is a **biennial**. A perennial can last many years—that is, unless you do something to your perennial to cause it to die in the first or second year.

Tender perennial is a term used to describe a plant that is considered perennial but it just won't make it through the winter outside in your area. For example, lantana (Lantana camara) is perennial in zones 8 through 11 but would be considered tender in USDA plant zones 1 through 7.

You will frequently see perennials described as **herbaceous** or **nonwoody**. This is a key distinction that sets perennials apart from woody plants. Herbaceous plants have a durable root system and a tender top that tends to die back, usually in winter. This is a general rule of thumb. Some perennials, such as bugleweed or ajuga (*Ajuga reptans*), are evergreen; others, such as rosemary (*Rosmarinus officinalis*), live so long they develop woody stems. This type of perennial is sometimes called a **sub-**

shrub. **Woody** plants like trees and shrubs have a durable root system. Some have herbaceous canopies that die back in winter, but they usually don't die entirely to the ground.

This brings us to an important and necessary understanding. Gardening is enhanced by a general knowledge of horticultural science. It is not, however, a subject that can be contained by hard-and-fast rules. If you require strict adherence to rules, you are going to be one unhappy gardener. If you can live with guidelines, you'll do fine.

Understanding that perennials have to take a break and fade back to their root system will save you a lot of panic, especially if you are a novice gardener. When I worked as a gardener at a retirement home many years ago, one of the residents gave me a hardy cyclamen tuber (*Cyclamen colchicum*) to plant in the facility's flower bed. It came up with lovely green foliage traced with silver markings. In June those butterfly flowers, their reflex petals such a delicate pink, were a beauty to behold. Then, in the heat of August, the foliage began to yellow and fade. I felt like such a failure as a gardener—until I did a bit of research and discovered the plant was doing exactly what it was supposed to do. Sure enough, it came back again the following year.

This brings us to another general rule of thumb. All bulbs, corms, tubers, and rhizomes are a special category of perennials that have unique root systems to ensure survival. Not all perennials have root systems made up of bulbs, corms, tubers, or rhizomes. And, if that isn't confusing enough, some perennials have seem to have both, such as the tuberous root system of dahlias (*Dahlia* spp.) and the food storage nodules on liriope (*Liriope muscari*) roots.

The lesson from this story is know your perennial. Research its basic characteristics and requirements or find an experienced gardener willing to take you under his or her wing.

Let's Get Dirty

Once you've researched your perennial, the time is at hand to add it to your landscape. The majority of perennials have very simple requirements:

- The location should receive six or more hours of sunlight.
- Perennials want average soil with a pH range of 6 to 7.
- The soil should be amended and loose so that it drains well.

This is what all of my gardening books told me so many years ago. After my first season of frustration, I learned that gardening books are a lot like cookbooks. The authors tend to assume the reader knows more than he or she usually does. Do those six or more hours of sunlight have to come all at once? What, exactly, is average soil? What should I amend the soil with? How loose is loose enough?

First, consider the location of your perennial. Most perennials want lots of sunlight in order to make plenty of colorful foliage and bountiful blossoms. Some perennials do require shade, such as marsh marigold (*Caltha palustris*) and ferns. Others, such as bleeding heart (*Dicentra*) or columbine (*Aquilegia*), prefer dappled shade. Imagine a sunny day when the sun peeks in and out from behind clouds and you have a sense of what "dappled" means.

However, when we think of perennials, we tend to think of those that need to bathe in the sun all day—or at least for six hours. These include popular perennials such as irises, daisies, peonies, daylilies, sedum, and so on.

Just remember, six hours of sunlight from 9 a.m. until 3 p.m. is different from six hours of sunlight from noon until 6 p.m. Afternoon sun is more intense. Check the plant zone guidelines for your area. I live in zone 7b and have found that if I am planting a perennial that is reaching the southern limits of its range, I need to find a spot that will provide some relief from the blistering afternoon sun. For example, bluebells (*Mertensia*), a perennial that grows in zones 3 through 8, may tolerate full sun in New York, but in my North Carolina Piedmont landscape it is definitely a plant for shaded areas.

As for the soil, this is what years of gardening have taught me: "average" soil probably doesn't exist in your landscape. It certainly isn't purchased in a bag. The ideal soil for perennials will be a balance of fine soil particles (also known as clay), large particles (a variety of stony granules like tiny pebbles or sand), and organic material (frequently called humus).

In my area of the South we are blessed with red clay—great for making bricks but by itself not so good for growing much of anything. Other growing areas of the country may have different-colored clay, but it is still a tightly packed material made up of fine mineral particles that doesn't drain well.

Another large segment of the country has very well-drained, sandy soil. It is usually nutritionally poor. A few lucky places in the United States have what is called **loamy** soil. Loam has a relatively high amount of humus. It may be clay-based or sand-based, but it has sufficient organic material already available in the mix. Gardeners in the rest of the country secretly envy and hate those who live on loamy soil.

Perennials want a combination of clay, sand, and humus. Clay provides nutrients, and sand provides pathways for air and water. Humus fixes the shortcomings of both materials and adds nutrients to the soil. Organic material spaces out fine clay particles, giving plant roots access to the nutrients they need. Organic material in sandy soil holds on to some of that moisture so that plants don't dry out so quickly.

*Like most plants, perennials can be started from seeds.
However, it's a slow process. A better way to increase your
population of perennials is through division—digging the plant up,
sorting out the root mass or tubers and replanting.*

When I taught adult classes on gardening some years ago, someone in the room would invariably ask why he or she couldn't just combine sand and clay to come up with a growing medium. The problem is, if all you have is sand and clay, the end result isn't a growing medium. It's a brick.

It is possible to have too much organic material. Gardeners find this out when they dig a hole, pour in a lot of soil amendment from the garden center and set their new plant directly in that amendment. The outcome is usually root rot. Organic material holds water. Too much organic material is like planting in a sponge.

So how much is the right amount? Get ready for another rule of thumb. The best recipe in my garden is two parts parent soil to one part organic material. Your mixture will vary, depending on the quality of your parent soil. A simple test I learned years ago from a state extension agent involves picking up a handful of soil before you plant. Squeeze it tightly in your hand. Hold your hand out at chest level and drop the soil. If it holds together in a tight wad, you need more organic material. If it breaks into clumps, you probably have a good mix.

What kind of soil amendment is right for perennials? Any decomposed, organic material will work. Decomposed or aged organic material will usually have a pH of between 6 and 7, perfect for perennials. You can use aged manure from any source, rotted leaves or grass clippings, bark remnants, or aged sawdust. All of these will improve the tilth or texture of your garden soil, provide good drainage, and create an environment that promotes a healthy community of earthworms and other microorganisms that will help plants thrive.

Perennial at Last!

Once you have set your perennials, keep an eye on them the first year and water as needed. If you are planting container plants from a nursery, there is no need to fertilize on installation. The potting soil will have enough fertilizer. Wait to feed until next season as new growth begins to break the ground. If you are dividing perennials in your landscape, feed lightly on installation and again when the plant breaks dormancy next year. Remember, perennials are lean feeders. Too much fertilizer will make for plenty of foliage but few, if any, flowers.

With that, you're all set! You're ready for an adventure in perennial gardening that can be at times frustrating, invigorating, worrisome, and fretful, but most of the time oh so soul-nurturing and heart-warming in its satisfaction.

Resources

Landendorf, Sandra F. *Successful Southern Gardening: A Practical Guide for Year-Round Beauty*. Chapel Hill: University of North Carolina Press, 1989. Pages 153–75.

Loewer, Peter. *Tough Plants for Tough Places*. Emmaus, PA: Rodale, 1992. Pages 83–176.

McHoy, Peter. *Anatomy of a Garden*. New York: W. H. Smith Publishers, 1987. Pages 55–59.

Reilly, Ann. *Gardening Naturally*. Des Moines, IA: Better Homes and Gardens Books, 1993. Pages 15–49.

Quick and Easy Plant Propagation

≈ by Jill Henderson ≈

In all my years as a gardener I have never met another gardener who didn't want more plants to fill gaps, make new beds, or share with friends and family. Of course, every gardener knows that starting herbs and flowers from seed is a great way to obtain an abundance of plants for the garden. And while a vast array of them are traditionally started from seed—and actually grow best when they are— there are others that either can't be started from seed at all or are very difficult to germinate.

Seed Isn't Always the Answer

Let's look at herbs like dill, basil, and cilantro as examples of why seed isn't always the answer to our propagation needs. These annual leafy herbs are exceptionally easy to start from seed, come true to type, and are typically not conducive to any other form of propagation. On the other hand, herbs like true French tarragon rarely flower and almost never produce viable seed. In the same vein are herbs like rosemary, whose seeds are difficult if not downright frustrating to germinate, and when they do germinate, the little plants take such a very long time to reach a harvestable size that it is almost not worth it. Then there are herbs like mint, which comes in hundreds of scents, flavors, and forms—all of which readily cross-pollinate with wild and cultivated mints growing nearby. For the gardener, this means that the seeds you gathered from your prized pineapple mint likely won't produce plants that taste—or sometimes look—anything like the parent plant. Not only that, but you'll have to wait quite a while before you realize that they aren't the same, and there's nothing more frustrating than wasted time and energy.

Indeed, when it comes any member of the mint family, including nearly all minty-type mints, oregano, thyme, marjoram, and sage, cross-pollination is not only the norm but also something you want to avoid like the plague. Let's use the two varieties of oregano I grow in my own garden as an example. One bears pretty pink flowers most of the season, but the leaves have almost no flavor. I call these plants "ornamental oregano" and use them as pretty, flowering ground cover throughout my many gardens. The second oregano is an exceptional culinary variety that bears white flowers and has superbly flavorful leaves. The problem with having two very distinct varieties of the same species growing and flowering in close proximity to one another is the inability to stop insects from cross-pollinating the two. If I allow both of these plants to flower, set seed, and self-sow year after year, I will most likely wind up with beds full of mixed hybridized oregano plants that may or may not bear the qualities I love about each of them as individuals. This natural process of hybridization occurs between many types of cultivated varieties of common herbs, just as it does with common garden vegetables and even flowers. If you let two distinct varieties of watermelon in your garden flower and set seed, there is a very good chance that the seeds that each produces will be a hybrid of the two parent varieties and will most likely not come true to the traits of either. Sometimes hybridization, whether natural or cultivated, can be a good thing. In fact, hybridization is one reason we have so many varieties of plants in the first place. But when it comes to the qualities we treasure in certain plants, accidental hybridization is not the gardener's friend.

There is yet one more drawback to using seed to start certain herbs: the natural genetic variability within each and every seed. This inborn trait to produce slight variations in each plant is what ensures that wild plants (which modern herbs practically are) have the ability to adapt and survive wherever they land. So while each seed will likely produce plants of a similar form, not all of them will smell or taste exactly the same, which is why you often hear herbalists admonishing newcomers to smell and taste potted herbs before they buy them. From one packet of seed, you might get 100 plants that are fine and flavorful enough but only a few that are exceptionally flavorful or medicinally potent. And when you finally find that one incredibly remarkable herb and want to replicate it, you won't be able to do it using seed. Only vegetative propagation, or cloning, can do that.

For herbs like mint and many others, the only way to get an exact replica of an existing herb is through vegetative propagation methods such as cuttings, division, and layering. Not only are these methods faster, cheaper, and more productive when used to multiply existing perennial herbs, but oftentimes they are the only way to replicate the wonderful qualities you love about the mother plants. So if you don't want to spend a fortune on nursery stock, fuss with pots and poorly germinating seed, or wait for slow-maturing plants to get exactly what you want, step out into your garden and I'll tell you the quick and easy way to propagate the plants you already have.

Sometimes Division Is Good

One of the easiest and most straightforward methods of vegetative propagation is root division, which is the simple act of dividing a mature perennial herb into two or more plants. An herb is considered mature when it has grown for at least two full seasons and is healthy and well-established. A plant that is not well-established is one that has grown for a year or more in the same place but has never attained its mature size or is perpetually small, weak, or sickly. An herb like this should be dug and replanted in a more favorable location but not divided. In time it may grow into a healthy mature plant that can be divided. But if it doesn't, it's best to start over with a fresh, new start.

To divide an established herb, begin by watering it the night before. A well-hydrated plant digs more easily and resists shock better. You don't want the soil to be soggy, just moist. Also, divisions are best performed in the cool hours of the day—either early morning or after the sun dips below the horizon in the evening. Next, gather up a few tools, including a freshly sharpened shovel or spade, a small knife, a pair of scissors, and a tarp or sheet to work on. If you plan to pot up one or more of your new divisions, have your potting and tagging supplies at the ready. If you plan on planting your new division right away, dig and amend the hole before you begin to avoid drying out the roots.

Air propagation is a method of cloning difficult-to-root trees, shrubs, and ornamentals using plastic air propagation balls or moist sphagnum moss bound with plastic, which are wrapped around a living branch or stem. Once roots have formed in the moist medium, the branch is cut from the mother plant just below the rooted area and the new cutting planted.

Before you put shovel to earth, take some time to evaluate the mother plant. If you're digging up the entire plant, you will want to get as much of the root system as you possibly can, both wide and deep. Doing so reduces the time it takes for both the mother plant and the new divisions to regrow lost root mass and become firmly established in their new soil. The number of divisions you can take from one plant depends entirely on how large you want each division to be and how fast you'd like the division to grow once replanted. Large divisions with bigger root structures look better and grow faster, while small divisions afford many more new but smaller plants for filling spaces, selling, sharing, or trading. Just remember that each division must have a healthy network of roots attached to at least two healthy, leafy stems. Without these, the plant will not be able to sustain itself and may die of shock after transplanting.

For plants that grow from a dense crown, such as lemon balm, hyssop, savory, or tarragon, there are a few ways to approach division. The first, and my personal favorite for very large plants, is to divide the plant prior to digging it up. Simply place your shovel blade in the center of the plant and use the weight of your body to thrust the blade quickly and cleanly through the crown and as deep as you can into the root ball. Next, loosen the soil around the plant and carefully lift the two divisions before making any further cuts or replanting. If the plant is not huge to start with, you can simply lift the entire plant and its root ball. Place the mass on a firm surface, either upright or on its side, before dividing. If you want to get the most divisions possible or are working with a small or delicate plant, use a sharp knife and cut from the surface down through the roots. This methodical approach definitely gives the gardener more control over where the crown is cut and the proportion of roots to each stem or crown. Herbs that grow in large masses and have creeping root systems or rooting stems, such as thyme, mint, or catnip, can also be divided as previously described, but unless I want a very large division, I find it much easier and neater to cut "plugs" from the middle of the bed using a sharp trowel or knife. This also reduces the unnecessary destruction of foliage in the bed.

For herbs with large fleshy roots or rhizomes like ginger and turmeric, dig up the whole plant and trim the foliage to a manageable size, if needed. Mature rhizomes will have natural folds and segmentations that are easily broken off and replanted. Just be sure to set them back in a horizontal position with any "eyes" or stems facing up. Horseradish can be treated similarly except that the root segments are replanted vertically, with the pointed end facing down. The best times to divide rhizomes are during the fall harvest or in early spring as soon as the first leaves begin to appear.

Garlic is a specialized bulb with many toes or cloves within each bulb that are easily separated from one another. To divide garlic, begin by selecting the largest, healthiest bulbs. Then, break the individual toes away from the root scar, taking care not to break open their papery coverings. Next, pick out only the largest toes for replanting and use the rest in the kitchen. If you stick to this method of only planting the largest toes, the overall size of your garlic will grow over time. Plant each toe six inches deep with the pointed end facing up and mulch heavily. Garlic grows best when planted in early fall and over-wintered for harvest the following summer.

Layering Is Slow but Rewarding

Layering is another method of vegetative propagation that involves rooting actively growing stems while still attached to the mother plant. This system is ideal for plants that have not reached a mature size appropriate for dividing or for sensitive plants that are slow to establish, such as lavender, sage, savory, hyssop, rosemary, and tarragon. Layering is most successful in the spring or early summer before the stems become woody. It is okay if the portion of the stem attached to the mother plant is a little woody, but the middle of the stem should still be green and flexible for this method to work well.

Start by selecting one or more long, flexible stems at various points around the mother plant. Loosen the soil below where each stem will lay and strip off all but the topmost leaves. Gently lower the stem to the ground, taking care not to break it off of the mother plant, which is needed to nourish the layered stem while it is forming its own root system. Push the center of the stem a few inches into the soil, allowing the leafy portion to stick out. Then cover it with an inch or two of soil and pin it down with a heavy rock or brick. Some herbs root up in just a month or two, while others might take most of the season. You will know when the stems have rooted by removing the rock and very gently tugging on the leafy end. Be careful, though! Uprooting a lightly rooted layering will set it back considerably. To ensure a vigorous new start that can survive the winter, I prefer to leave the stem attached to the mother until spring. At that time, the layered stem is cut from the mother plant and transplanted to its new location.

When it comes to herbs like mint, thyme, oregano, and marjoram, which naturally root wherever their stems touch the ground, you can expedite the process by removing any mulch from under the stems, loosening the soil a bit, and pinning a group of stems down with a rock. If kept watered, these stems should root up within three or four weeks and be ready to transplant by midsummer or fall.

Stem Cuttings Make for Many

While division and layering are two very easy and effective methods of propagating new plants for your garden, rooting stem cuttings is faster than layering and more productive and less damaging to the mother plants than divisions. Additionally, both woody and herbaceous herbs respond well to this method.

To propagate new plants from stem cuttings, start by selecting young, healthy, and actively growing stems that are not yet woody. This detail is much more important when rooting cuttings than when layering stems because only young stems have the right hormones to be able to produce new roots. You'll want to gather cuttings from the very ends of the branches. Use a very sharp knife or razor blade and make the cut as clean and smooth as possible. I prefer to take only one cutting from the tip of each branch, but some species will allow you to take many more than that. If you take more than one cutting per branch, do what tree grafters do and mark which end is up and which end is down. Cut the down ends at an angle and the up ends straight across. This way, no matter what happens to the leaves, you'll always know which end is which.

Next, strip the leaves from the lower two-thirds of the stem. Pour out a bit of fresh, clean rooting liquid or powder into a small disposable container. Never dip stems directly into the original bottle or you run the risk of introducing bacteria that will destroy the hormone's effectiveness. Once you have dipped the cutting, stick it three inches deep into a premade hole in a pot filled with moist, soilless potting mix. If taking many cuttings at once, use a box or flat and space the cuttings six inches apart. Moisten the potting mix, but don't flood it, which will wash the rooting hormone off your cutting. Keep the flat out of direct sunlight and keep the soil moist, but not soggy, for the next four to eight weeks.

Cuttings do best when kept in relatively humid conditions. If you don't have a greenhouse, try setting your pots or flats inside a clear, lidded storage tub at least twelve inches deep. You can punch holes in the bottom of the tub or elevate flats on pea gravel to allow for good drainage. Loosely cover the top of the tub with the lid, venting as needed by turning it at an angle to the tub's rim. New cuttings should be kept out of direct sunlight until they grow a few roots. Use shade cloth or simply set them in an area of bright, but not direct sunlight. Once the cuttings begin to grow new leaves, begin allowing the soil to dry slightly between watering. And as plants become more vigorous, very slowly move the cuttings to progressively sunnier areas to harden them off.

Of course, there are quite a few herbs that root very well in a plain old glass of water on the kitchen windowsill. Try this out on herbs like lemon balm, sage, catnip, and mint. Once the stems have several long roots, be sure to transplant them to a pot for a while before transplanting them into the garden. This is because water-borne roots are not structurally the same as soil-borne roots. Give your new cuttings a little time to acclimate to living in the soil before thrusting them into the garden environment. A few weeks should give them plenty of time to do this. However you decide to approach it, you can begin propagating the plants you already have in your garden right now. And the next time you see a plant in a friend's garden that you'd love to grow, you can offer to trade them one of your beautiful homegrown starts for one of theirs and perhaps teach them how they can generate tons of new plants the quick and easy way.

Zinnias: An Herb That Became a Favorite Flower

⪙ by James Kambos ⪙

B y the first week of July, my herb and flower garden is splashed with color. The monarda raises its shaggy red flowers atop fragrant stems here and there. The shasta daisies with their white and yellow flowers always look crisp and fresh. Towering above the coreopsis, the sweetly scented flowers of tall purple phlox look relaxed no matter how hot it is. But, beyond the daylilies in the lower end of my garden, standing bold and tall, are my favorites—the zinnias. Beneath the July sun, the rich colors of their petals still seem to hold the warmth of Mexico and the American Southwest, the regions where they originated.

Yes, it's true they make no apology about being bright and showy.

Some people have even said "brassy." But for me it's not summer without zinnias!

Zinnias belong to the Asteraceae family, along with asters and daisies. Their genus is *Zinnia*, which contains about twenty species. Only three species are garden worthy: *Zinnia elegans*, *Zinnia angustifolia*, and *Zinnia haageana*. There are at least a hundred varieties available, and the list continues to grow.

A Forgotten Herb

Most of us know the zinnia as a cheery, bright annual flower that has been around since Great-Grandma's day. However, the zinnia is also considered an herb because it was once used as a dye plant. No matter what color petals are used to create the dye, all zinnias yield a dye that is yellow to warm gold in color. The only color zinnias don't come in is blue. Some varieties even come in green, or actually, a pale chartreuse.

I frequently refer to zinnias as a "forgotten herb" because few people know about its history as a source for dye. Most of the herbalists that once used zinnias to make dye are long gone. So, the zinnia is an herb as well as a pretty annual flower.

Zinnia History

Zinnias date back to the 1500s when the Spanish discovered them growing as a wildflower in Mexico. At the time, they were considered a weed. Then around 1750 the German ambassador to Mexico sent some seeds belonging to this wildflower to a German doctor, Johann Gottfried Zinn. Dr. Zinn was a brain and eye specialist, but he had a passion for botany. He studied these seeds and wrote the first scientific study about these nondescript Mexican flowers. Eventually, these plants were named zinnias in Dr. Zinn's honor.

Later, in the 1850s, the French developed a double zinnia form. Soon the plant world took notice. In the early 1920s the first dahlia-type zinnia was developed in America by Luther Burbank.

It didn't take long after that for American seed companies and their researchers to create many beautiful new forms of zinnias. What began as a weedy Mexican wildflower became one of America's top-selling annual bedding plants by the late twentieth century. Sales of zinnias are rapidly increasing. In fact, a major garden center in my area actually ran out of zinnias during the 2017 planting season. Many zinnia suppliers have begun reporting that zinnia plants are now a leading moneymaker for them.

Planting and Growing Zinnias

Few herbs or flowers give back so much beauty with so little effort as zinnias do. Give them average to fertile soil, sun, and occasional deadheading, and zinnias will make their way with little help from you.

Zinnias may be planted in two ways. You may sow the seeds directly into the garden, or you can buy established plants in plastic pots available at garden centers. I use both ways depending on my needs. For planting in the cutting garden or for large areas, I prefer seeds. Zinnia seeds sprout quickly and are economical. If I need some quick color or if I have some bare spots after the growing season begins, then I'll use potted zinnias. Either way, zinnias should be planted after all danger of frost has past. In my Ohio garden this is usually early May.

To direct sow the seeds into the garden, weed and loosen the soil. Add topsoil or compost if needed. Level the soil with a hoe. Scatter the seeds evenly, cover lightly with soil, and keep the seed bed moist until the seeds sprout. I've even scattered the seeds on top of the prepared soil without covering completely, and they did fine.

To plant potted zinnia plants, simply dig a hole large enough for the plant. Then remove it from the pot and place in the planting hole. Firm the soil around the base of the plant and water.

Zinnias also make a great companion plant in the vegetable garden. A few zinnias, or a row of them, planted among your vegetables help deter many destructive insects and worms.

No matter where you plant them, zinnias attract bees and butterflies, which are beneficial to the garden. Deadheading is recommended to encourage flower production, but I let a few of my zinnias go to seed to attract goldfinches—they love the seeds.

Zinnias are not attractive to deer.
They can safely be planted in areas that
have a large deer population.

About the only problem zinnias are sometimes afflicted with is powdery mildew. This is a fungal disease that causes a white powder-like growth to form on foliage, stems, and sometimes flowers. To prevent this, be sure your zinnias are well spaced and get good air circulation. Another preventive measure is to water zinnias early in the day. This will allow the plants to dry thoroughly.

A Few Zinnias to Get You Started

There are about a hundred varieties of zinnias available. They come in a rainbow of colors and a variety of shapes. Some are dahlia shaped, some are double, and some even have spidery cactus-shaped petals.

It's easy to find a zinnia you'll love. Since I can't write about all of them, I've come up with a list of my favorites. These are zinnias I've grown. I've seen how they perform in heat, drought, and humidity. They're winners!

The zinnias I've selected will keep your garden colorful from early summer to hard frost. You'll also have enough for cutting.

'California Giant': This is probably the zinnia Grandma grew along a fence. Stems grow three to four feet, and the flowers can grow up to five inches across. It usually comes in a seed mix of red, yellow, orange, white, pink, and purple. The flower form is slightly flat and open. This heirloom variety has been adding charm to gardens since 1926.

'Enchantress': The flowers of this stunning pink zinnia are held above sturdy three-foot stems. This is the zinnia that will have people saying, "I can't believe that's just a zinnia!"

'Oklahoma Mix': This zinnia was bred for its superior cut-flower qualities. It produces loads of flowers on thirty-inch stems. Flowers are semi to fully double and one and a half to two and a half inches wide. Colors include white, salmon, yellow, and pink. It's extremely resistant to powdery mildew.

'Persian Carpet': Also known as Mexican zinnia (*Zinnia haageana*), this extremely drought-resistant zinnia grows on stems only sixteen inches tall. Its two-inch flowers are usually

bicolored in shades of red, burgundy, yellow, and gold. The foliage is narrow. It looks great at the edge of a flower bed or in a wildflower garden. I plant mine near a clump of thyme, and they look great together.

'Profusion': This zinnia hybrid is a powerhouse of vigor, disease and heat resistance, and bloom. Colors include cherry, white, yellow, orange, pink, and apricot. The two-inch flowers almost cover its attractive narrow leaves. They're fantastic massed in the landscape or singly in front of the border. It also does well in pots. It grows to eighteen inches with a twenty-inch spread. 'Profusion' does very well in very hot areas, such as along pavement. No need to deadhead.

'Star': This hardy zinnia smothers itself with two-inch flowers from summer to fall. Its flowers come in white, yellow, and orange. It grows to about fourteen inches, with a mounded spreading shape about a foot wide. 'Star' is lovely planted at the edge of a raised bed where it can cascade over the side. It's not bothered by heat or drought, and deadheading is not required.

The herbalists of long ago valued the zinnia for the yellow-gold dye its petals gave. That dye probably brightened the lives of the pioneers as they moved west. Thanks to the magic of plant breeders, the zinnia is still brightening our lives today. Whether in the garden or in a vase, zinnias will always be valued for their beauty and charm.

Extending the Harvest Season

~ by Kathy Martin ~

About ten years ago my husband built a cold frame tucked up against the south side of our urban house. I had tried for years to overwinter potted rosemary in the house—each time it dried up and died. In my new cold frame, I planted a large rosemary and left it outside for the winter. It was the most amazing plant that year. It overwintered beautifully in the shelter of the cold frame, and I harvested fresh rosemary all winter, even when I had to dig down under the snow to open the frame. After overwintering, the plant was huge. It was very happy the next summer. So was I. I still remember the taste of those rosemary-spiced winter meals!

There are several ways to extend the herb harvesting season. These include fall and winter sowing of annual herbs and overwintering of perennial herbs. I prefer to grow and overwinter herbs outside in the garden.

Fall sowing is the simplest as it requires no cold protection. The timing of sowing is based on the date of the average first fall frost and is set such that plants are mature and ready for harvest during the last few weeks before frost. Winter sowing and overwintering require protection from the winter cold. The timing of winter sowing is based on the date when days become too short to support plant growth. Sowing time is set so that full-sized plants can be harvested all winter. I'm referring to "overwintering" here as an approach to extending the outdoor harvest of fresh perennial herbs by growing them with cold protection—like the rosemary I overwintered years ago in our cold frame

Many herbs can be overwintered inside, but often overwintering outside is the best option. It can provide more space, reduce the costs and time of setting up plant shelves and lighting indoors, and provide a healthier and more humid environment for many herbs. Bringing outdoor perennial herbs inside for overwintering brings the challenges of low indoor winter humidity and controlling any insect pests that may have been on the plant.

Fall Sowing

One approach to vegetable gardening is to plant in the spring, harvest all summer, and then clean up and put the garden away by midfall. However, the crisp fall days can be a great time to garden. Not only are temperatures cooling, but there are fewer bugs, fewer weeds, and less need for watering. Also many herbs and vegetables do best in the cool weather of fall. These crops can be set out in late summer, filling in spaces left by summer crops such as basil, potatoes, garlic, onions, and zucchinis.

Fall growing generally does not require any protection from the weather. Sowing is timed so that crops are harvested before the average first killing frost date. However, nature doesn't always follow average dates. Some light covering may be needed on chilly nights. Old sheets or blankets or heavy row cover draped over the plants will do the job.

Annual herbs are best for fall sowing. My favorites include cilantro, dill, and mustard greens. I have sown fall salad mixes that include misuna, lettuce, tatsoi, and escarole. Cilantro and dill are great to plant repeatedly, and their leaves become plentiful in the cooler weather and shorter daylight of fall. They can spice up fall meals. Having fall dill and cilantro is also perfect for making end-of-the-harvest pickles or salsa fresca. Other herbs for fall sowing include basil, borage, chervil, and calendula.

Winter Sowing and Overwintering Herbs Outside

Winter sowing extends the time that fresh herbs are available. Plants are available for harvest throughout the entire winter, plus there is a burst of new growth in very early spring. In areas that freeze, overwintering requires protection from the cold, snow, and winds. Cold frames, tunnels, and greenhouses are the most common approaches. The first two, cold frames and tunnels, are low cost, easy to set up, and flexible for different uses year to year. These are the two discussed here.

The harvest time of virtually any herb can be extended with a cold frame or tunnel. Most can also be overwintered even in the coldest climates, with the exception of tender, warm-weather herbs such as basil.

Annual herbs can be winter sown, while perennial herbs can be moved to or grown in the protected area. Annual herbs to winter sow include cilantro, dill, fennel herb, mustard greens, bunching onions, arugula, spinach, endive, escarole, and parsley. Tarragon and rosemary are tender perennial herbs and, with some luck, the same plant can be overwintered many years. Parsley is a biennial herb and can be overwintered once or winter sown. Parsley is very hardy and in milder winters or winters with good snow cover, it will overwinter with no protection, giving an early fresh spring harvest. Bunching onions, arugula, spinach, endive, and escarole aren't herbs, but it's a shame to write about winter sowing without mentioning these, especially spinach. These vegetables overwinter beautifully and can provide homegrown greens all winter.

Hardy herbs will generally survive the winter, but often not in a condition for harvesting during the darkest and coldest time of the winter. By placing these in a winter tunnel or cold frame, fresh leaves can be picked all winter. Hardy perennial herbs that I grow include sage, lots of varieties of thyme, oregano, chives, mint, chamomile, marjoram, and winter savory.

Building Cold Frames and Winter Tunnels

A cold frame is usually a wooden box covered with windowpanes or clear plastic. The frame rests directly over the soil. Cold frames can be purchased premade or constructed with a wide range of materials. A simple cold frame can be made using the following steps:

1. Build a box about 3 feet by 6 feet from untreated lumber. The 6-foot lengths will be the back and front of the frame. The back of the box should be about 18 inches high, sloping to about 14 inches at the front. The slope

will position the top at an angle that enables more sun to reach the plants. The angle will also allow the cold frame to shed rain and snow.

2. Hinge an old window frame over the top of the cold frame, attaching it in the back along the highest side. Alternatively, fiberglass or clear plastic can be supported by panes without glass and used for the top. The insides of the cold frame can be insulated with rigid foam. Weather stripping along the top edges will also help to insulate the interior. In extreme cold or snow cover the cold frame with a tarp, heavy burlap, or an old blanket.

3. Position the cold frame so that it faces as close to south as possible. Positioning the frame next to a building will also help by trapping heat and protecting it from cold winds.

The cold frame my husband made was a fairly temporary structure with dimensions of about 6 by 12 feet. In a cold frame this big, I had to be able to get inside to reach all areas. He made the back about 4 feet high and the front about 2 feet. The frame had greenhouse plastic on the top panel, which generally lasted for two years before it grew brittle and needed replacement. The sides were all-purpose, 4-millimeter plastic sheeting from Home Depot supported on a wooden frame. Tears were mended with duct tape. We added rigid foam insulation in the coldest times of winter.

The frame was located in a very protected and warm spot. It was up against our white-painted house, facing southwest. Another house was nearby but not close enough to block the sunlight. Even without a cold frame, this spot cooled down slowly in the fall and warmed up fast in spring. I had to remember that a closed cold frame can build up a lot of heat on a sunny day. When temperatures went above 40 degrees Fahrenheit (4 degrees Celcius), I opened the frame to the air.

I used a remote thermometer to watch the temperature inside the frame since it was close to the house. The lowest temperature I recorded inside the frame was about 28 degrees F (-2 degrees C). This was on a very cold night that went into the teens outside the frame. I had covered the frame with a tarp. During the day, I pulled off the tarp and let the sun warm the soil as much as it could.

I had visions of rebuilding my cold frame someday. Perhaps a brick base and glass panes. Cables for heating the soil. But we moved away before I could rebuild it. At our new house I set up a winter tunnel instead of a cold frame.

A winter tunnel is easier to construct than a cold frame. It is a flexible, removable structure that can be easily repositioned to other locations. A winter tunnel can be made by following these steps:

1. Secure a 10-foot-long, ½-inch PVC pipe to two sides of a garden bed about 4 feet wide, forming an arch about 4 feet high. Repeat, placing pipes about 2 feet apart down the length of the bed. Secure the pipe by affixing a pole or board down the length of the bed at the top of the arches.

2. Cover with plastic, securing the edges with weights such as rocks, boards, or sandbags. For my tunnel, I use standard clear 6 millimeter greenhouse plastic, 12 feet wide, from an online garden supply store.

3. If winter temperatures regularly fall below 25 degrees F (-4 degrees C) or so, an extra layer of protection may be needed. Insulating row cover such as Agribon can be used on short hoops placed inside the plastic tunnel. Use

9-gauge wire to make the interior hoops. The cushion of air between the two layers will add a large degree of additional cold protection.

My winter tunnel is in the backyard of my house. It covers one of my 1-foot-high raised beds. The PVC pipes are secured to the outside of the raised bed with hardware brackets. It has protected my plants during cold snaps as low as -12 degrees F (-24 degrees C). It's stayed up under snow covers of three feet or more. On warmer days I lift up the plastic from the south side and allow air circulation. I've had trouble with critters like voles and chipmunks, so I dug in ¼-inch hardware cloth 8 inches deep around the base of the bed, and this has solved that problem—so far.

Try using a remote thermometer to watch the temperature inside the cold frame or tunnel. You'll be able to watch the low and high temperatures and know when to either add layers or open the frame.

There can be a lot of flexibility in setting up a winter tunnel. A friend of mine built a tunnel she called a "tent house." It was a tent of clear plastic vinyl over a series of two 1-by-2-inch boards that had been connected to form a peak at the top. Like me, she also used insulating row cover as a second layer over the plants inside during the coldest times.

When to Sow for Fall and Winter Harvesting

The trick to planting in the fall is to count backward from the average first fall frost date in your garden. To figure out when to plant a certain herb or vegetable, check the seed packet for its number of days to maturity. Then add about two weeks to account for the fall factor. The **fall factor** represents the slowing of plant growth as light fades and temperatures cool down. Subtract this number of days from your first fall frost date to find the time when you should sow (see sample table on page 41).

Leafy greens are generally best for fall growing. They mature fast and thrive in the cooler temperatures. Great crops to sow include cilantro, dill, mustard greens, lettuce, spinach, endives, and escaroles, arugula, and Asian greens. If you have space in a window at home, you may want to start seedlings in pots so you can water them evenly while the sun is still hot. Transplant to the garden after about three weeks.

Sometimes local nurseries will put some fall transplants out for sale, but availability is unreliable. If you're willing to search, you may or may not be rewarded. Lack of availability of fall seedlings is great reason for sowing your own. The goal with winter sowing is to have your plants ready for harvest before the low light of winter stops their growth. In this condition, if plants are protected from the weather (cold, wind, and snow), they can provide a fresh harvest all winter.

The time to sow annual herbs for overwintering outside depends on your latitude, which determines when your daylight will fall below ten hours per day. Most plants don't grow at all with less than ten hours of sunlight. It's not a sudden change, but as daylight decreases, plants gradually stop growing. To have a crop that you can harvest all winter, annual seeds need to be sown at a time that allows them to reach their full size before the low sunlight stops their growth. The date when the hours of sunlight fall below ten a day for your city can be found online. The US Naval Observatory offers a tool to generate a table for your area here: http://aa.usno.navy.mil /data/docs/Dur_OneYear.php.

To determine winter sowing times, you'll need to count backward from the date your day length falls below ten hours per day and then add a **winter factor** of about three weeks. As with calculating fall sowing times, check the seed packet for the plant's number of days to maturity, add about three weeks, and then count backward. A table with some winter and fall sowing times is below:

Sample Sowing Times for Fall and Winter Planting					
		Days before frost or 10-hour day		Sowing dates for Boston area	
Herb	Days to Harvest	Fall	Winter	Fall	Winter
Basil	70	85	95	July 17	Aug 7
Borage	50	65	75	Aug 6	Aug 27
Calendula	50	65	75	Aug 6	Aug 27
Chamomile	60	75	85	July 27	Aug 17
Chervil	60	75	85	July 27	Aug 17
Chives	80	95	105	July 7	July 28
Cilantro	50	65	75	Aug 6	Aug 27
Cutting Celery	80	95	105	July 7	July 28
Dill	40	55	65	Aug 16	Sept 6
Parsley	80	95	105	July 7	July 28
Shiso	80	95	105	July 7	July 28
Spinach	40	55	65	Aug 16	Sept 6

Spinach, generally considered a vegetable, is included here because it is an ideal plant for fall and winter sowing. It is very fast growing and cold tolerant.

Don't worry if your winter sowing is later than these times. The young plants will perk up in the spring and begin growing once daylight exceeds ten hours and above-freezing temperatures are maintained in the cold frame or winter tunnel. Overwintering these small plants will give an early spring harvest that can't be beat!

Hardy perennial herbs that are already established plants can be dug into the soil of a cold frame or winter tunnel for overwintering. Their leaves will generally remain tender and ready for harvest for at least a good part of the winter. Try thyme, oregano, and sage. Tender perennials can also be overwintered in a well-protected cold frame or tunnel. Try rosemary or tarragon.

For both fall and winter sowing, there are mobile apps and online sites that can do the backward counting (subtracting dates) for you. There are also apps that will calculate fall and winter planting dates for specific crops and specific locations. They are great fun to use and help you experiment with extending your herb harvest.

Agastache: An Herb for the Perennial Border

by Diana Stoll

Once hyssops caught the attention of hybridizers, it didn't take them long to enter the gardening spotlight. The genus *Agastache* offers much to gardeners: colorful flowers over a long period of bloom; vertical form, fine texture, and fragrant foliage; nectar for hummingbirds, butterflies, bees, and other pollinators; low water needs; and, of course, all its utilitarian herbal uses.

Growing Agastache

Agastache is a genus mostly native to the southwest portion of the United States and Mexico. Many are fair-weather perennials unable to survive winters in zones cooler than zone 8, but some are cold hardy in my zone 5 garden, where their aromatic foliage

and spikes of tubular flowers delight hummingbirds, butterflies, bees, and other pollinators as much as they please me.

They have an upright growth habit with slightly serrated leaves similar to the foliage of catmint. The tops of the leaves are gray-green; the undersides are often washed with white. Sturdy stems bear flower spikes packed with tiny tubular florets that bloom from the top down. Flowers may be blue, lavender, purple, pink, peach, yellow, orange, or white. If spent blooms are deadheaded regularly, expect continued flowering on most varieties from midsummer until first frost. Without deadheading, plants produce seeds and flowering comes to an end sooner.

The genus *Agastache* is a member of the mint clan and shows off the family's characteristic square stems and leaves that smell like black licorice. Commonly called hummingbird mint or giant hyssop, this group of plants has grown under the radar of many gardeners until they recently caught the attention of hybridizers. New cultivars with impressive flower and foliage colors along with increased winter hardiness are now available.

Plant hyssops in the sunniest spaces in the garden. They can tolerate a bit of shade but reach their blooming potential in full sun. Well-drained soil is a must—the roots of *Agastache* rot in wet, poorly drained soil. If the soil doesn't drain well, amend it with organic matter or grow the plant in raised beds.

Keeping plants well watered during their first season in the garden is important to help roots settle into their new homes. Once established, they are drought tolerant, but in periods of prolonged drought water deeply and then wait until the soil dries to water again.

Hyssops require very little care. They rarely, if ever, require fertilizer. If plants indicate the need, apply a balanced, all-purpose fertilizer in early spring. Gardeners prone to loving their plants too much should note over-fertilizing will cause lax stems that flop.

Instead of mulching with hardwood mulch or shredded leaves, use crushed gravel. Even tidy gardeners who like to cut back perennials before winter should put the pruners away before cutting back hyssops. Plants survive winter best when their foliage is left standing. Cut them back to a few inches above the ground in early spring.

When flowering starts to decrease, it may be time to divide plants. Hyssops are easy to divide. Dig up a clump and separate the root mass into sections—each with several healthy buds—discarding parts that have become woody. Replant divisions as soon as possible.

Hyssops spread by self-seeding and by rhizomes.
Share seedlings with friends or let them remain
where Mother Nature planted them.

Propagate hyssops by scattering seeds in the garden in fall or by starting seeds indoors in spring. Seeds need light to germinate, so don't cover them with soil, and keep the soil moist but not wet until seeds sprout, usually in a few weeks. As seedlings grow, transplant them into larger pots. They might bloom the first year, but many will wait until the second year for their first flowering.

Sterile hybrids that do not produce seeds can be propagated by semi-ripe cuttings in late summer. Cut four- to six-inch pieces of the current season's growth. The base of each cutting should be hard, but the tip should be soft. Put cuttings in a plastic bag right after pruning to keep them as moist as possible. Remove the soft tips and the leaves at the bottom, dip the cuttings in rooting hormone, and plant them in mix of well-drained potting soil and perlite. Water them thoroughly, cover pots with plastic wrap, and move them to a bright, warm location out of direct sunlight. When roots develop, new growth will appear.

Benefits of Agastache

Agastache offers a bounty of benefits to wildlife. The flowers provide nectar to a wide variety of bees, butterflies, moths, and hummingbirds. Some report that hummingbirds favor red-flowered hyssops and swallowtail butterflies prefer hyssops with blue flowers, but unless the birds and butterflies in my garden are either starving or colorblind, the color of the flowers doesn't seem to matter. In fall goldfinches snack on their seeds.

As attractive as hyssops are to winged wildlife, they are rarely bothered by four-legged garden foes. Deer and rabbits find the scent of their foliage offensive and look elsewhere for snacks. If provided the growing conditions they prefer, hyssops are relatively free of disease too. Give them plenty of air circulation to avoid powdery mildew and rust, and plant them in well-drained soil to reduce the possibility of crown and root rot.

In North America, Native Americans recognized the value of *Agastache* long before it made its way into the perennial border. They used this herb for everything from making tea and breath freshener to healing wounds and curing coughs. Today herbalists utilize hyssops for many of the same remedies and continue to discover more therapeutic uses. I don't often head to the herb garden for pharmaceutical purposes, but I do prefer rubbing the foliage of hyssops on my skin to reaching for a spray can to repel mosquitoes.

Make space for *Agastache* in herb gardens where it can grow alongside other herbs with fragrant foliage—lavender, thyme, rosemary, and sage—and gather leaves for making tea, seasoning food, or crafting potpourri.

Whether they are grown as annuals in containers or as perennials, hyssops add color, texture, and vertical accents. Flower arrangers should include a few plants in their cutting gardens. A seasonal bouquet of dwarf sunflowers, zinnias, celosia, and hyssop would most certainly get any husband out of the doghouse.

Include them in butterfly gardens with asters, goldenrod, and milkweed. Combine them with joe-pye weed, ironweed, and sunflowers in meadows. In late-summer containers partner hyssops with zinnias, marigolds, garden mums, and ornamental cabbage.

To find the *Agastache* planted in my landscape, one should just follow the parade of bees to the perennial border. Bees of all sorts buzz about from bloom to bloom, barely noticing the hummingbirds and butterflies that stop by to drink from the nectar-rich flowers.

Hyssops are wonderful neighbors to other perennials, content playing a supporting role or taking the lead. Partner them with medium-sized ornamental grasses like 'Thundercloud' switchgrass or 'Karl Foerster' feather reed grass. The flowering spikes of hyssops blend beautifully with the seed heads of the grasses.

Recreate a little patch of prairie when hyssops are joined in the border by goldenrods, coneflowers, bee balm, black-eyed Susan, and little bluestem. Or plant them with asters, Russian sage, and sedum, and the garden will bloom in a magnificent fall finale.

Favorite Species

An entire book could be written about the many different species of *Agastache*. These are just a few of my favorites.

Agastache foeniculum, most commonly called anise hyssop but also known as blue giant hyssop, fragrant giant hyssop, lavender giant hyssop, and licorice mint, is native to the Upper Midwest and Great Plains into Canada. It grows two to four feet tall and a foot wide. Lavender-blue flower spikes atop sturdy stems bloom from mid-summer until fall. Anise hyssop is a mainstay in herb gardens but is also beautiful in the perennial border mingling with pink-flowering coneflowers.

There are many garden-worthy cultivars of *A. foeniculum*. 'Alabaster' has creamy-white blooms on plants growing three feet tall. Wouldn't this be an ideal addition to an evening garden featuring white-flowering plants?

The sultry dark bronzy-green foliage of 'Bolero' is a beautiful backdrop for the brilliant rosy-pink flowers loosely held on two-foot stems. Plant it beside a pink-flowering aster for a plant combo that glows. 'Purple Haze' lives up to its name. Its flowers top two-foot plants in a cloud of lavender from July until frost. The lavender-blue blooms contrast beautifully with the chartreuse foliage of 'Golden Jubilee'. An All-American Selection Winner in 2003, it grows up to three feet tall and nearly as wide.

Agastache rugosa, commonly known as Korean hyssop, purple giant hyssop, and wrinkled giant hyssop, grows up to two feet tall and nearly as wide. Deep lavender-blue flowers bloom all summer long if deadheaded. Its glossy green foliage is very fragrant. Partner it with a yellow-flowering yarrow like *Achillea* 'Moonshine'. Both *Agastache rugosa* and *A. foeniculum* tolerate humidity better than other species.

Agastache 'Blue Fortune' is a hybrid of *A. foeniculum* and *A. rugosa*. Its soft blue flowers are a butterfly favorite in my garden. It grows three feet tall and eighteen inches wide. 'Blue Fortune' and pink garden phlox are a pretty partnership.

Another cross between *A. foeniculum* and *A. rugosa*, 'Black Adder' shows off deep smoky blue flowers on purple stems from midsummer through September. Plants grow up to three feet tall and two feet wide.

If this variety is too tall, consider *Agastache* 'Little Adder'. Performing in the small but mighty category, it reaches just eighteen inches. Position it at the front of a perennial border where it can flaunt its purple flowers from July until frost.

A. rugosa is one of the parents of the 'Kudos' series of hyssops. 'Kudos Coral' flaunts orange buds that open to coral-colored blooms, 'Kudos Ambrosia' parades flowers of soft orange and rosy-pink stroked with white, and 'Kudos Mandarin' shows off orange blooms that sparkle in the garden. They all grow about eighteen inches tall and wide.

Agastache rupestris may get its common name, sunset hyssop, from the color of its flowers. Burnt orange and salmon blooms capture the colors of a sunset on its petals. Plants begin blooming in August and continue into fall. The narrow gray-green leaves are surely the inspiration for another of its common names, threadleaf giant hyssop. Native to Arizona and New Mexico, it grows approximately two feet tall and wide.

Agastache cana grows up to three feet tall and two feet wide. Common names for this hyssop, native to New Mexico and Texas, include Texas hummingbird mint, mosquito mint, and wild hyssop. Plants are enveloped in rose-pink flowers from late summer into fall. Pair it with *Geranium* 'Rozanne' in a playful combination.

Agastache × 'Desert Sunrise' is a hybrid of *A. rupestris* and *A. cana*. A giant of the group, it reaches four feet tall and boasts reddish-pink flowers touched with orange. Let it mingle with coneflowers in a bird and butterfly buffet beginning in late summer.

Cooking with Agastache

Agastache foeniculum can also be used in the kitchen. The leaves can be used fresh or dried to make tea. Just a few fresh leaves chopped and added to green salads and fruit salads give them a cool, minty flavor. Season chicken, fish, or rice with leaves, but use them sparingly so their flavor doesn't overpower the recipe.

Make anise hyssop honey. Pour warm honey over dried leaves and give them several weeks for the hyssop's flavor to infuse the honey. Tiny individual flowers can also be added to fruit salads or baked into cookies. Garnish cold drinks with spikes of flowers.

Whether using the foliage for cooking or crafting, harvest leaves when the flowers have just finished blooming, when the oil content in leaves is at its peak. To dry flowers, strip the leaves from their stems or hang the entire stems in a dry, dark place.

Resources

Armitage, Allan M. *Herbaceous Perennial Plants: A Treatise on Their Iden-tification, Culture, and Garden Attributes*. 3rd ed. Brentwood, TN: Cool Springs Press, 2008.

Anisko, Tomasz. *When Perennials Bloom: An Almanac for Planning and Planting*. Portland, OR: Timber Press 2008.

"Plant Finder." Missouri Botanical Garden. Accessed January 10, 2018. http://www.missouribotanicalgarden.org/plantfinder/plant findersearch.aspx.

How to Attract Hummingbirds with Sage

❧ by Kathy Vilim ❧

If you wish to invite hummingbirds into your garden, you will be putting out the welcome mat by planting sage. Sage (*Salvia* spp.) is a wild native herb genus that happens to be the favorite nectar plant of hummingbirds. When we think of sage, we usually think of it as an herb with culinary and spiritual uses. Besides having aromatic medicinal and edible properties, the best thing about sage is it attracts pollinators, particularly hummingbirds.

Why Garden for Hummingbirds?

We have all heard about the decline in pollinators in recent years. This goes beyond vanishing bees. There are hundreds of different species of hummingbirds in the Americas, yet BirdLife International identifies around 10 percent of these extant species as being at risk of extinction. One reason for this is due to chemically treated meadows and farmland, where hummingbirds used to be able to stop and feed while migrating back and forth between the United States and Mexico. Another source of decline is due to ever-increasing development, the paving over of wild places. Keeping pollinators vibrant and thriving is one very good reason for environmentally conscious gardeners to provide for hummingbirds where they can: in their own gardens.

But why do hummingbirds prefer sage to other flowers? Sage comes in a variety of colors, including red. While hummingbirds may have a poor sense of smell, they can see red and other vibrant colors (which they associate with nectar), like purple and blue, whereas bees cannot. In addition, it is sage's leaves, not its blossoms, that hold its fragrance, another deterrent for the bees, as they use smell to find nectar-rich blossoms. This gives "hummers" the first shot at red salvia's nectar, thereby helping secure a food source.

The long, tubular flowers of sage tell the hummingbird, "This is your nectar source." The shape makes it difficult for bees to get inside. Soft petals gently curve in such a way that the hummingbird's needle-like beak hits the inside of the flower. In sage's pollination system, a unique lever causes the stamens to move and the pollen to be deposited on the pollinator. Sage and hummingbirds enjoy a special relationship, as the plant is bird-pollinated: **ornithophily** is the pollination of flowers by birds.

The nectar of sage contains sucrose, which is a high-octane fuel source not found in just any flower, and the hummingbirds need this. After sugars, the other important part of nectar is its amino acids, such as lipoic acid, which may add a preferred taste. Hummingbirds are so tiny that they don't have places in their bodies to store fat, yet they need energy for zipping around. Their hearts beat very fast performing their antics. They also have a big migration to fuel up for—the long journey to Mexico.

The *Salvia*-Hummingbird Relationship

Salvia plants are beloved by California gardeners because they are drought tolerant, grow without any fuss, and have a long bloom time. But more than that, we enjoy watching hummingbirds in our gardens. Where there is sage, there are hummingbirds! Because of our mild winters, Californians can see hummingbirds all year round, but you don't have to live in California to plant sage or to see hummingbirds. No matter where you live in the United States, you can find native species of hummingbirds and native species of *Salvia* plants growing wild and coexisting. Sage provides nectar for the hummingbirds, and hummingbirds pollinate their blooms. It is as if hummingbirds and sage were made for each other, existing in a symbiotic relationship.

Native species of sage plants will be blooming when the hummingbirds are fattening up to leave on their long journey to Mexico and when they return from their winter migration. In California, where the hummingbirds do not leave for migration but instead stay put for the whole winter, a variety of native *Salvia* species provide for continuous bloom. To find the varieties native to your area of North America, visit the Biota of North America Program's plant atlas: http://bonap .net/Napa/TaxonMaps/Genus/State/Salvia.

When, Which, and Where?

When can you expect to see hummingbirds in your garden? That depends on where you live and whether your species of hummingbird migrates for winter. Some birds will not arrive in the Northeast and Midwest until May. The approximate arrival times of the major species of hummingbirds (such as ruby, Anna's, Allen's, black-chinned, and rufous) can be found in migration maps online on sites such as Hummingbird Central.

If you live east of the Mississippi, the hummingbirds you will see are the ruby-throated hummingbirds; they are the only hummingbirds that nest east of the river. The ruby-throated hummingbirds are a migratory species (trans-gulf migrants), so you will have to wait until spring for their return. How long you will have to wait depends on that year's weather and when the hummingbirds decide to leave their winter home in Mexico. Each hummingbird leaves when it wants, acting as an individual rather than following a collective mind.

Interestingly, hummingbirds are able to remember last year's journey and follow the same path, enjoying the same nectar source from one year to the next, even returning to the same feeder! Flights are usually during daytime, and hummingbirds fly low so they can find flowers.

Hummingbird Migration

The hummingbird's migration is an amazing, perilous trip. Many birds die trying to make the trip every year. Some of the birds have taken to flying from Florida to Texas, hugging the coastline, rather than make direct flights some 500 miles across the Gulf of Mexico (at approximately 25 miles per hour). Some species, like the tiny and fragile rufous hummingbirds, travel an impressive 3,400 miles up the West Coast from Mexico to Alaska and the Pacific Northwest to breed in springtime. This is the longest known migration of any of the hummingbirds. In midsummer the male rufous will turn back south again, traveling through the meadows of the Rocky Mountains. Occasionally, a few rufous hummingbirds will spin off eastward to be seen in Midwest gardens, though this is rare.

In contrast, some western species, such as Anna's and Allen's hummingbirds, don't migrate at all. Instead, they make their homes along the Southern California coast. Where winters are mild, there's no need to leave! California gardeners will plant sage for the hummers, and, as nature has provided, there will be a choice of native sage species to prolong bloom time. We need to feed our flying friends all year long! Many native plant gardeners report having made friends with certain individual birds. I myself have found tiny hummingbird nests in my garden—and I mean tiny, like the size of a penny!

Hummingbirds as Garden Friends

Once the ruby-throated hummingbirds return from Mexico, if you want to entice them to stay in your garden and sit for a while, consider if your garden is a suitable backyard habitat for hummingbirds. In order to live happily, they need what most animals need: a place to rest, a place to hide from predators, clean drinking and bathing water, food (nectars and tiny insects), and a place to nest (trees away from the house and human traffic). They also need tree branches to perch on; they spend more time sitting still than we realize. I enjoy watching them from my own garden bench below the trees.

When you water, creating a spray with your hose, hummingbirds appear instantly as if desperate for a shower. But they are very fragile, only able to tolerate the gentlest of sprays. This means they will fly to the edges of your water spray—no use moving closer to them, as they will just fly away! When you plant your sage garden, why not plan it around a water feature, such as a small water fountain? Hummingbirds are attracted to moving water and love to take showers.

There is the whir of an approaching hummingbird, but they also have a call. Did you know that not all species of hummingbirds make the same calls? You can hear the hummingbirds in your region by searching the species on the National Audubon Society website.

In my Southern California garden in the Santa Monica Mountains we have Anna's hummingbirds. They do not migrate, but stay all winter and all year long, so I have had a chance to make friends with them and recognize their calls. Occasionally, an invading rufous hummingbird will appear, usually in February, to challenge the Anna's source of nectar. Then I will hear the rufous's call. The rufous has a bright golden head, an extraordinarily beautiful sight especially when the sun hits it. But Anna's hummingbirds will fight to the death to defend their supply of *Salvia*. It can get pretty intense sometimes between the males. They will even fight over the hanging feeders. Rufous is a migratory species just passing through on their way back to the Northwest after wintering in Mexico.

There is no lack of native sage growing wild in the chaparral outside my garden. We have many different varieties of *Salvia* growing there, with different bloom times and a variety of colors. With all this wild sage around, how do I attract hummingbirds to *my* garden? My garden holds something else for the hummingbirds: I planted with a water feature in mind, and they appreciate it especially in summer when there is no rainfall.

The following is my partial regional list of *Salvia* species. For a complete list of all the different sages native to your area, take advantage of the USDA PLANTS website, which offers photographs of the plants.

Sage for Hummingbirds of the Eastern Region

The ruby-throated hummingbird, *Archilochus colubris*, is pretty much the only hummingbird you will see east of the Great Plains in the United States. These birds can be found from Canada in the north, down to Florida's Panhandle, and west to the Mississippi. They are migratory. The following are sage options for the ruby-throated hummingbird:

The Southeast

Plant anise-scented sage, *S. guaranitica*. With black and blue flowers, this sage is popular throughout the Southeast partly because it adapts to damp conditions. Anise sage requires rich soil and lots of sun, and it smells like licorice.

The Eastern Region

Try the fragrant pineapple sage, *S. elegans*. One of the last hummingbird plants to bloom in autumn, pineapple sage is a major attraction for migratory ruby-throated hummingbirds as well as migratory hummers that wander in from the western states.

The Eastern and Central Regions

Azure sage, *S. azurea*, also known as pitcher sage and big blue sage, is a tall, delicate perennial found growing commonly in short grasslands throughout the eastern and central parts of the United States. An early flowering variety, it continues to bloom through autumn in Florida. The native habitats for blue sage include prairie, plains, meadows, pastures, savannahs, and the edge of woodlands. It is also of special value to both native bees and bumblebees.

Sage for Hummingbirds of the Western Region

There are by far a greater number of different hummingbird species (over two hundred true natives) in the western states than in the eastern states, with Tucson, Arizona, being the best place to view them. The most common western species of hummingbird, Anna's hummingbird and Allen's hummingbird, do not migrate but instead live along the California coast all year long. Finding nectar for these birds in the winter is not a problem. As there are many hummingbirds staying put through winter, there are that many varieties of sucrose-rich native sage plants growing for them. The following are just a few of the many native coastal varieties.

Coastal California

Island pitcher sage, *Lepechinia fragrans,* is native to Southern California's Channel Islands and is a threatened species. The plant is rugged with fragrant furry leaves and gorgeous pink flowers. Unlike most *Salvia* species, it prefers moisture and shade.

Salvia 'Dara's Choice' is a California native with rich blue flowers in spring and early summer. Great ground cover for slopes, sunny neglected areas, and problem spots, 'Dara's Choice' can be used in mixed borders of drought-resistant plants. A hummingbird- and honeybee-friendly plant, this lovely low-growing sage is thought to be a cross between black sage (*S. mellifera*) and creeping sage (*S. sonomensis*).

Try sacred white sage, *S. apiana*: bees, hummingbirds, and spiritual blessings join together where this elegant shrubby sage grows. An important ceremonial herb to indigenous Californians, white sage should be grown in every sage garden. Its stiff leaves appear silvery white, and its flowers bloom soft white on long spikes.

Cleveland sage or California blue sage, *S. clevelandii,* is a must-have sage for the California native plant garden. This tall, drought-tolerant chaparral plant has deep blue flowers. Use it in back of a border in a dry garden.

Sage for Hummingbirds Traversing Western Regions

Rufous hummingbirds travel exclusively through the western states, even traversing the Rockies. Unlike Anna's and Allen's hummingbirds, rufous birds do not make a home in California in the winter. Instead, they prefer to make the longest trip of all the migratory hummingbirds, some 3,400 miles from Mexico up into Canada. Some fly as far south as Panama. They are commonly seen nesting in the Pacific Northwest in summertime. Rufous is easily recognizable by its handsome, golden-colored head.

The Rocky Mountains

Mountain sage (*S. microphylla*) and autumn sage (*S. greggii*) are woody perennials that offer an assortment of primary reds and rosy shades. These have compact growth and are native to Arizona, Texas, and Mexico. They are at home in dry, hot summers and attract bees, butterflies, and hummingbirds. Plant this for the broad-tailed hummingbirds flying along the Rockies in the Southwest.

Mojave sage (*S. mohavensis*) is a California native that thrives in the Southwest (in elevations between five to ten thousand feet) and is a Santa Fe gardener's dream. It requires little water and little maintenance and is therefore good for xeriscaping. Mojave sage produces showy bluish-purple flowers all summer long and is sometimes called the giant flower sage because its blooms are larger than most other sages.

The Deep Southwest

Autumn sage varieties are mounded woody perennials and are the most widely grown types of *Salvia*. They are known for flowering from early summer through fall and preferring dry ground and open spaces in Texas and southeastern Arizona. Here are some options for planting in hot areas, such as Texas: 'Furman's Red' sage (*S. greggii* 'Furman's Red'), cedar sage (*S. roemeriana*), Huntington Gardens orange mountain sage (*S. regla* 'Huntington Gardens Form'), and 'Lowry's Peach' or autumn sage (*S. greggii* 'Lowry's Peach'). 'Wild Pink' Lemmon's sage (*S. lemmonii* 'Wild Pink') is an aromatic, highly drought-tolerant shrub that flowers abundantly and is also found wild in New Mexico.

Desert Regions

Pineapple sage grows well in Arizona. In Arizona's deserts specifically, plant red Davinson's sage (*S. davidsonii*). Other sages that do well in desert regions include red autumn sage, Lemmon's sage, Mojave sage, and Carl Neilsen sage (*S. mohavenis* × *clevelandii*).

How Do I Plant Sage?

No matter where you live, planting sage is not difficult. Just remember it is a "wild" native plant and, like all natives, it does not want to be pampered. It does not want amended garden soil or special soil additives, though it can tolerate sharing most native garden soils. Native sage species are naturally tolerant to the rainfall in your area and so need little to no water once established. In California where the ground is sandy, the water drains quickly away from sage's roots, and it prefers that; it doesn't like soggy roots.

You can buy sage from native plant nurseries. To find one near you, check with your local branch of the North American Native Plant Society. Before choosing a plant from a native plant nursery, consider how much space you have to work with. Some species of sage, like the woody, mounded autumn sage, grow into big bushy plants, while others have compact growth habit. I have even seen sage growing up against houses touching house roofs, like small trees!

There are many colors of blooms, with red being a hummingbird favorite, of course. You can create a sage garden using different colors or a border of all one color. Feel free to mix sage with other perennial natives too so that there is always something blooming for hummingbirds and for you. A native plant garden will attract the small insects that are also necessary for the hummingbird diet. Check bloom times on different species to make sure they are blooming when the hummingbirds are home. Plants can also be arranged around a water feature, such as a small fountain.

I used to garden just for beautiful flowers; for many years, I was content with gardening just to enjoy them. But now I find that I need to have that other element: the wildlife. Wildlife such as birds complete my garden now. I enjoy watching them eat and nest; they are my friends, entertaining me with their antics or quietly keeping counsel with me when I need it. It's just not the same when they are not around.

Selected Resources

BirdLife International Data Zone search. Accessed January 29, 2018. http://datazone.birdlife.org/species/results?cmn=&cty=0&fam=80&gen=0&kw=&reg=0&spc=&thrlev1=&thrlev2=&so=rl.

Blackstone, Ellen. "Create Hummingbird Haven Native Flowering Plants." Narrated by Mary McCann. Produced by John Kessler and Chris Peterson. *BirdNote*, 2015. Podcast, 1:43. Last modified April 2017. http://www.audubon.org/news/create-humming bird-haven-native-flowering-plants.

Bruneni, Susan. "May: Mojave Sage: *Salvia pachyphylla*." Santa Fe Botanical Garden. May 2012. https://santafebotanicalgarden .org/may-2012/.

"Migration Secrets Revealed." *Birds & Blooms*. Accessed September 16, 2017. http://birdsandblooms.com/birding/birding-basics /migration-secrets-revealed.

"Seeing Red and Loving It: Hummingbirds and *Salvia microphylla*." Flowers by the Sea. Accessed September 16, 2017. http://www .fbts.com/everything-salvias/seeing-red-and-loving-it-humming birds-and-salvia-microphylla.html.

Fruiting Vegetables and a Few Other Nuts

⤚ by Charlie Rainbow Wolf ⤙

Mention fruit, and most people think of juicy berries, crisp apples, sweet melons, or the succulent varieties of citrus fruit. However, what's classed as a fruit covers far more than that. From a botanical point of view, a fruit is defined as having seeds on the inside. If we look at fruit from that angle, then it includes what I refer to as "fruiting vegetables": tomatoes, cucumbers, peppers, squash, and pumpkins, to name a few. There are heirloom and hybrid varieties, some of which can be grown in pots or on patios. Some are weird and wacky while others are more standard, more traditional to the stereotypical varieties.

Tomatoes

I've started with tomatoes because where we live, this seems to be the stalwart that everyone grows. From the elderly who just want to feel the dirt under their fingernails to the young ones who are only just learning about life cycles and the food chain, tomatoes are popular. Determinate tomatoes are easier to plan than indeterminate ones. An indeterminate plant will just keep growing until the first frost, while a determinate one usually provides some kind of idea as to how big that particular tomato plant will be at maturity.

Not all tomatoes are red, either, even though that's usually the standard that comes to mind. There are pink ones as well as yellow ones, which are less acidic than the red ones and appreciated by those with digestive issues. White, purple, and green varieties are also available. In our garden, our favorite cultivar for standard tomatoes is *Lycopersicon lycopersicum* 'Black Prince', a wonderfully dark and fleshy heirloom variety.

We also plant the little grape and cherry tomatoes too. For cherry tomatoes, we don't think you can beat *L. lycopersicum* 'Chocolate Cherry'. The fruit is a deep brown-red, about the size of a shooter marble, and so fleshy and sweet. In contrast, the yellow pear tomato (*L. lycopersicum* 'Yellow Pear') is marigold yellow and produces two-inch pear-shaped fruits that are juicy and sweet. Both of these tomatoes are indeterminate; give them plenty of room to spread, and you'll be rewarded with fruit on the vine until the first frost.

One of the most effective ways to ensure that your tomatoes get their water requirements is to drill several quarter-inch holes in a five-gallon plastic bucket (up the sides and through the bottom) in the ground. Put a large tomato cage (or make your own from some flexible wire fencing) around it, and then plant three or four tomatoes around that. Stake your tomatoes to encourage them to grow up the fencing, and keep the bucket full of water. Water will leach out of the bucket into the soil, keeping the roots of the plants nice and moist. The bucket will catch the rainwater too. For sweeter tomatoes, sprinkle some baking soda on the soil around the plants.

It's possible to grow tomatoes in straw bales, but after a couple of years, we abandoned this idea. For one, it's a lot of work to keep the bales hydrated enough to really get good juicy fruit on the vines. For another, our plants got top heavy, and wanted to topple out of the bales. We put trellises behind them, and they were reasonably happy with that, but we've had better luck throwing the plants right into the soil than growing them in straw.

Don't think that you have to limit your tomatoes to just salads, juice, and pasta sauce. When frost is predicted, grab all the tomatoes off the vines and bring them inside. Some will ripen on the windowsill. Making fried green tomatoes is another way of using the fruit before it spoils. Green tomato chutney makes a wonderful pickle relish for hot dogs or grilled cheese sandwiches. Tomato wine is a bit bland and acidic (just trust me on this one), but tomato jam—made with green tomatoes, lemons, ginger, and sugar—is a marmalade-like preserve and absolutely delicious!

Peppers

Just like there is a rainbow of tomatoes to grow, there's a rainbow of peppers too. From the palest creamy yellow to the darkest purple, these fruiting vegetables will certainly add color to your garden—and your table. Because they're easy to grow and freeze well, we usually grow a large plot of sweet peppers. Sweet peppers, bell peppers, and other capsicums are all the same thing and members of the species *Capsicum annuum*. They can be large or small, ornamental as well as edible, mild or hot. Jalapeños, poblanos, and chili peppers all fall into this category.

Don't throw away those disused CDs! Hang CDs,
aluminum pie plates, or take-away dishes from strings
between your trellises and garden supports. Shiny objects
make the garden look busy and will help to deter pests
from helping themselves to your garden.

While there aren't as many oddities in the pepper kingdom, they can still be found. Our favorite is *Capsicum annuum* var. *annuum* 'Peter Pepper'. It's a hot pepper with an interesting and rather phallic shape that comes in red or yellow. Because of the heat factor, we include it for ornament rather than consumption. It certainly provides a talking point in the vegetable garden!

Peppers are easy to grow. Follow the advice on your seed packet and start the seeds inside about a month before the last frost date in your area. Plant them out and let them take off! There's not a lot of hardening needed when it comes to peppers, nor do they demand specific soil conditions. They like to be moist but not soggy, with a ground temperature above 60 degrees. Peppers are good garden buddies with tomatoes and parsley. We put cinnamon basil in with ours.

For me, the best thing about capsicums is that it's possible to use them as both a vegetable and a fruit. Cooked, they add mild sweetness to curries and stir-fries; raw, they provide a delightful crunch to salads or with dips and sauces. If you're fond of pickles, make a sweet relish to eat with cheese and crackers. The red and green ones make a particularly festive-looking sweet and tart preserve for Christmas and the holiday season.

Cucumbers

This is another one of the default fruiting vegetables that we grow. Our favorite is *Cucumis sativus* 'Straight Eight'. We've found this heirloom variety to be an extremely vigorous grower, with a heavy yield of straight, succulent cucumbers around eight inches in length, just as the name implies. The nice thing about these is that if we can't get to them all and leave some on the vine, they don't get woody. We've had some nearly two feet long, yet they've still been juicy and sweet. We trellis them; keeping the fruit off the ground and hanging helps to keep it straight.

Some varieties of cucumber also fall into the weird and wacky category too. There's *C. sativus* 'Lemon', which grows fist-sized fruits that have bright yellow skins and watery pale green flesh that is sweet and refreshing. Cucumbers need a lot of water to keep them flavorful, and although we've grown them in straw bales previously, we now trellis them.

Another cucumber oddity is the mouse melon, which really isn't a cucumber at all. It belongs to a different Cucurbitaceae genus, *Melothria scabra*. These little "sour grapes" are gaining in popularity, and I'm not surprised! They're unusual, easy to grow, taste like slightly tangy cucumbers, and look like miniature watermelons clinging to the vines. How cute is that?

Planting radishes in with your cucumbers helps deter cucumber beetles, which will decimate all your hard work in a hurry if they decide to infest your plot. Another way of controlling some garden pests is to spray the plants with sugar water, like you'd put out for hummingbirds. An added advantage to this is the sweetness draws the pollinators.

It's hard to preserve cucumbers after the growing season, but it is possible. In addition to all the usual pickle and relish recipes, cucumbers make an interesting wine. They can be frozen in slices or pureed to make vitamin water and smoothies. Don't dismiss cucumber sorbet, either; cucumber and mint are a delightfully unusual addition to a salad as well as a light and intriguing dessert.

Squash

Squash is mostly divided into two varieties: summer squash, which includes zucchini and crookneck squash and is harvested in the summer months; and winter squash, which includes butternut and acorn squash, is harvested in the autumn, and has a longer shelf life. Like tomatoes and cucumbers, squash comes in traditional heirloom varieties, hybrids, and some pretty weird alien-looking stuff too.

Everyone seems to grow zucchini, and there's a reason for that. It's so versatile! It comes in many types, but our favorite is *Cucurbita pepo* 'Black Beauty'. This is an heirloom variety, and we like it because there are so many ways to use it. The small fruits are harvested and added to stir-fries and salads. Slightly larger fruits are battered and shallow fried. Let the fruits go even larger and you've got what my English husband refers to as a "marrow." Take out the seeds and stuff the marrow with meat and potatoes or vegetable rice, then bake it in the oven for a wonderfully warming dish. Even the flowers are edible, and they are very tasty stuffed with mushroom and cashew paté. Peel and seed the fruits to make a puree that freezes wonderfully for future use in zucchini bread or vegetable soups and stews.

For summer squash, we usually go with crookneck. Another type of *C. pepo*, crookneck can be used in much the same way as a zucchini (or courgette, according to my other half!). It's easy to grow and doesn't spread or vine like some of the other varieties we cultivate, and its bumpy yellow skin is a nice contrast to the smooth dark green of the zucchini.

One problem we seem to have when growing these is the squash beetle. It will flatten a plant overnight, or at least it seems that way. We grow the squash away from the straw bale gardens, because apparently the beetle blighters like to breed in the bales! Straw is not a recommended mulch for squash plants and other cucurbitas. We use neem oil and eucalyptus soap to try to keep a handle on the bug population, and some gardeners I know put a board or a shingle in their garden overnight and then dispose of the larvae collected on it the next morning. Squashing squash bugs is the most effective way of keeping them off the plants, but it's time-consuming. For companion plants, add radishes and nasturtiums to the bed.

Winter squash comes in such a wide variety of shapes and colors—and unusual names—that we've not had time to try them all. 'Red Warty Thing' (yes, that really is a winter squash name), 'Chicago Warted Hubbard', and 'Turk's Turban' are just three of the intriguing types we hope to try one day. We had success with 'Blue Hubbard' (*Cucurbita maxima* 'Blue Hubbard') apart from when it came to cracking open the fruit. If you struggle with carving a pumpkin, you might want to steer clear of this one—or at least invest in a strong machete! Our favorites for winter are acorn squash *C. pepo* 'Bush Table King' and *C. pepo* 'Waltham,' a butternut variety. The acorn squash is lovely when stuffed with curry and apricots and then slow roasted in the oven. 'Waltham' is delicious in so many recipes. I cube it, toss it in crushed garlic and sesame oil, and bake it until it starts to turn golden brown.

Gourds

Gourds are used for many purposes by crafters, from bird-houses to dippers to carvings, but some of them are actually edible too! They are yet another member of the Cucurbitaceae family, some with hard exteriors and some with soft. History reveals that gourds have been used for centuries as utensils, containers, toys, and even musical instruments.

Gourds are popular in the garden because they're so very easy to grow, and you can do so many fun things with them. Bottle gourds (*Lagenaria siceraria*) are used for birdhouses, containers, and even pipes. Luffas (also spelled loofahs) are also made from gourds: the fibrous inner fruit of *Luffa aegyptiaca* is dried to use as a scrubbing sponge. My seed packet says that luffas are also edible when they're young, peeled, sliced, and stir-fried. There's really no limit to what can be done with gourds once you get your imagination on fire.

We found the edible gourds most interesting because even though they are related to cucumber and squash, they don't seem to have similar insect problems. We've grown *Cucurbita moschata*, which is listed as a squash but seems to behave more like a gourd. Eaten young, it's very zucchini-like but maybe not as juicy. Other edible gourds include cucuzzi (*L. siceraria*), which is a summer harvest, and *C. maxima* 'Galeux d'Eysines', which grows like a warty winter squash and produces pink fruits weighing in at over twenty pounds!

Nuts

Are nuts and seeds considered fruits? If you look at the botany, many of them are! The shell of the nut surrounds the seed within, just like the flesh of tomatoes and peppers do their seeds. What makes nuts different is the way the seed is protected. Cashews, pecans, walnuts, and almonds are inside a protective casing, which itself is surrounded by a fruit. Think of a peach: crack open the stone inside the peach, and there's an almond-like nut in it.*

The inconvenient thing about nuts is that they take so long to grow! It's not like you can plant them in spring and harvest them in the summer. Many nut trees take years before they start to fruit. However, if you've got the space for them to grow and the time for them to reach maturity, adding a nut or two to the garden brings long term-rewards, both in the fruits and with the added benefit of a shade tree.

Roses

Roses are a fruit. Have I gone crazy? Not at all! Although the beach rose (*Rosa rugosa*) is mainly grown for ornamental purposes, it does fruit! After it flowers, it produces rose hips, deep orange in color, approximately the size of a large grape and full

---

* It's not a good idea to eat a large quantity of peach kernels. They contain traces of a substance called amygdalin, which is a form of cyanide. You'd have to eat a lot of them to be in any real danger, but forewarned is forearmed.

of vitamin C. Rugosa roses come in different-colored single or double blossoms. They're hardy, they're fragrant, and they add interest and protection to the perimeters of the garden.

Rose hips—sometimes called haws—have a myriad of uses. We've made rose hip wine, rose hip jam, and rose hip jelly. They're delicious when steeped with hibiscus flowers as a tea. Rose hip syrup is a popular tonic believed to help boost the immune system, and it's easy to make. Bring rose hips, water, and sugar to a boil, simmer until it thickens, then strain and pack into sterilized bottles.

I can't leave roses without mentioning that, like squash blossoms, the flowers of the rugosa are also edible. Use them candied or crystallized with sugar on sweets and desserts, steep them to make rosewater for Turkish delight, or use them in ice cream and sorbets. Rugosa roses are very vigorous growers, with roots that travel and thick spiny branches, but their rewards are so vast that we wouldn't be without them in our garden!

Resources

Burge, Weldon. *Grow the Best Peppers.* Vol. 138 of *A Storey Country Wisdom Bulletin*. Pownal, VT: Storey, 1995.

Goldman, Amy. *The Compleat Squash: A Passionate Grower's Guide to Pumpkins, Squashes, and Gourds.* New York: Artisan, 2004.

Leavons, John. *How to Grow More Vegetables: (And Fruits, Nuts, Berries, Grains, and Other Crops) Than You Ever Thought Possible on Less Land Than You Can Imagine.* Emeryville, CA: Ten Speed Press, 2004.

Riotte, Louise. *Carrots Love Tomatoes: Secrets of Companion Planting for Successful Gardening.* Pownal, VT: Storey, 1998.

Page, John. *Grow the Best Tomatoes.* Vol. 189 of *A Storey Country Wisdom Bulletin*. Pownal, VT: Storey, 1998.

Verrier, Suzanne. *Rosa Rugosa.* Buffalo, NY: Firefly Books, 1999.

Cooking

Stinging Nettles

⁂ by Suzanne Ress ⁂

Having grown up in the north-eastern United States, I was well aware of the threat, whenever I ventured into the woods, of poison ivy contacting my skin. But it was not until I was an adult, living in northern Italy (where there is no poison ivy), that I fully realized the lesser, but still quite nasty, survival tactics of the stinging nettle plant.

Stinging nettle (*Urtica dioica*) grows throughout North America and Asia, as well as in Europe. It is perennial but dies down to the ground in the cold months and is reborn every spring, spreading over an ever-greater area by underground rhizomes. It often grows along streams and river-banks and in uncared-for places such as empty lots and beside hedges and walls. It starts out small in the early spring and reaches a height of two or three feet by the time it blooms in late summer.

Its pointy heart-shaped leaves are serrated and seem dry, almost crackly, with a deep green on top and lighter green underneath. When the plant blooms, its flowers are small light green clusters.

If your bare leg brushes against a stinging nettle plant by mistake, you won't know it right away—it takes about twenty seconds before the plant's poison, injected into your skin by hundreds of miniscule hypodermic needle-like structures on the leaves called trichomes, takes effect. At first you'll feel a burn and then about thirty seconds later an irritating tingle that can last several hours. The nettle plant has injected into your skin a mixture of neurotransmitters (histamine, acetylcholine, and serotonin), which cause inflammation and pain, and acids (formic, tartaric, and oxalic), which are believed to cause the extended duration of the tingly feel.

I applaud the first daring soul who found a way to eat stinging nettles. Not only are they edible, but they are also a delicious spring treat packed full of nutritional value. A small portion of nettles (100 grams or 3.5 ounces cooked) contains only 42 calories but has 28 percent of the US recommended dietary allowance of fiber, 40 percent vitamin A, 48 percent calcium, 14 percent magnesium, 9 percent iron, 9 percent potassium, 39 percent manganese, and a whopping 623 percent vitamin K, which is necessary for blood clotting.

Traditionally, nettles have been used to treat urinary tract infections, stimulate appetite, help milk flow in nursing mothers, reduce rheumatic problems and susceptibility to colds, staunch diarrhea, and purify the blood as a general spring tonic.

Young spring plants, gathered with gloves on your hands, can be used raw, dried to make teas and infusions, or cooked and used in almost any recipe that normally calls for spinach.

Once the plants are near to blooming, leave them alone. Although they can still be eaten cooked, they lose their tender delicacy, so allow them to bloom and be wind-pollinated for next year's crop.

In Scotland spring nettles have long been used to make an oatmeal and nettle porridge called "nettle kail," considered very healthy and used to treat all sorts of ailments.

When you collect wild nettles, make sure they have not been sprayed with pesticides. Avoid picking nettles that grow along roadsides, where, in addition to having possibly been sprayed, they will have absorbed toxic fumes and who knows what else. It is especially important when you are going to consume the nettles raw that they are clean. As usual, wear gloves to collect them and take only the tops of young spring plants.

Nettle Tea

The simplest stinging nettle recipe is tea. In the months of March, April, and May in the Northern Hemisphere look for the young plants low to the ground, and, using your gloved hands, pinch off only the top clusters of leaves. A couple of handfuls of leaves will be enough for a pot of tea.

Steep the fresh leaves in freshly boiled water for 8 to 10 minutes, and then strain and enjoy as is or with honey, lemon, sugar, or milk. The used leaves will not sting.

Nettle Pesto

2 cups (packed) fresh nettle leaves

½ cup walnut halves

2 spring onions, white parts only, sliced

½ clove garlic

½ cup extra-virgin olive oil

½ cup grated parmigiano reggiano

Salt and pepper

Wearing rubber gloves, place all the nettle leaves, stripped of their stems, in a food processor, and add the walnut halves, spring onions, garlic, and a couple tablespoons of the olive oil. Pulse until everything becomes finely chopped, and then slowly add the rest of the oil while pulsing until it becomes a course paste. Now scrape it into a bowl and stir in the grated parmigiano and the salt and pepper to taste.

Immediately before using, add 1 to 2 tablespoons of boiling water (from the pasta or vegetables you are cooking to use it on) to thin and heat it. Do not directly heat the pesto! Mix in freshly cooked hot pasta or vegetables such as cubed boiled potatoes, green beans, or zucchini. Stir well and serve. This pesto can also be used as a sauce for fish, meat, poultry, or tofu.

Although the nettles are used raw, their sting is rendered innocuous by the chopping, which destroys the leaves' trichomes.

Nettle and Onion Dip

Revitalize the beloved classic onion dip by making it with healthier ingredients.

2 cups packed fresh nettle leaves

1 cup plain Greek yogurt

1 cup crème fraîche

½ ounce onion soup mix (about ½ envelope)

Bring a small amount of water to simmer in a saucepan with a lid. Wearing gloves, toss in the nettle leaves, cover, and simmer about five minutes. Drain them well and let cool. Squeeze out any excess liquid with your hands (you don't need gloves once they are cooked), and chop them on a cutting board.

Put the yogurt and crème fraîche into a bowl and mix well. Add ½ ounce onion soup mix and stir thoroughly, and then stir in the chopped, cooked nettle leaves. Cover and refrigerate for a couple of hours. Serve with crudités or potato chips.

Nettle Soup

2 tablespoons butter

3 potatoes, cut into small cubes

1 quart vegetable broth

2 cups packed fresh nettle leaves

2 tablespoons freshly snipped chives

Freshly ground pepper

Gently melt the butter in a soup pot. Add the cut-up potatoes; stir them around and sauté gently for about 5 minutes. Add the broth and turn up the heat to medium. Bring the soup to a gentle simmer and let it simmer this way for 7 minutes. Using a potato masher or a fork, mash up about half the potatoes to thicken the soup. Wearing gloves, toss the nettle leaves into the pot. After 3 minutes at a simmer, turn off the heat, stir in the snipped chives and some freshly ground pepper, and serve piping hot with fresh crusty bread. Serves 2 to 4.

Beans with Nettles

  2 tablespoons olive oil

  1 clove garlic, minced

  2 cans (12 ounces each) white beans, great northern or
     cannellini

  ½ cup dried tomatoes, roughly chopped

  2–3 cups packed fresh nettle leaves

Heat the olive oil in a big frying pan and briefly sauté the garlic, being careful not to let it brown. Add the beans and some
of their liquid (reserve the rest in case you need it). Throw in
the dried tomatoes and simmer gently for a few minutes to
blend the flavors and soften the tomatoes. Add more bean liquid if necessary. Then, wearing gloves, toss in the nettles, stir
it all together, and put a lid on the pan. Simmer 5 minutes
more. Season with freshly ground pepper and serve. Serves 4.

Mushrooms and Nettles

  2 tablespoons butter

  2 to 3 cups button mushrooms, sliced

  ½ clove garlic, minced

  2 to 3 cups packed fresh nettle leaves

  Salt and pepper

Melt the butter and sauté the mushrooms together with the
garlic, until the mushrooms are soft and brown and have given
up their liquor. Wearing gloves, toss in the nettle leaves and
sauté 5 more minutes. Add salt and pepper to taste. Serves 2.

Nettle Kraut

Fermented vegetables are easy to make, tasty, and useful in
maintaining a healthy digestive tract. Adding nettles to sauerkraut makes it especially vitamin and mineral rich.

1 head Chinese cabbage

2 cups packed freshly picked nettle leaves

1 tablespoon noniodized salt (sea salt or Himalayan)

Cut the cabbage in half lengthwise, then in quarters. Remove the cores and then slice it finely by hand. Put the sliced cabbage into a large bowl. Wearing rubber gloves, slice all the nettle leaves, in bunches, into strips. Add these to the bowl. Sprinkle on 1 tablespoon salt, and, with your gloved hands, massage the salt thoroughly into the vegetables. The slicing and rubbing action will remove the stinging trichomes from the nettle leaves. Leave the vegetables for 10 minutes and then check to see if liquid has formed in the bowl. If not, add another ½ tablespoon of salt and massage again.

Once liquid has formed, still wearing your gloves, place 1 handful of vegetables at a time into a 1-quart glass mason jar, pressing it down with a pestle after each handful. Pack all the vegetables tightly into the jar, leaving at least 2 inches of space at the top, and then lay, but do not screw, the lid on.

Once or twice a day press the vegetables down again with a pestle, making sure the liquid covers the vegetables. After 7–14 days, depending largely on air temperature, the kraut should be sufficiently fermented. Screw on the lid and store in the refrigerator for up to 6 months. Serve as a side dish or condiment as you would regular sauerkraut.

Nettle Frittata for Two

2 tablespoons butter

1 medium onion, chopped

2 cups packed fresh nettle leaves

5 fresh eggs, beaten

Salt and pepper

Heat the butter in a frying pan until melted, then add the chopped onion. Cook gently until the onion begins to look soft and slightly clear. Then, wearing gloves, add all the nettles and stir them around for 1–2 minutes until they wilt.

Turn the heat up to medium and pour in the eggs. As the edges of the frittata begin to cook, lift them gently with a spatula and tilt the pan so that the uncooked egg in the middle runs underneath. Continue this way for about 5 minutes until the frittata is nearly cooked. Then season with salt and pepper and cover the pan for 2 more minutes so the top of the frittata will cook completely. Voilà! Serve hot.

Risotto with Nettles

This is a classic spring dish in northern Italy.

    2 tablespoons olive oil

    1 onion, finely chopped

    1 garlic clove, minced

    2 cups Arborio rice

    ½ cup dry white wine

    1 quart vegetable broth

    2 cups packed fresh nettle leaves

    1 tablespoon butter

    ½ cup freshly grated parmigiano

    Freshly ground pepper

Heat 2 tablespoons olive oil in a large, wide pan and add the chopped onion. Sauté gently until it is limp and nearly clear. Then add the minced garlic and sauté for 1 more minute.

Pour all the rice into the pan. Stir it thoroughly and then leave it to toast for 1–2 minutes.

Toss in ½ cup good dry white wine and let it evaporate, enjoying the perfume.

Next, pour in 1 cup broth and stir the rice. When the broth has been absorbed, pour in a second cup, and then, after it is absorbed, ⅓ cup broth and all the nettles. Wearing gloves, stir the nettles into the rice, and when the liquid has been absorbed, add 1 more cup of broth. By the time this final cup of broth has been absorbed by the rice, about 18 minutes should have passed since you put in the first cup. Don't overcook the rice!

Turn off the heat and add 1 tablespoon butter, grated parmigiano cheese, and some freshly ground pepper. Leave the risotto to rest, uncovered, for 5 minutes. Give it a good stir and serve. Serves 4.

Buon appetito!

Resources

Culpeper, Nicholas. *Culpeper's Color Herbal.* Edited by David Potterton. New York: Sterling, 2002.

Rodale's Illustrated Encyclopedia of Herbs. Edited by Claire Kowalchik and William H. Hylton. Emmaus, PA: Rodale, 1998.

Stewart, Amy. *Wicked Plants: The Weed That Killed Abraham Lincoln's Mother & Other Botanical Atrocities.* Chapel Hill, NC: Algonquin Books of Chapel Hill, 2009.

How to Make Chèvre: Easy and Rewarding Cheese Making at Home

⫷ by Corina Sahlin ⫸

My head rests against my goat's side, and the only sound I hear is milk squirting into the stainless steel bucket. I love this morning routine: stumbling out of bed, walking to the barn through grass wet with dew, hearing the goats chewing hay and greeting me excitedly because they know their breakfast is coming. I was born and raised in Southern Germany, where cows and goats graze on alpine pastures and award-winning cheese and yogurt are made in mountain huts of wood and stone. I was brought up with the tastiest, freshest cheese and milk you can imagine, and I suppose that's why I always wanted to raise my own goats.

This dream came true after I moved to America when I was twenty years old. Ten years later I met and married my husband, and we homestead on five acres in the Pacific Northwest wilderness, where we raise goats, pigs, ducks, chickens and three homeschooled kids. Over the fifteen years of living on our homestead, I have made thousands of pounds of cheese, and I want you to know that you can make cheese too. I mean that! I have taught hundreds of people how to make cheese, both on my homestead and online. Almost all of them successfully make cheese with store-bought milk. Many people wouldn't dream of attempting to make cheese because they think it's too complicated. Once you make one batch of cheese, you will become addicted to the alchemy of the cheesemaking process—and the delicious taste!

In this article I will teach you how to make chèvre, a French-style soft goat cheese and one of the easiest cheeses to make. You can make it with cow milk, but then it's not called *chèvre* (meaning "goat" in French) but farmer's cheese. Chèvre is a creamy, spreadable cheese that tastes wonderful with herbs and spices added to it. You can also use it for desserts paired with fruit, and it can be used like cream cheese, since it has the same consistency. My vanilla cheesecake made with chèvre is out of this world!

Common Misconceptions about Making Cheese at Home

You might assume you need your own dairy animals or raw milk to make cheese. That is not true. Although I raise my own dairy goats and use their raw milk for making cheese, most of my students buy pasteurized cow milk at the store and make wonderful cheese with it. Of course, if you can purchase milk from a local farmer, that's even better!

You might worry that you need to buy expensive equipment to make cheese, but this could not be further from the truth. In fact, many people already have the utensils they need in their kitchen: stainless steel pots, stirring utensils, a knife, a colander . . . Instead of buying expensive molds and cheese presses, you can easily make your own. (I have a YouTube tutorial on how to do this on my channel.)

You might think making cheese is a really complicated, scientific process. Nah! People have made cheese for thousands of years—first sloshing around milk in containers made from animals' intestines and then with soured milk pressed between cloth under heavy rocks. With good instructions, making cheese is as easy as reading and following a recipe.

You might be scared of making your family and friends sick with your homemade cheese. Salmonella, *E. coli*, food poisoning . . . Many folks are really scared about food safety—as they should be. It's smart to be safe when it comes to food. People are intimidated by canning, but if you follow good instructions and practice sound sanitation, making and preserving your own food is safe.

Benefits of Making Cheese at Home

Cheese making is a fun, rewarding, and empowering skill and a way to take charge of your food supply. Do you want to feed your family cheese made with milk that may have antibiotics, growth hormones, and pesticides? We don't. It is a good idea to support organic farmers by buying their milk in the store or directly from their farm. Organic milk makes healthy, tasty cheese! But have you looked at the price tag of some organic cheeses out there? They are high, and they should be because a lot of resources, knowledge, and skill go into this cheese.

Making your own cheese saves you lots of money, and I also believe that making my own cheese gives me a better-tasting product. It's fresher, creamier, and better than store-bought. Also, I can make some really unique cheese, such as chèvre flavored with sage, nettles, or caraway seeds—combinations you can't find at the store.

One last benefit of making your own cheese at home is impressing your family and friends! People will think you're the Big Cheese when you whip out a chunk that you made all by yourself. Let's get started!

Step-by-Step Instructions for Making Chèvre

I will show you how to make this yummy cheese with either five quarts of milk (which will make about two pounds of chèvre) or two quarts of milk if you don't want to use as much milk. Before we get started, let me tell you some tips.

Although I make every other type of cheese raw (I also make gouda, cheddar, manchego, and tomme), I pasteurize the milk for this cheese. It sits around at room temperature for a long time, so the risk of bacterial contamination increases, and pasteurization makes it safe. Its shelf life is longer that way as well—you can keep it in the fridge for two weeks.

I pasteurize the milk at a low temperature (145 degrees Fahrenheit), which is better than high pasteurization temperatures. This lower temperature preserves beneficial enzymes and keeps the proteins in the milk intact. It's the closest to a raw milk product you can get. If you buy pasteurized milk at the store, please don't purchase ultra pasteurized milk. This process heats milk at very high temperatures, which damages the calcium and proteins needed for cheese making and hinders the coagulation process.

Chèvre freezes well, so when you make a batch, eat some right away fresh and then freeze the rest in half-pound packages. Make sure you freeze it unsalted without any herbs and spices added. Thaw it at room temperature and then add seasoning.

For many years I made chèvre with cheesecloth, but now I use special chèvre molds for draining the whey. Buying molds is more expensive than buying cheesecloth, but it's worth it. I get more consistent results with the chèvre molds, whereas draining with cheesecloth can leave the cheese rubbery because it drains unevenly. If you are in love with chèvre and feel like you will make it a lot, it's worth buying chèvre molds. If you just want to try to make this cheese to see if you like it and you don't want to invest in molds, use cheesecloth.

I recommend visiting www.cheesemaking.com and www.getculture.com for purchasing cultures, rennet, cheesecloth, and molds. This is what you will need to make a regular batch of chèvre (directions for a smaller batch are in parentheses):

5 quarts goat milk (or 2 quarts), not ultra pasteurized
Thermometer
¼ teaspoon MM 100 culture, freeze dried (or ⅛ teaspoon)
⅓ cup cool water (or ¼ cup)
3 drops rennet (or 1 drop)
1 teaspoon salt (or ½ teaspoon)
Stainless steel pot to fit the amount of milk
8 chèvre cheese molds (or 4) or muslin cheesecloth
Eye dropper

If you choose to pasteurize the milk, heat it to 145°F and keep it at that temperature for 30 minutes. Cool it down to 80°F. I put the pot of milk in a sink filled with cold water. If you are in a hurry, change the water frequently or add ice to the water bath.

Sprinkle MM 100 culture over the milk and let it rehydrate for two minutes, then stir it into the milk. Use ¼ teaspoon MM 100 culture with 5 quarts of milk, or use ⅛ teaspoon MM 100 culture with 2 quarts of milk.

Add rennet: for 5 quarts of milk, add 3 drops of rennet with a clean eyedropper or syringe to ⅓ cup cool water. Take 2 tablespoons of this diluted rennet mixture and stir it into the milk for 30 seconds. For 2 quarts of milk, add 1 drop of rennet to ¼ cup cool water. Take 2 tablespoons of this diluted rennet mixture and stir it into the milk for 30 seconds.

Cover the pot and let it sit at room temperature for 8 to 12 hours. At the end of that time, a firm curd will have formed (it looks like thickened yogurt), and you will see some clear whey on the top of the curd. I often start this cheese in the morning, and then it's ready to drain in the evening. Or I start it in the evening, and it will sit overnight, ready to be drained in the morning. Do whatever works for your schedule.

Next, drain the curd. If you use chèvre molds, carefully place curd into them with a ladle. Try to be as gentle as possible with this step. Fill the molds all the way to the top. When you get to the bottom of the pot, there will be a lot of whey. Drain this out into a bowl to save the whey for other uses (make bread with it, feed it to the chickens, or dilute it with water and water your plants). Make sure to catch every last bit of the curd to place into the chèvre molds. If you use cheesecloth, make sure you use a very fine cheesecloth called butter muslin. Some people use a clean pillowcase cloth. Drape the cloth over a colander sitting on a bowl to catch the whey. Carefully pour the curds into the cloth. Be gentle.

Let the cheese drain for 8 to 12 hours. The longer it drains, the drier it will be. If you want your cheese more moist, drain it for a shorter time. When you like the texture, put it into a bowl and add 1 teaspoon salt for every 2 pounds, or just add salt to taste. Mix it with fresh or dried herbs. The options are endless! I like using garlic powder, chopped chives, or parsley and spreading it on bread or crackers. I also use chèvre in lasagna instead of ricotta cheese. You can use it in recipes asking for cream cheese or add fruit to it and make it into a dessert.

Herbed Chèvre

1 tablespoon lemon zest, minced

¼ cup minced fresh parsley

1 tablespoon minced fresh thyme (or 2 teaspoons dried)

1 tablespoon minced fresh oregano (or 2 teaspoons dried)

1 tablespoon minced fresh rosemary (or 2 teaspoons dried)

⅛ teaspoon freshly ground black pepper

8 ounces chèvre

Mix the lemon zest and all herbs and spices together. Form the chèvre into a log and roll it in the herb mixture.

Honey Lavender Chèvre

2 tablespoons honey

8 ounces chèvre

1 tablespoon fresh lavender blossoms

Mix the honey into chèvre and then roll it into a log. Sprinkle lavender over it.

Parsley, Marjoram, and Dill Chèvre

    1 tablespoon chopped fresh parsley

    1 tablespoon chopped fresh marjoram (or 2 teaspoons
        dried)

    2 teaspoons chopped fresh dill (or 1 teaspoon dried)

    Black pepper to taste

    ¼ cup toasted walnuts or almonds (optional)

    8 ounces chèvre

Stir together all ingredients and serve packed into a bowl or
formed into a log or balls. You could even top the cheese with
some chopped toasted walnuts or almonds.

Vanilla Cheesecake

This recipe is adapted from a vanilla bean cheesecake featured
in a Williams and Sonoma baking book and makes one nine-
inch cheesecake.

For the crust:

    1 cup honey graham cracker crumbs (about 9 crackers)

    4 tablespoons unsalted butter, melted

    2 tablespoons sugar

    ¼ teaspoon grated nutmeg

    ½ cup walnuts, pecans, or almonds

For the filling:

    2 pounds chèvre (unsalted, unseasoned), at room tem-
        perature

    1 cup sugar

    3 large eggs, at room temperature

    1 tablespoon vanilla extract

    Juice of 1 lemon, strained

For the topping:

> 2 cups sour cream
>
> ¼ cup sugar
>
> 2 teaspoons vanilla extract

Make the crust first. Preheat oven to 350°F and move the oven rack to the middle. In a food processor or blender, break the graham crackers into fine cracker crumbs, then add butter, sugar, nutmeg, and nuts. Process until everything is finely ground and mixed thoroughly.

Butter the bottom and sides of a 9-inch springform pan. Pour the crumb mixture into the pan and press it evenly into the pan bottom with your hands. Bake the crust until it turns darker brown and smooths out, about 10–12 minutes. Transfer the pan to a wire rack and let it cool completely. Reduce oven heat to 325°F.

To make the filling, use a hand mixer to mix the chèvre on low speed until creamy. Add the sugar and mix slowly until smooth. Turn off the mixer and scrape down the bowl and beater with a rubber spatula. Add the eggs one at a time, beating on low speed after each addition. Scrape down the bowl and add vanilla and lemon juice. Mix again on low speed until smooth and creamy. Don't mix too much; otherwise, the cheesecake will sink in the middle after it's baked.

Place the springform pan with the cooled crust on a half sheet pan and pour the batter on top of the crust. Cover the cake pan with a pot lid or another cookie sheet to insulate the cake while it bakes. Bake the cheesecake until the center jiggles very slightly when the pan is gently shaken, 45 to 50 minutes. If the center looks soupy, cover the cheesecake again and bake for a few minutes more.

Meanwhile, make the topping. In a small bowl, combine the sour cream, sugar, and vanilla. Stir well. Cover with plastic wrap and set aside at room temperature until needed.

Remove the cheesecake from the oven and uncover it. Carefully pour the topping around the edge of the cheesecake. Using a small spatula, gently spread the topping out evenly over the entire surface of the hot cheesecake. Do not press down too hard or the topping will sink into the cake.

Cover the cheesecake again, return it to the oven, and bake for another 5 minutes just to set the topping. Transfer the cheesecake to a rack and let it cool covered for 1 or 2 hours. Remove the lid or sheet pan. Cover the cooled cheesecake with a large plate and refrigerate overnight. If you are in a hurry to eat it, put it in the freezer for 2 hours.

To unmold, release the springform pan sides, opening them wide so that they fall away from the cake. Set the cheesecake on a serving plate and serve chilled. Store in an airtight container in the fridge for up to 5 days—but I guarantee you it won't last that long!

Hidden Treasures of the Garden: The Joys of Root Vegetables

by Dawn Ritchie

A love of the soil was instilled in me as a youngster. It began with a simple gesture. An invitation to tug at a sprig of green shooting up from the ground. Out came a long, glistening carrot, surely as surprised as I, to witness its first glimpse of sunlight. With a quick brush of the fingers, the dirt was swept away and my mother bade me eat that carrot right there. Unwashed, unpeeled, wild, and feral. The sweet, crunchy flavor thrilled my immature palate. It was still of the earth.

Root vegetables are the garden's hidden treasures, brimming with flavor, nutrition, and the inexplicable secrets of the soil, where mysterious invertebrates make their lairs. There's something about root vegetables that brings out the untamed in us. Maybe it's because we instinctually know, deep in our un- spoken DNA, that we are all a part of the earth and will one day belong to it too.

The Joys of Root Vegetables

Roasted, fermented, boiled, grilled, poached, pickled, deep fried, broiled, baked, mashed, grated, sliced, and raw. These culinary approaches all work for root vegetables, but when it comes to soups, it's a marriage made in heaven. We'll explore that, but first, heat up your oven.

Roasted Roots: The Mélange

A sure-fire winner when you are serving a hot meal is the low-impact, time-saving medley of root vegetables that I call the mélange. Primarily because I enjoy saying *mélange* in a bad French accent, but, truthfully, this dish of roasted roots deserves that affectation because it can accompany virtually any main entrée, be it meat, fish, chicken, or vegetarian. It also creates lovely eye candy when dressed around the entrée.

6–8 multicolored carrots (red, yellow, orange, and purple)

3 leeks (white ends and 2 inches of green)

8–10 cloves garlic

8 shallots

1 onion

1–2 turnips

½ rutabaga (optional)

1 parsnip

3 potatoes (choose colorful varieties or French finger-lings)

2 beets (try a combination of yellow beets, 'Chioggia', or traditional 'Detroit Dark Red')

4 tablespoons extra-virgin olive oil

Sea salt

Freshly ground pepper

Sprig of fresh thyme for garnish (pinch of dried will substitute)

Clean, peel, and slice the vegetables lengthwise. This creates a more sophisticated presentation than cubed vegetables. Leave skins on the potatoes.

Gently toss the veggies in a bowl with extra-virgin olive oil, a generous sprinkling of sea salt, and freshly ground pepper until fully coated. Toss beets last.

Spread the mixture on a foil-lined cooking tray. Roast in a 400° oven for 30 minutes or until caramelized, stirring occasionally. Keep an eye on it; some ovens are hotter than others. There's a fine line between caramelized vegetables and burnt vegetables.

Finish with a sprig of fresh thyme. A drizzle of balsamic vinegar doesn't hurt either. Serve warm. Serves 4 as a side dish.

Planting a Root Vegetable Garden Is an Act of Freedom

With the first blush of spring, something sparks our senses. We have an innate hankering to dig and plant. Legions of vegetable gardens are born during this frenzy, only to be abandoned to the weeds when vacation activities take hold.

Herein lies the advantage of planting a root plot. They are slow growers. The longer you leave them in the ground, the sweeter the vegetable and heartier the harvest. Plant seeds and bulbs in the spring and reap the rewards in the fall just as the impending fallow of winter has you gazing wistfully at that garden again.

I have planted root plots and left them to the whims of Mother Nature all summer long and have still gleaned a harvest. Root vegetable plots are pure freedom. Plant one!

What to Plant

Plant what you enjoy eating and one thing each season that you've never tried before. Always expand your horizons. Must-haves include onions, shallots, carrots, beets, turnips, radishes, potatoes, leeks, and garlic. For the more adventurous: Jerusalem artichokes, daikon, ginger, rutabaga, parsnip, celeriac, turmeric, and more.

Preparing the Soil

Root vegetables require good tilth. Their roots grow downward. If the soil is too compacted, vegetables will either eject themselves upward or remain stunted. Gardeners with compacted soils have three options: use a double dig method to pull out hard pack and dig in fresh compost, sand, and organic matter that will allow for aeration; build a raised bed; or use pots.

Seeds

Direct seeding is the best option for most root vegetables. For around ten dollars you can buy enough seeds for several seasons of radishes, carrots, beets, rutabagas, parsnips, and turnips. Compare that to what you pay for a single bunch in a store.

These are the descriptors to look for on seed packets: non-GMO, heirloom, organic, open-pollinated. You won't always get all these goodies altogether, but non-GMO is crucial. Begin with a seed that has not been genetically modified to withstand pesticides. "Better that a crop fail than be compromised from the start" is my motto.

You can purchase seeds or acquire them for free through seed libraries and neighborhood seed exchanges. An internet search will reveal those seed swaps. They occur early, before planting season. Swaps are excellent sources, not only because the seeds are free but also because they are most often collected by passionate organic seed savers who source rare and heritage varieties.

Seeds lose their effectiveness after several seasons.
Plant twice as many old seeds as new ones.

Bulbs

Some root vegetables are better begun by planting bulbs, tubers, corms, or crowns. You can purchase onion seeds, for instance, but the failure rate for direct seeding is high. They'll need to be started indoors about two months before the last frost.

It's best to buy "sets" if you are a beginner. These are those little mini onion and shallot bulbs that you see hanging in bags at garden centers, sure to guarantee a crop.

If you choose to grow horseradish or ginger, you'll want to get a piece of root. Plant the wider end toward the sunlight for horseradish. Be forewarned, however: these roots are travelers. They trek underground and can overtake your whole plot if you don't isolate them.

Radishes

These fellas are your first harvest. Pop those seeds in the ground as soon as soil is workable. Don't settle on just the standard round cherry radish. Try something exciting, like the 'French Breakfast' radish—a long, sleek, mild radish. Also, plant daikon. It comes up later in the season and is shockingly huge. The black Spanish radish is hot (!) and considered a liver cleanser. You'll also find heirloom Chinese watermelon radishes that have a shocking-pink interior, icicle radishes, and colorful Mardi Gras radishes. Who knew the radish family could be such a party? Don't limit yourself. Go wild! Make happy salads.

If a seed potato has multiple eyes (little sprouts coming out of the potato), you can cut it up and plant each chunk with an eye separately. For every seed potato you plant you'll reap an average of eight.

Potatoes

Buy certified seed potatoes from a garden center or seed catalog. Look for gourmet and heirloom varieties. You'll see the wisdom of this when you make your mélange. Purple and red potatoes really perk up a dish. Don't plant potatoes purchased at grocers. They are often sprayed to prevent them from producing eyes that could become offspring.

Plant potatoes deep. Dig a trench, lay a seed potato in, eyes pointing upward, and cover with several inches of soil. As stems grow up to ten inches, mound soil up around the base

leaving the leaves exposed to sunlight. It's called "hilling up."
The higher the hills, the more potatoes. Harvest in late fall.

Leeks

Leek, oh glorious leek! What a blessing you are for gourmets everywhere. Leeks also arrive late in the fall and, along with the potato, make a soup that angels have surely sung about. With a little butter, cream, leeks, potatoes, and chicken stock, you can produce this delectable chilled soup called *vichyssoise*. A dash of fresh chive atop and you are a celebrity chef.

Vichyssoise

The prevailing wisdom in making this soup is to use a two-to-one ratio of leeks to potato: two leeks, one potato. Extrapolate from there. Personally, I prefer more tender leeks and usually go three to one. The soup is quick to make but needs time to chill.

Leeks

Pat of butter

Potatoes

¼ cup heavy cream per multiple of 2 leeks to 1 potato ratio

1–1½ teaspoon salt

Chicken stock or water to cover, plus several inches

Clean and finely chop the white part of the leeks only. Peel and chop potatoes.

Sauté leeks in butter in a soup pot on medium low until translucent. Do not brown! Add potatoes, 1 teaspoon of salt, and enough stock to cover plus 2–3 inches. Boil until potatoes are fork soft (about 30 minutes).

Puree (I use my smoothie blender). Add ¼ cup heavy cream for each multiple of the 2 to 1 ratio of leeks to potatoes, to the consistency you prefer. I like a thinner soup; you may prefer thicker.

This soup has a subtle flavor. Serve cold with chopped chives dressing the top. Divine!

Carrots

Sandy, loamy, deeply dug soil makes carrots happy campers. Space rows twelve inches apart and seeds one inch apart. Carrots also grow well in deep twelve- to fifteen-inch pots. Keep watering consistent. 'Imperator' is the standard carrot you find in stores, and 'Nantes' is perfect for home gardens. But add colored carrots to your seed purchases. They are less sweet but visually interesting.

If you're not a digging enthusiast, plant 'Paris Market' carrots, which produce hilarious round balls about an inch in size. They are perfect additions for your roasting pan of beef or chicken, just after juices are flowing. Add other root veggies and you have a one-pot meal.

Carrots are best eaten roasted or raw and are not so fabulous boiled, unless you are making a curried carrot or carrot ginger soup.

Carrot Ginger Soup

    8–10 carrots

    1 onion

    1 clove garlic

    1 thumb peeled fresh ginger root, minced (or 1 teaspoon ground ginger)

2 tablespoons olive oil

1 teaspoon salt

6–8 cups broth of your choice

1 tablespoon of lemon or orange juice

Dollop of crème fraîche (optional)

Sauté vegetables in oil in a soup pot. Add salt. Add broth and cook until fork soft. Add more broth for a thinner soup. (If you add too much fluid, don't worry—you can always cook it down. Just stir often and keep an eye out for burning.)

Puree with stick blender or food processor in batches. Season to taste. That splash of lemon or orange juice brightens the flavor. For a creamy touch, top with crème fraîche. Serve warm. Serves 2.

I serve this soup with toast points and chèvre drizzled with garlic-infused olive oil. Yum!

Garlic

Fall is the season to plant garlic. It rests underground during winter and sends up green shoots in spring. Leave it to grow all summer long and harvest in the fall after leaves wilt. For bigger garlic bulbs, snap off the garlic scapes before they produce flowers. You'll know what scapes are when you see stems shoot up and twirl between the leaves. Your garden is dancing! Don't throw them out. Chop finely and add to stews or salads.

When the harvest comes in, it is time to make garlic aioli (garlic mayonnaise). Mash 3–4 garlic cloves with a mortar and pestle. Slowly add a steady, thin drizzle of olive oil, pinch of salt, and dash of lemon juice until emulsified. The longer you pound, the better. It's a workout! Perfect on boiled or poached veggies with fish, aioli will rock your world.

Horseradish

Kick those free radicals to the curb with this high–vitamin C condiment that delivers flavor and mega health benefits. Horseradish is not only the perfect accompaniment to roast beef and oysters on the half shell, but it is also a powerful antioxidant. It belongs to the genus *Brassica,* and the broad leaves are also edible in small measure. But too much of a good thing could mean tummy aches for some due to the spicy enzymes.

Plant horseradish root in the spring and isolate it to a corner if you have a small garden. Horseradish is a perennial. It returns year after year. Harvest the spindly roots in autumn. Peel, pulverize in a food processor, and incorporate with a two-to-one water and vinegar solution, a touch of salt, and pinch of sugar, and you have produced flavor and heat for your winter dishes. Amazing on hamburgers and toasted brie sandwiches.

Beets

The beet is a marvelously versatile root vegetable that can be enjoyed hot or cold or even fried as chips. The leaves are packed with nutrients and are fabulous in salads, soups, and stews. Plant in spring and harvest baby beets and greens throughout the summer and full-sized beets in the fall.

Caution: Beets stain linens, stone countertops, and fingers. Wear rubber or latex gloves during prep to keep your fingers from turning red. Wipe up spills quickly.

If you've never had borscht—the mother of all root vegetable soups—now's the time. I had my first taste of the ruby-red potage on a Russian cruise ship—the MS *Aleksandr Pushkin*—en route to Europe in my youth. Authentic and memorable.

Borscht is easy to make and uses numerous other root vegetables right when the harvest is overflowing. Traditionally, onions, potatoes, beets, and carrots, but anything else you dare—turnips, broad beans, and so on. I always add cabbage to stay with tradition. In this basic recipe, the earthy flavor of beets is ameliorated by a strong dose of red wine vinegar that freshens. With a finishing dollop of sour cream and a fistful of crusty bread, you have a satisfying fall soup course fit for peasant or king.

Borscht

　　1 onion, finely chopped

　　1 carrot, peeled and shredded

　　1 tablespoon butter

　　6 cups beef broth (beef base bouillon in a pinch)

　　1½ cups shredded cabbage

　　½ tomato, peeled, seeded, and finely chopped

　　3–4 beets, peeled and cubed or sliced lengthwise into
　　　　bite-size pieces

　　1 potato, peeled and cubed

　　1 clove garlic, minced (optional)

　　1 bay leaf

　　3–4 tablespoons red wine vinegar

　　1 teaspoon salt

　　Large dollop of sour cream to finish

　　½ teaspoon fresh dill

In a medium saucepan, sauté onion and carrot in butter. Pour beef broth into a pot and simmer. Add the vegetables, garlic (optional), and bay leaf and cook on medium low for 35–40 minutes. Remove bay leaf. Add vinegar. Season with salt to taste.

Serve with sour cream topped with fresh dill. Attractive and satisfying. Serve hot or cold. Serves 3 to 4.

Food for Thought

❧ by Monica Crosson ❧

"Sometimes," my mom would say to me when I was a child, "I think I'd forget my head if it weren't attached." This was usually communicated to me during times she was experiencing stress. Those late nights when she would be simultaneously decorating three dozen holiday cupcakes for my class, cleaning up for a 4-H meeting to be held at our home the following day, and putting the finishing touches on costumes for a church pageant. And as a child, I would agree because she was old (all of about 35), and losing your mind is what happens when old age hits you.

I never thought I would have to worry about what I later came to know as "brain fog" or "fuzzy thinking." I was the child my parents referred to as their human day planner. "Monica," my mom would say while preparing dinner with a phone wedged between her cheek and shoulder, "Don't let me forget about the baby shower next Thursday."

"Got it, Mom," I would answer.

I never forgot a name, birthday, event, or item on the grocery list that I kept filed in the little Rolodex in the back of my mind. You need the phone number of our local bakery? let me think about it . . . Yep, here it is. Another thing I was exceptional with was directions. I had a knack for memorizing landmarks when we traveled as a family.

But something happened in my late forties, around the time menopause crept up on me. My Rolodex containing a lifetime of names, birthdates, phone numbers, freeway exits, and events began to blur. I started forgetting items from my internal grocery list. Then baby showers and barbecues would sometimes slip right by me, leaving me feeling like a complete idiot when I showed up with belated gifts days or weeks later. And forget about learning names! The pièce de résistance came when I took my daughter to South Seattle for a house concert. It was dark when we left, so it was hard for me to find the landmarks I had so clearly memorized. To top it off, my cell phone had died, so my backup plan of using its GPS to get us back to the freeway had failed. I drove around and around, mumbling about streets that, under the glare of sodium lights, seemed like they should have led me back to the freeway.

"Are we lost, Mom?"

I started to cry. "I don't know. This is so stupid. No, we're not lost—I'm just confused. I should be able to get out of here. I don't know what's wrong with me lately. I'm such a basket case. I swear I'd lose my head if it weren't attached."

Chloe laughed.

"What's so funny?"

"Well, you're starting to sound like Grandma."

"I do sound like my mom." I cried harder. "Grandma was right, though—age makes you crazy."

"We should ask for directions, Mom." My daughter patted my hand.

"Why didn't I think of that? Oh, Chloe, I just thought of something. What if I have dementia?"

Chloe shook her head.

Fog on the Brain

I ended up doing a little research and found out that, no, I didn't have dementia and that cognitive issues, such as memory loss, lack of concentration, disorganization, and lower attention span are very common among women going through menopause.

In fact, studies show that women struggle the most with memory loss during the first year after their last period, according to the *Harvard Gazette*. And though experts don't know why menopause brings on cognitive issues, it is believed to be due in part to declining estrogen levels. According to research, estrogen works with areas in the brain that affect verbal memory and executive function. In addition, all those other neat side effects of menopause, such as hot flashes, depression, and trouble sleeping, can also affect our ability to focus.

It's not just menopausal women who experience brain fog—the hormonal fluctuations during pregnancy can also impair cognitive abilities. Elevated cortisol levels in people who suffer chronic stress affect reasoning and memory. And chronic fatigue syndrome, a puzzling medical condition that usually strikes women between the ages of thirty and fifty, can cause reduced cognitive abilities accompanied by extreme lethargy, muscle aches, a recurring sore throat, and tender lymph nodes in the neck and armpits. Let's not leave out the multitaskers. People who have too many irons in the fire are also susceptible to cognitive issues.

There is no miracle drug for brain fog, but there are things we can do to alleviate the symptoms naturally, including relaxation, deep breathing, exercise, reducing stress, limiting alcohol and caffeine use, getting enough sleep, and eating a healthy diet rich in antioxidants.

Brain Food

The food we eat plays a vital role in our cognitive health. Our brain matter is mostly made up of lipids (fats); the rest is made up of glucose, amino acids, proteins, and micronutrients. Foods high in antioxidants and omega-3 fatty acids not only help create and maintain new cell membranes, but they may also help prevent degenerative brain conditions. If eaten continuously, foods high in trans fats, found most often in fried and processed foods, can compromise brain health and worsen memory.

Another thing to consider is our stress factor: our bodies don't like stress. When we're stressed out, little chemicals prompt our immune system to kick in and fight back through inflammation. While inflammation is the body's natural response mechanism that helps protect and repair it, chronic inflammation can cause harm. It's been linked to autoimmune diseases like multiple sclerosis, anxiety, and high blood pressure. So how does this link to food? Through our gut!

Our gut produces hormones that help keep our body's immune responses and inflammation under control. Also, gut hormones that enter the brain influence cognitive ability. So, sticking to a diet rich in vitamins, minerals, and antioxidants is good not only for our bodies but our minds as well.

Here is a list of foods that may help alleviate brain fog:

Beets: Most people I talk to have bad memories of these jewel-toned root vegetables that have lingered from a childhood of beets that came out of a can and tasted like tinny dirt. Which is too bad, because beets are one of the most healthful foods you can eat and are super easy to grow. Beets are chock full of vitamins, minerals, and cancer-protecting antioxidants. They also contain natural nitrates that increase blood flow to the brain. Try baking beets to bring out their sweetness, add them to salads, or make them into chips.

Broccoli: Vitamin K and choline make this vegetable a perfect brain food that helps keep your brain sharp. It also contains high amounts of vitamin C and is full of fiber. Broccoli is great in stir-fries, soups, or salads.

Blueberries: These sweet little powerhouses are one of the most highly concentrated sources of antioxidants and contain vitamin C, vitamin K, and fiber. They are also a good source of gallic acid, which helps protect our brain from deterioration and stress. Try them in a smoothie, sprinkle them over your morning cereal, or eat them frozen for a cool summer snack.

Celery: Who knew a vegetable that packs so few calories could be so good for you? With high amounts of antioxidants and polysaccharides, celery acts as a natural anti-inflammatory. When cooking with celery, don't forget the leafy tops. They add a great flavor to soups and sauces.

Coconut Oil: This versatile oil works as a natural anti-inflammatory, can help with memory loss, and helps destroy bad bacteria in your gut. Use coconut oil in baking, soups, or smoothies.

Dark Chocolate: Yes! I love it when one of my favorite foods is good for me! Chocolate's anti-inflammatory and antioxidant secret is flavonols. They can also help lower blood pressure and improve blood flow to both the brain and heart.

Leafy Greens (Spinach, Chard, Kale): Your mom was right about eating those greens! Loaded with vitamin K and A, leafy greens are great for fighting inflammation and for keeping bones strong. Also, a recent study shows that people who eat one or two servings of greens per day may experience lower mental deterioration. Use generously in lasagnas, salads, and stir-fries.

Olive Oil: Polyphenols found in olive oil may improve learning and memory and help reverse age-related changes to the brain. The best way to take advantage of olive oil's benefits is by using it at room temperature. It begins decomposing at high temperatures. Use in dressings, marinades, and sauces.

Pumpkin: A wonderful antioxidant and a great source of fiber, pumpkin is an anti-inflammatory that is beneficial for tissue repair and stress. The fruit also contains L-tryptophan, which aids in depression. The seeds are chock full of zinc and magnesium, which play an important role in stress and cognitive health. Use the fruit for pumpkin pie or in soups and stews. Sprinkle the seeds over yogurt or use in baking your favorite bread.

Rosemary: A favorite herb in Mediterranean cooking, rosemary contains carnosic acid, which helps protect the brain from neurodegeneration. High in antioxidants and anti-inflammatory properties, it's good not only for the brain but for your eyesight as well. Use rosemary in soups and stews, with potatoes, or baked with roasted garlic in bread.

Salmon: High in omega-3 fatty acids, salmon is the ultimate food for brain power. Eating salmon regularly can help increase focus and improve memory. Try salmon smoked or grilled.

Tomatoes: What makes tomatoes a super brain booster is the lycopene, a phytonutrient that gives tomatoes their bright red color. Lycopene may delay the onset of Alzheimer's disease and dementia by correcting brain cell corruption and protecting healthy cells. Use in sauces or slice for salads or snacking.

Turmeric: Turmeric is an ancient root that has been used for centuries for its healing properties. Known to increase oxygen intake, turmeric may help you stay alert and process information. Curcumin, a chemical compound found in this root, helps make it a powerful anti-inflammatory as well. Use turmeric in chicken dishes or in tea.

Walnuts: With a high amount of vitamin E, antioxidants, and minerals, walnuts make a great snack that can also improve your brain power. Use them in trail mixes, add them to baked goods, or throw a few in a smoothie.

Cognitive Health Garden

Many of the foods included in my list can be easily grown in your backyard garden or in containers on a patio or balcony. Imagine stepping just outside and gathering nutritious and healing foods to add to your recipes. Here are my picks for your very own garden for cognitive health:

Beets: Preserve beets by pickling them in a brine of honey and cider vinegar for snacking all year long. 'Red Ace' is a fast-maturing variety that boasts red-veined greens. This variety is sweet and may become a new family favorite.

Blueberries: Ranking number one among fruits and vegetables for antioxidant activity, blueberries are a must for any backyard gardener, and dwarf varieties that can be planted in containers make it possible for anyone to enjoy their benefits. 'Top Hat' is a compact two-foot plant perfect for containers. White flowers in the spring turn to dusky-blue fruit in the late summer.

Broccoli: A member of the cabbage family, one ounce of broccoli has an equal amount of calcium to one ounce of milk. 'Arcadia' is a great cold-tolerant variety with large, domed heads and excellent side-shoot production.

Chard: 'Bright Lights' is a beautiful, lightly savoyed variety that has beautiful stems of pink, yellow, red, and white. It is a consistent grower and slow to bolt.

Celery: Are you up for a gardening challenge? Give celery a try. This marshland plant is a heavy feeder and requires a lot of attention, but the rewards are definitely worth it. 'Tango' is known to perform better under less than desirable conditions, 'Tango' is a vigorous plant that grows stalks that are less fibrous than other varieties.

Don't think you have enough room to grow your favorite squash? Not to worry, trellising your vining plants is a great space saver.

Kale: 'Siberian,' though not quite as cold hardy as other varieties, is a vigorous, high-yielding variety sweeter than most.

Leafy Greens: Greens are easy to grow and pack a nutritious punch. Best of all, you can find varieties that can be grown for every season.

Pumpkin: 'New England Pie' pumpkin produces fruit weighing four to six pounds with bright orange stringless flesh. Because it's not as sweet as other varieties, it works great for both sweet and savory dishes.

Rosemary: If you live in a warmer plant hardiness zone (zone 8 and over; see page 221), rosemary can be grown as a fragrant hedge. For colder zones, try growing it in a container. 'Tuscan Blue' in warmer climates will grow four to six feet tall and three feet wide. It boasts beautiful dark blue flowers and has excellent flavor.

Spinach: 'Indian Summer' is a hybrid variety with smooth leaves that is slow to bolt and a three-season producer. 'Teton' is a hybrid that can be grown all year long in mild-winter areas. This beauty has deep green leaves and is slow to bolt.

Tomatoes: Nothing beats the flavor of homegrown tomatoes, and they're perfect for containers. 'Amish Paste' is a beautiful heirloom 'Roma'-style tomato juicier than most paste tomatoes. It can be used in healthful sauces or sliced and tossed into your favorite salad. It's large for a sauce tomato, averaging eight to twelve ounces.

Be Good to Yourself

Once I realized that my bouts with brain fog were a normal part of the aging process, I was better able to take control of the situation and create a game plan to alleviate my symptoms. Taking daily walks, shifting my diet, and letting go of extra, unnecessary obligations all helped me relieve stress and nurture my maturing body and mind.

So, whether you are dealing with hormonal changes due to pregnancy or menopause, are experiencing unexpected life changes that create stress, or have too many irons in the fire, remember to take care yourself with nutritious food and self-love. Your body and your mind will thank you for it.

Selected Resources

Bridger, Haley. "Changes in Memory Tied to Menopausal Status." *Harvard Gazette*. September 27, 2016. https://news.harvard.edu/gazette/story/2016/09/changes-in-memory-tied-to-menopausal-status/.

Farr, Susan A., et al. "Extra Virgin Olive Oil Improves Learning and Memory in SAMP8 Mice." *Journal of Alzheimer's Disease* 28, no. 1 (2012): 81–92. doi:10.3233/JAD-2011-110662.

Goldhill, Olivia. "Brain Food: 6 Snacks That Are Good for the Mind." *Telegraph*, January 23, 2015. https://www.telegraph.co.uk/news/science/science-news/11364896/Brain-food-6-snacks-that-are-good-for-the-mind.html.

Gómez-Pinilla, Fernando. "Brain Foods: The Effects of Nutrients on Brain Function." *Nature Reviews Neuroscience* 9, no. 7 (2008): 568–78. doi:10.1038/nrn2421.

Weber, Miriam, Mark Mapstone, Jennifer Staskiewicz, and Pauline M. Maki. "Reconciling Subjective Memory Complaints with Objective Memory Performance in the Menopausal Transition." *Menopause* 19, no. 7 (2012): 735–41. doi:10.1097/gme.0b013e318241fd22.

Herbal Tonic Syrup

☙ by Emily Towne ❧

Human creativity has brought to life a dazzling array of botanical flavors and combinations. The vital role of plants in our lives has been embedded in our cultural evolution since before recorded history; the role of herbs in beverages has never been more powerful nor their ever-evolving story so intriguing. Herbal tonic syrups bring to life the brilliance of our collective botanical history, giving us a product that is at once ancient and unapologetically modern. Many herb-based beverages that began as curatives endured and evolved over the centuries into some of the contemporary beverages we know today, alcoholic and otherwise. Tonic syrups are part of this heritage.

Historical Origins of Tonic Water

First, the cinchona bark. When the bitter bark of the Peruvian cinchona tree, chewed by indigenous peoples to cure fevers, was shared with Europeans in the 1600s, a long and circuitous journey that would endure for centuries had begun. *Cinchona* is genus of flowering evergreen shrubs and trees native to tropical America, several members of which are used for medicine. Chewing its bitter bark extracted quinine, an alkaloid that treats malaria. Quinine became the go-to malaria medicine around the world and is still used today. It is listed by the World Health Organization as an essential and safe medicine. Synthetic quinine was developed during WWII.

In the 1800s British officials stationed in Colonial India, where malaria was endemic, began to add soda water and sugar to their doses of bitter cinchona bark powder. This magic trick gave us tonic water. To further increase palatability, adding readily available gin and lime was the obvious next step, creating the iconic gin and tonic still enjoyed around the world today.

While few of us have had cause to use quinine as a curative, most of us have enjoyed a gin and tonic with its quintessential bitter flavor. Commercial tonic waters contain synthetic quinine, though a few companies use the real thing. Most commercial tonic waters also contain high fructose corn syrup or other synthetic sweeteners, citric acid, sodium benzoate, and natural flavors. These modern ingredients make for a shelf-stable mass-produced product, but they are also largely derived from genetically modified corn, which also contains pesticide and herbicide residues. For these reasons, many have found the impetus to seek out more authenticity.

Tonic Syrups and Creative Cocktails

The rejection of factory-made, mass-produced products combined with a penchant for handcrafted goodness led to do-it-yourself tonic waters. The unending search for novel flavor experiences fueled the addition of herbs and exotic botanicals into the mix, thus creating beautiful and delicious tonic syrups, the next step of this enduring botanical journey. Readily available ingredients from local and online sources have opened up a world of flavor options to craft bars, distilleries, do-it-yourselfers, and farm-to-table restaurants, which are producing their own signature herbal tonic syrups. Herbs, berries, barks, seeds, flowers, grasses, and spices have never been more creatively employed. Far from their roots as a bitter medicinal, these sweet, nuanced syrups are a delight to the most sophisticated palate. They can be customized to individual preferences with truly endless possibilities. Combined with club soda or another sparkling water of choice, we've entered a new era of gin and tonics, craft cocktails, and creative nonalcoholic beverages.

Various brands of tonic syrups are available commercially, but why not seize the opportunity to create your own unique elixir? Mix up a batch and enlist a friend to help you taste-test it. Nothing ensures quality quite like doing it yourself.

Learning to make your own tonic syrups is a satisfying way to expand your herbal repertoire and fuel your creative urges. Once you have established the basic concepts of formulation and technique, you are on your way to creating your very own signature recipe. Through trial and error, I created the recipe on page 123, which has a nuanced flavor profile as well as a delightful color. Store-bought tonic syrups are a luxury item to purchase, as are many of the ingredients to make your own. However, most items on this ingredient list go a long way and allow you to make multiple batches once you've made the investment. I enjoy using home-grown herbs, which cuts down on what I need to purchase.

Creative cocktails and nonalcoholic beverages are both easily concocted using this tonic syrup. In keeping with the spirit of tonic's origins, I use gin as my spirit of choice for this article. Many gins are very juniper-forward in flavor, but there are other options as well. Feel free to use your favorite and experiment. To accompany the tonic syrup recipe here, I prefer an overtly floral gin (imagine drinking a flower), such as gins by Uncle Val's. Other good options include gins from Pinckney Bend, which are complex and citrus-rich, and Prairie Organic Spirits, which are certified organic and have more subtle flavors with notes of melon and pear. These smaller-batch gins support American farmers and use clean ingredients.

Herbal tonic syrups make great gifts!
Bottle them in a pretty bottle, add your own creative
label, and share with friends. Maybe they will
thank you with a creative cocktail.

The following tonic syrup recipe contains prominent citrus notes, so I generally opt for herbs and flowers for a garnish rather than the traditional slice of lime. Any edible flower, herb, or spice may be added as a garnish. My favorite is a sweetly aromatic nasturtium flower floating serenely on the surface of my orange-hued cocktail. It is pleasure for the eye, nose, and palate. Also delightful are sprigs of lavender, rosemary, and leaves from the herb garden, such as mint, basil, or stevia, slapped in your open palm to release their essential oils before placing them on the surface of the cocktail. Juniper berries, peppercorns, or whole cloves add aromatic pungency, while rose petals and cucumber slices introduce floral delicacy. The idea is to complement the botanical tones of the particular gin with a well-chosen garnish.

Choosing Quality Ingredients

Tonic syrups are comprised of three basic components: cinchona bark, herbs and botanicals, and sweetener. The first two components are combined together in one step; the sweetener is added later to that mixture.

In order to create the highest quality product, you must source top-notch ingredients. When possible, I opted for organic ingredients, sometimes from my own garden. This is especially important when choosing citrus in order to avoid pesticide residue and wax coatings. Only the zest of the citrus is used; I juiced the remaining citrus for later use so as not to waste its goodness.

All of the recipes in my research included citric acid as an ingredient. Citric acid comes as a white powder resembling sugar and is often added to products as a preservative or flavor enhancer. I sourced a version that was not genetically modified, readily available online, and experimented with amounts. I found that less is better. Too much citric acid resulted in an extremely sharp, overtly citrus product that masked the more delicate flavors of the botanical ingredients. I also tried a batch with no citric acid but ruled it out as too bland.

What differentiates tonic syrup from simple syrup or other flavored syrups is the inclusion of cinchona bark, which provides quinine's essential bitterness. This slight bitter flavor is what makes tonic water so appealing and what pairs so well with spirits. Cinchona bark is available from a number of online sources and comes in cut pieces, as a powder, or as an extract. Powders have more surface area and therefore less can be used, but they are also more difficult to strain out of the final product. I used the cut bark, which is chunky and easier to strain. I used *Cinchona officinalis*, which is the most readily available variety and lends a beautiful red-orange tint to the finished product. I strained the final product through a sieve lined with butter muslin. Coffee filters may also be used.

For the sweetener component, I used unbleached, minimally processed (without bone char) granular sugar, which lends a slight tint to the syrup. Any sugar of preference may be used. Some recipes call for agave syrup, but I chose not to use it in order to keep my tonic syrup less processed. I experimented with a basic simple syrup, which is a one-to-one ratio of sugar to water, but felt that it was not quite as sweet as I would like it to be in the finished cocktail. I ended up with a richer sugar syrup that more fully enhanced the flavors of the herbs and botanicals.

Making a Batch in Your Home Kitchen

There are quite a few ingredients in this recipe that were fun to source and experiment with. If you are not able to find them locally, try online. Some ingredients can be substituted, or omitted, but the final results will not be the same. The cinchona bark is essential as it provides the bitterness of quinine and is what makes it tonic syrup. Several ingredients came from my own herb garden and my personal cache of dried flowers, which I preserve all season long. Make sure to allow plenty of time to make the recipe. I find that it helps to first assemble and measure all the ingredients and zest the citrus before mixing everything together. Be prepared to fall in love with the intoxicating aroma that will fill your kitchen!

Herbal Tonic Syrup

    1 inch piece of cinnamon stick

    ¼ teaspoon rosewater

    1 dried whole peony flower

    5 dried fragrant whole roses

    3½ cups water

    ⅓ cup cinchona bark

    ⅓ cup chopped lemongrass (fresh or dried—I used dried)

    Zest of 2 oranges

    Zest of 3 lemons

    Zest of 3 limes

    4 whole allspice berries

    4 whole cardamom pods, slightly crushed

    1 tablespoon dried lavender flowers

    1 tablespoon dried hibiscus flowers

    5 juniper berries

    ¼ teaspoon grains of paradise

    ¾ teaspoon orris root

    1 tablespoon citric acid

    ¼ teaspoon salt

Set aside the cinnamon stick, rosewater, peony, and roses. Add the rest of the ingredients to a medium cooking pot. Cover the pot with the lid slightly askew to capture steam. Bring the pot to a boil over a medium to high heat, stirring well to mix all ingredients. Maintain a medium boil for 5 minutes, stirring occasionally and being careful to not scorch ingredients. Reduce heat to a low simmer and simmer for 15 more minutes with lid askew, stirring occasionally. Add the cinnamon stick, rosewater, peony, and roses and continue to simmer for 5 more minutes. Remove from heat and stir well. Allow it to steep in the covered pan for another 30 minutes, up to 60. Strain mixture through a sieve lined with butter muslin or a coffee filter. Allow it to sit for 20 minutes to completely drain. Restrain the liquid through another clean filter if necessary. Pour it into clean glass jar.

Sugar Syrup

Boil together 3 cups sugar with 2½ cups water until sugar is dissolved (about 5 minutes), stirring occasionally. Remove from heat and pour into a separate glass jar.

In a clean jar, combine 2 parts herbal tonic syrup with 1 part sugar syrup. Taste and adjust to your preference. Herbal tonic syrup may be stored in a glass jar or other fancy bottle of your choice. Keep refrigerated. This syrup will keep in the fridge up to 2 weeks.

Gin and Herbal Tonic Syrup Cocktail

To a tall, chilled glass with ice, add 1 shot gin and 1 shot tonic syrup, and then top off with club soda. Adjust amounts of each ingredient to individual preference. Garnish with flower or herb of your choice. Sip away!

Nonalcoholic Tonic Syrup Beverage

Add 1–2 shots herbal tonic syrup to club soda or any sparkling water of your choice. Flavored sparkling waters, such as lemon or lime and coconut, are a nice choice. Garnish and enjoy!

Introduction to Bento Making

❧ by Deborah Castellano ❧

The simplest definition of a bento is any food that is eaten from a box. While the word *bento* is Japanese, it can also be applied to American-style food for lunch. The easiest example of a bento to conjure in our minds is the bento box lunch special that comes in a large tray at a Japanese restaurant and has rice, some kind of sushi, some kind of fried meat or teriyaki protein, little dumplings (*shumai*), and usually some orange slices. Delicious and fun, but a lot of prep when you don't work in a restaurant. There is also the style of bento for which the goal is to make something incredibly artistic but edible using the bento box as the canvas. This is also time-consuming, though beautiful to look at. And then there is the

most common use of the word *bento*, which means a packed lunch using a small box that's pretty on the eyes and nutritious in the tummy. If you have a child who is a picky eater, bentos are meant to entice them to eat things they would usually turn their noses up at. Bentos are also great for adults to be mindful of portion control.

You don't need an actual bento container to make a bento meal. There are lots of companies that make little plastic dressing containers that can be used for your lunch sauces. If you do want to get in there and use a modern authentic bento box with as many little compartments as you could possibly wish for, Amazon has a wide range of bento boxes, many for less than twenty dollars. Bentgo makes some cute boxes for adults and children alike. In the land of bento accessories, you can usually find cute reusable plastic toothpicks at baking supply shops. Little cookie cutters go a long way to add some fun, reusable silicone cupcake liners in different colors and sizes will spice up a bento box nicely, and *onigiri* (rice ball) molds are available very inexpensively online as well. If you live near a Japanese market, shop for bento boxes and accessories as well as some bento staples if you are making Japanese-style bento boxes for your lunch.

When assembling your box, choose a protein, such as a hard boiled egg, salmon, wedge cheese, rotisserie chicken, deli meat, almonds, dried meat, bacon, leftover meatballs from the night before—whatever sounds good to you. Then choose a starch, such as rice, bread, pasta, or leftover mashed potatoes. Then choose a vegetable, such as cherry tomatoes; carrots or cucumbers cut into shapes; snap peas; zucchini spirals; mushrooms; and fresh herbs such as parsley, fennel, basil, chives, dill, or rosemary to make your bento look and taste more interesting. Finally, choose some delicious fruit for your bento, such as blueberries, strawberries, pineapple, grapes, or bananas. Think about your bento box and the accessories you have for it. How can you put it together in a way that will be visually interesting to you while still giving you (or your family) enough energy to make it until dinner? Remember, how you choose to arrange the food makes it more fun to eat.

Tomato and Sausage Kebab Bento

1 link sausage of your choice (Italian pork sausage, breakfast sausage, chicken sausage, tofu sausage, etc.)

6 cherry tomatoes

6 basil leaves

3 strawberries, halved

½ banana, sliced

Edamame (soybeans), shelled with a little salt

Sliced cucumbers

Cook the sausage in a skillet or on the grill. Slice the sausage. Use toothpicks to spear the cherry tomatoes, basil, and the sausage into mini kebabs. Do the same with the strawberries and bananas. Place the edamame in a silicone cupcake liner and the sliced cucumbers in another.

California Sushi Bento

1 tablespoon rice seasoning (see page 130)

2 cups cooked brown rice

½ cup canned crab

½ avocado, cut into crescents

½ cucumber, cut into circles

Soy sauce

1 lemon wedge

1 tablespoon rice vinegar

Mix the rice seasoning with the rice. Make a bed in your bento box with your rice. Arrange the cucumber in a row on top of the rice. Arrange the avocado and crab in rows as well. Add a lemon wedge and a small container with soy sauce.

Bento Roll-Ups

4 slices of your favorite deli meat, vegetarian soy deli slices, cheese, or vegan cheese

Blueberries

Cherry tomatoes

¼ cup vanilla yogurt

1 dash cinnamon

Roll the deli meat or veggie slices and stand them up in the box (cut in half if need be). Around the rolls, arrange silicone cupcake liners and put blueberries, cherry tomatoes, and yogurt that you've sprinkled with cinnamon into each.

Stars and Moon Bento

2 slices of cheese or vegan cheese

Round crackers

1 dash cinnamon

1 apple, sliced into crescents

1 tablespoon nut butter or sunflower butter

1 clementine, peeled and sectioned

Cut stars out of the cheese and alternate them with crackers. Sprinkle cinnamon on the apple. Put the apple slices, nut butter, and clementines each into a silicone liner. Dip the crackers or apples into the nut butter.

Everything but the Wine Bento

    Carrot sticks

    Sugar snap peas

    Raspberries

    Grapes

    Baby kale

    Parsley

    Cubes of your favorite cheese

    Small breadstick crackers

    Small slices of salami

Put the carrots and snap peas into a cupcake liner and the raspberries and grapes into another. Put down a bed of baby kale and parsley into the bento and arrange cheese, crackers, and salami on top.

Traditional Bento Staples

Now that you've played with some basic recipes and ideas, let's delve deeper into bento so that you have even more recipes to add to your repertoire. Rice is typically at the very beginning of bento box making. I will give you some standards and some variations that I like. Let's start simply, with some easy mix-and-match ideas you can use to make a healthy Japanese-style bento.

Sushi Rice

    1 cup sushi rice

    2 cups water

    ¼ cup rice vinegar

    2 tablespoons sugar

1 tablespoon sesame oil

1 teaspoon salt

Rinse the rice in a colander under some cool water until the water is clear. Combine rice and water in a medium pot and put on medium heat on the stove. Bring to a boil and then cover and cook on low heat for about 20 minutes or until the rice is tender and the water has been absorbed. Remove rice from heat and let it sit uncovered while it cools.

In another saucepan, mix the rice vinegar, sugar, sesame oil, and salt together on medium heat until the salt and sugar have dissolved. Once the mixture is dissolved and the rice is cool enough to touch, start adding the mixture to the rice little by little while stirring. Keep stirring until the rice has absorbed most of the liquid. Optional: add rice seasoning to the rice for added color and zest!

Rice Seasoning

¼ cup raw white sesame seeds

¼ cup raw black sesame seeds

3 sheets *nori* (seaweed), shredded into small pieces

1 tablespoon sea salt

3 tablespoons tomato flakes

Mix all the ingredients in a 1-pint mason jar, sealing the lid and shaking it. Then pour the ingredients into a dry skillet on medium heat. Shake the skillet until your ingredients are all toasted, let the mix cool, and put it back into the mason jar.

Cauliflower Rice

1 tablespoon sesame oil

2 cups riced raw cauliflower, drained

1 tablespoon rice vinegar

3 tablespoons rice seasoning

Heat the sesame oil in a large skillet on medium heat. Add the riced cauliflower to the skillet. Use a spatula to move the rice around constantly while cooking for about 5 minutes. Add the rice vinegar. Cook for another 2–3 minutes. Add the rice seasoning. Remove from heat and serve.

Teriyaki Tofu

1 block extra firm tofu, pressed to remove excess liquid

Salt to taste

Oil for frying

1 teaspoon honey

1 teaspoon low-sodium soy sauce

½ teaspoon sesame oil

Slice the tofu into ¼-inch pieces. Sprinkle salt on both sides of the tofu to your taste. Heat an oiled frying pan to medium heat. Pan fry the tofu until it is golden brown on both sides. Whisk together the honey, the soy sauce, and the sesame oil in a bowl. Heat the sauce in the pan on low and add the tofu, coating the tofu on both sides in the sauce. Remove from heat and serve.

Sesame Noodles

¼ cup low sodium soy sauce

1 teaspoon sriracha

2 tablespoons rice vinegar

4 tablespoons sesame oil

1 tablespoon garlic paste

12 ounces whole wheat noodles, cooked and drained

4 green onions, diced

In a small bowl, whisk together the soy sauce, sriracha, rice vinegar, sesame oil, and garlic paste. Pour over the noodles. Sprinkle the green onion on top. Makes 4 lunch-sized portions.

Baked Chicken Katsu

    1 tablespoon olive oil

    1 cup panko bread crumbs

    ½ pound thin chicken cutlets

    Salt and pepper to taste

    2 tablespoons flour

    1 large egg

Preheat the oven to 400°F. In a bowl, combine the olive oil with the panko bread crumbs. In a frying pan on medium heat, fry the breadcrumbs until golden brown. Put them in a paper towel–lined bowl to drain. Let cool. Make a few slits in your chicken cutlets so they won't curl up. Salt and pepper the cutlets to taste. Put the flour in a small bowl with a little salt and pepper. Beat the egg in another small bowl with some salt and pepper. Dredge your chicken in the flour and then dip it on both sides in the egg. Dip the chicken into the panko, pressing on the chicken so the panko sticks. Put on a baking sheet in the oven for 20 minutes. Remove from heat and serve.

Overnight Pickled Plums

    1 pint mason jar and lid

    ½ cup rice vinegar

    ¼ cup white vinegar

    ¼ cup dark brown sugar

    2 tablespoons salt

    ½ pound small ripe plums, cut in half

2 cloves

1 star anise pod

1 teaspoon cinnamon bark

½ teaspoon pink peppercorns

1 teaspoon fennel seeds

Run the mason jar and lid through your dishwasher or boil for five minutes. In a saucepan, combine rice vinegar, white vinegar, sugar, and salt until dissolved. Let cool for 30 minutes. In the mason jar, add the plums, cloves, star anise, cinnamon, pink peppercorns, and fennel seeds, being sure to leave at least 1–2 inches of room at the top. Pour the liquid into the jar, leaving a little room at the top. Seal the jar. Put in the refrigerator for at least 1 night, preferably 3. Good for 2 weeks; keep refrigerated.

Curry in a Hurry

1 apple, diced

2 purple carrots, diced

1 sweet potato, sliced

¼ cup canned chickpeas, drained and rinsed

1 quart vegetable stock

3 tablespoons sesame oil

4 tablespoons flour

1 tablespoon soy sauce

2 tablespoons mild yellow curry powder

Put the apple, carrots, sweet potato, chickpeas, and vegetable stock in a pot. Cook on medium heat until vegetables are tender, about 20 minutes. Make a roux in a small saucepan by heating the sesame oil and slowly adding flour to it until it forms a soft ball. Add the soy sauce and the mild yellow curry powder. Add a little bit of the vegetable stock at a time to the roux until the ball starts dissolving. Once it's a thick liquid, add it to the vegetables and stock. Simmer for 20 minutes. Serve over a bed of rice.

Japanese Soft-Boiled Eggs

- ½ cup water
- 2 teaspoons honey
- 2 tablespoons rice vinegar
- 2 tablespoons low-sodium soy sauce
- 2 eggs

Combine water, honey, rice vinegar, and soy sauce in a small glass container. Bring a small pot of water to a boil on medium heat. Carefully put the eggs in the pot. Reduce heat. Cook for 7 minutes. The eggs shouldn't move in the pot. If they do, the water is too hot. Carefully take the eggs out and submerge in an ice bath for 3 minutes. Gently peel the eggs. Submerge your eggs in the small glass container with sauce. Cover and put the container in the refrigerator overnight. Cut eggs in half lengthwise to serve them the traditional way. Eggs will be good for 3 days; keep refrigerated.

Health
and
Beauty

Four-Tier Herbal Formulary

❧ by Holly Bellebuono ❧

One of the most eye-opening (and lighthearted) assignments I give my students in my herbal medicine school is to open their medicine cabinets, pull out any tinctures or herbal remedies they have purchased, and review the label. From the list of ingredients, they try to determine if the manufacturer used a method or reason for including the herbs in the bottle. Often, my students puzzle over a long list of herbs that appear to serve the same function or seem to be fillers or included for taste. They learn that there is actually a very logical method for including herbs in a remedy, and while most commercial producers ignore this, herbalists can easily apply this method—what I call

the four-tier formula—to make better and more effective healing remedies.

Despite its high-school-chemistry-sounding name, **formulary** is simply a way to structure your thoughts when combining herbs into a remedy; it's a way to categorize a plant's actions to determine if it should be used for a client or patient for a particular illness or situation and then combine herbs based on those actions. Formulary involves pharmacology, anatomy, and chemistry, as well as intuition and a connection to the person in need. It is a very creative and fulfilling endeavor; there are as many ways to do it as there are herbalists and healing traditions. Many traditions, including Ayurveda and Traditional Chinese Medicine, have perfected their own healing philosophies and methods for formulary, using a solid understanding of how herbs work in a formula. Many also include the ideas of using simples (one single herb at a time) or polypharmacy (the practice of combining more than one herb to create a blend). No one formula is right for every culture or every person, though the four-tier formula is a good starting point when learning how to think about creating your own blends or including herbal medicine in your practice.

Given that there are so many plants to choose from, my students find it immensely helpful to use the four-tier formula structure to narrow down the vast possibility of herbs to a concise few. Many of my students have been relieved to learn how to think about formulary this way because it gives them a practical platform for organizing all those useful herbs. Overwhelmed herbalists ask, "Should I include this herb because it seems relevant? Or perhaps this one? My client needs a soothing demulcent herb. Should I give her mallow or aloe or slippery elm? How do I know which herb will be most beneficial?

Could eight herbs be better than four? Can there be too many, or should I throw in everything but the kitchen sink?" The sensible structure of the four-tier formula helps narrow down all those potential herbs to the few that will be most effective.

For the practitioner who is new to herbs or wants to increase his or her knowledge of using plants for health, formulary can seem overwhelming. We have access to literally hundreds, if not thousands, of herbs around the world that have dozens of actions, chemicals, and stories attesting to their uses; combine this with the fact that an herb can be used in one way in Western herbalism and in an opposite way in India's Ayurveda, and there are countless ways a new herbalist might be confused when creating a new tea blend or tincture. Which herbs are best for which ailments, and which are contraindicated? How much of this herb compared to that one? What about secondary symptoms and other issues? Here is where formulary shines and where the handed-down knowledge of plants really gets exciting. Blending different plants together to complete a whole medicine with a variety of attributes has long been hailed as a master's-level approach to herbalism, not to mention it's a lot of fun. Formulary brings together empirical knowledge of pharmacology, botany, anatomy, and, for holistic practitioners, a sense of self and intuitive integrity that is central to the healing arts.

Is there a "right" number of herbs in a formula? Some compound formulas combine every herb with a similar action, but remember that too many herbs in a formula can create a burden for the body to process and expel and can actually render a formula weak since the primary herbs are in lesser quantity. Rather than think about the ideal number of herbs, consider the action of the herb itself, the needs of the patient, and what herbalism has the most to offer:

- Specific curative effects for organs, body systems, and acute illnesses
- Sustainable modulating effects for chronic issues
- Preventive nutritive support for long-term nourishment

Four is not a magic number, but it allows the herbalist to bring in herbs with various actions as tonics, for specific disease support, for corollary issues, and with organ systems in mind. This framework provides a creative springboard from which almost any remedy can be created, a launching pad from which you can adjust or enhance any given treatment for the most effective and nourishing remedies possible. Feel free to use this as a base for your crafting to develop and pursue your own methods.

Four-Tier Formulary

First, begin with understanding an herb's many actions. Its **actions** are those properties or qualities that an herb has on an organ or system of the body. It's what an herb does. For example, motherwort (*Leonurus cardiaca*) has several actions: it is nervine, cardiotonic, and bitter. This means motherwort can be used in situations when someone is feeling anxious, is experiencing hypertension, or has indigestion. Ideally, motherwort's actions will overlap to help someone experiencing a range of related issues: motherwort is perfect for a person who is so nervous or anxious that she gets an upset stomach and a racing heart.

Plant actions are at the heart of herbal medicine and formulary. Learn that sage is astringent and antibacterial and antifungal. Learn that peppermint is aromatic and carminative and too many more actions to list. Slippery elm is demulcent; calendula is emollient. By educating yourself about an herb's actions, you will learn all the ways it can be used in various situations. I encourage my students to keep an action notebook with pages titled (in alphabetical order) astringent, bitter, carminative, emmenagogue, immunomodulating, sedative, tonic, and so on. There are scores of actions attributed to herbs, and keeping such a journal helps the herbalist categorize which herb does what and how its many actions overlap.

Once you know an herb's actions, you can apply the herb to the proper category in the four-tier formula, as follows:

Tier 1: Tonic
Tier 2: Specific
Tier 3: Corollary
Tier 4: Vehicle

These are straightforward categories that form the basis of every formula. In other words, each remedy you make will contain one herb that is tier 1, one herb that is tier 2, and so on, making for a four-herb remedy. As you become comfortable with this structure, you'll be able to add on and substitute to customize remedies for your clients and patients.

Tier 1: The Tonic

The foundation of my formula structure is nourishment, which is the **tier 1 tonic**. Tier 1 herbs are meant to be taken long-term to nourish, support, and sustain. Many tier 1 herbs are precisely those that we enjoy drinking as teas or infusions every day because they are delicious, mineral-rich, and "energizing" (though no tier 1 herbs contain caffeine). Examples of tier 1 herbs are lemon balm, nettle, red clover, alfalfa, ashwagandha, oatstraw and milky oat tops, gotu kola, vervain, ginkgo, red raspberry leaf, violet leaf and flower, holy basil (tulsi), and hawthorn. Tonics are safe, plentiful herbs that are not endangered or at-risk (consult United Plant Savers for more information about at-risk herbs); they contain few phytochemicals (such as alkaloids) that could render them "active" or "curative" medicines; and they almost always are rich in the nutrients our bodies need, such as calcium, potassium, iron, and magnesium.

Generally, tier 1 tonic herbs can be consumed safely, often as foods, and can be taken for weeks, months, or even years with positive effects. Why would a formula not include a more power-packing remedy for tier 1 when your client is suffering from a viral, bacterial, or fungal infection, a wound or injury, or a mental or other physical illness? Because your client is not only that infection or illness. By addressing the client as a victim, as the illness itself, or as a number (these are common habits in the modern system of allopathic medicine), your client loses self-respect, responsibility for healing, and the impetus and inspiration to get well. Instead, herbalism promotes the care of people, not diseases.

Generally, tier 1 tonic herbs are in the greatest quantity in the formula, usually twice as much as tier 2 herbs. For instance, if nettle is tier 1, it is listed as "2 parts" while peppermint, which might be the tier 2 herb, is listed as "1 part."

Tier 2: The Specific

Tier 2 specifics are the primary herb for any given condition or illness. Specifics are particular to a system of the body, directly influence the body's ability to deal with an illness, or are capable of ridding the body of a disease. Tier 2 herbs include goldenseal for bacterial infection, yarrow for fever, and elderflower or horseradish for sinus congestion. Tier 2 is the closest thing we'll come to in herbalism to a magic bullet. When people feel they are coming down with a cold and think, "I should take echinacea," this is a magic bullet approach. Instead, broaden your approach to include other herbs, one of which (echinacea) may be a tier 2 specific in the formula, working in concert with other herbs to address secondary or corollary symptoms and needs.

Start with the tier 2 specific and build the other tiers of the formula after that. Our minds tend to start with the "magic bullet" approach—the herb that seems most obvious—so let your mind do this and then broaden the formula from there.

The tier 2 herb is also being used with discretion in terms of quantity—often tier 2 herbs will be used in half the quantity as the tier 1 herbs, or even less, though they'll usually be in greater quantity than tier 3 or tier 4 herbs. It's also important to remember that tier 2 herbs won't be used for the same length of time as tier 1 tonic herbs; for example, a person may only need horseradish (tier 2) for a few days, while they'll need the tonic benefits of nettle or elderflower (tier 1) for weeks. Be sure to adjust the formula as needed so that the specific is only being taken when it's actually needed.

Tier 3: The Corollary

Tier 3 corollary herbs can be a versatile bunch. They may (1) address issues that come along with an illness, such as a sore throat from vomiting or painful urination from a urinary tract infection; (2) be bitters to support digestive health; or (3) be warming herbs to support circulation. This tier is sometimes called adjuvant, supportive, corollary, or secondary. Tier 3 herbs can either help the specific herb in its function (i.e., help tier 2), or they can address secondary symptoms that aren't addressed by the tier 2 specific. For example, in the case of a urinary tract infection, fighting infection is the job of the tier 2 specific, but addressing the pain is the job of the tier 3. Echinacea, golden-seal, or yarrow would be an appropriate tier 2, while mallow or calendula would be a tier 3.

In an example of a topical remedy, a formula may be created for a wound that includes calendula as tier 1, yarrow as tier 2, and red clover as tier 3. All three herbs are vulnerary, meaning they help heal wounds. But thinking of red clover as a tier 3 recognizes its soothing effects that are supportive, while yarrow is styptic.

Tier 3 herbs can be warming or bitter. Warming herbs and spices "open up" a person to herbal healing, speeding blood flow and improving both digestion and circulation so that the tier 2 herbs can work most effectively. Warming herbs, such as mustard, cayenne, ginger, clove, and cinnamon, are especially helpful in cold or stagnant conditions, and they can be added whenever there is mental fatigue, blockage, slow movement, or confusion. Bitters make a wonderful tier 3 addition because they naturally stimulate the body toward active digestion, supporting a process central to daily function and indirectly supporting other tiers in the formula.

Tier 4: The Vehicle

Finally, **tier 4** herbs are the **vehicle** or **carrier**, that special herb that has what herbalists call an "affinity" for a certain organ or system of the body. These herbs usher the real workers to the area of the body where they're needed, so to speak. In the case of UTI mentioned previously, I might use yarrow as the tier 4 because it is a diuretic and naturally goes to the urinary tract. Yarrow has multiple actions, making it an overlap herb and ideal for a UTI: it is antibacterial, diuretic, diaphoretic, and bitter. As a vehicle, it will usher other herbs to the urinary system; other vehicles for a UTI include pipsissewa, nettle, and dandelion.

The idea of a vehicle or carrier herb may seem vague at first, but it draws from a lengthy heritage of herbalism and observation of how plants act in the body; it refers to the many instances where plant chemistry closely matches body chemistry and certain herbs really do have a pronounced effect on certain organs or systems. For instance, feverfew and ginkgo act as vasodilators, opening the arteries and vessels and thereby increasing blood flow to the brain; as such, these herbs can be considered tier 2 specifics for a headache, but they can also be tier 4 vehicles when another herb is the specific. Similarly, raspberry has traditionally been considered in herbal medicine as having an affinity for the uterus; in formulas for pelvic inflammatory disorder or uterine cramping, raspberry can be an excellent choice as a tier 4 vehicle. External formulas (for salves or ointments) generally do not require a tier 4 herb.

If there are no practical vehicle herbs, you may leave out the tier 4 altogether or replace it with a tier 2 or tier 3 herb. Generally, the goal should be to use as few herbs as possible to achieve the greatest results. For this reason, look for those multipurpose herbs with actions that overlap—herbs that achieve many results in various body systems. The quantity of the tier 4 herb can be much smaller than the others, one-half to one-fourth the quantity of the tier 1.

Formula Examples

When developing formulas, keep in mind the herbs can all be in the same bottle but don't necessarily have to be. For instance, the tier 1 tonic may be given as a tea throughout the day, while all the other herbs may be in a tincture.

In the following examples, the healing arts practitioner has already learned the actions of the herbs used: we know that skullcap is mildly sedative and nervine, that willow is analgesic, and that feverfew is analgesic and has traditionally been used for its vasodilator effects as a vehicle for the head. Based on these actions and considering the person's symptoms, the following formula makes sense for a mild headache:

A Formula for a Mild Tension Headache

    2 parts skullcap

    1 part willow

    1 part lavender

    1 part feverfew

Similarly, we know that hawthorn, linden, and hibiscus are safe hypotensive herbs (they lower blood pressure) and nervine tonics, that dandelion is diuretic and as such can relieve pressure on the heart, that oats are calcium-rich and nervine, and that motherwort is a great overlap herb for the cardiovascular, digestive, and nervous systems. A couple of good formulas for high blood pressure would draw on these herbs in the following proportions:

A Formula for High Blood Pressure

    2 parts hawthorn

    2 parts linden

    2 parts dandelion leaf

    1 part oatstraw or milky oat tops

Another Formula for High Blood Pressure

    2 parts hibiscus

    1 part hawthorn

    1 part linden

    1 part motherwort

The following is an example of a four-tier formula without a vehicle herb. If desired, a fourth herb that supports the other tiers, such as holy basil (tulsi), dill, or catnip, could be added.

A Formula for Food-Triggered Gas

    2 parts chamomile

    1 part fennel

    1 part spearmint

Next, we'll see elderberry and sage both being used but in different ways; the first addresses sinus congestion, while the second is for a wet cough. Astringent sage is ushered to the sinuses using horseradish as the tier 4 vehicle, while the cough employs wild cherry. Be creative, as there is no one right method, and overlap herbs, such as sage, are very versatile. These formulas can be taken as a tea, tincture, or capsule:

A Formula for Sinus Congestion

    2 parts elderflower

    1 part elderberry

    1 part yarrow

    1 part sage

    ½–1 part horseradish

A Formula for a Wet Cough

    2 parts mullein

    1 part sage

    1 part coltsfoot or elderberry

    1 part wild cherry

Developing this type of formulary will help the healing arts practitioner build a strong foundation for clear, effective, and intuitive remedies. Formulary is one of the most interesting and enjoyable parts of herbal medicine—up there with spending time in a sunny garden or hearing from a client that they feel better. Using creative formulary is a rewarding and effective skill in your herbal repertoire.

Love in a Cup:
Abuelita's Healing Garden

❧ by Thea Fiore-Bloom ❧

I began to fall for big, tough, tattooed Rico right after he told me stories of the woman who raised him, his cherished *abuelita* ("little grandmother" in Spanish). Maria Estefana Santiago was an indigenous woman of the Zapotec people of Mexico who showed her love for her grandson Rico and granddaughter Elizabeth in her kitchen.

Like many boys in his village, Rico had to quit school at fourteen years old to work in the agave fields with his strict grandfather six days a week in order to bring in enough income for the family to survive in their cash-strapped, beautiful region of Mexico called Oaxaca (wa-HA-ka). But on days when there was a deluge of rain, Rico got a magical reprieve. On those mornings he would wake up to what would become two sense memories that would never leave him: the sound of rain plunking down on the tin roof of the *casita de adobe* (small adobe house) and the smell of warm *pan* (bread) and *chocolate* (hot chocolate) being readied by his abuelita in *la cocina* (the kitchen).

Rico still gets excited when he spies storm clouds on the horizon. I think it's because his brain now associates rain with love, in a *taza* (cup).

Oaxaca is a culinary capital of Mexico. Oaxacan cooking is so savory and exotic thanks in part to the traditional use of luxurious, little-known herbs and spices. To learn more about the cultural history and exceptional flavors that inspire Oaxacan cuisine, read Zarela Martinez's The Food and Life of Oaxaca, Mexico.

Abuelita served up more than chocolate in those cups. Most mornings the earthenware ceramic cups or bowls adorned with lemon-yellow flowers contained comforting herbal infusions. These preparations were part of the herbal legacy she inherited from her ancient foremothers and forefathers whose language she passed on to her trilingual grandchildren, who now speak Zapeteco, Spanish, and English.

Elizabeth believes those herbal preparations brewed by the gnarled hands of her abuelita "comforted the body but also healed the spirit." Why not give yourself or your family love in a cup by planting your own version of Abuelita's comfort garden?

The herbal infusions and poultices of Abuelita that Rico and Elizabeth have kindly shared with me are offered up here to comfort everyday aches and are not intended to be medical advice or cure serious illness.

Humble, Not Highbrow, Growing Advice

Little abuelita gardens in Mexico, like the abuelitas who create them, are *humilde* (humble, down-to-earth). You would be violating long-held grandmotherly traditions if you went and spent a bunch of money on fancy plants at a fancy nursery for fancy pots. The plants here will grow from seed or seedlings. Rico and I have road tested them all in our cozy patio comfort garden, dedicated to the memory of Maria Estefana.

In fact these hardy herbs and vegetables have been growing out of stone walls, homemade tire planters, and coffee cans on patios in Mexico for generations. The black-thumbed among you need not fear. These herbs will survive despite you.

Pick five of the ten below that appeal to you and plunk them down in one large container pot or windowsill planter with drainage holes and all-purpose soil in the spring after the last frost. Water whenever the soil feels dry to the touch, and you are good to go for a small summer or autumn harvest. If you have leftovers, hang plants to dry in a cool, dark place and store for winter tea.

Ten Herbs for Your Comfort Garden

1. Comfort for Tummy Trouble

If Rico or Elizabeth had a stomachache, then *chop chop*—relief would soon be at hand in the form a steaming cup of *té limon* infused with lemongrass (*Cymbopogon citratus*) snipped from its sturdy planter made from an old car tire that sat on the patio.

This is a wonderful scented grass to add exotic aromatic beauty to a humble kitchen garden. Try combining *yerba buena* (spearmint) with lemongrass for an especially pleasing, cheering, fresh cup of tea. Don't use if pregnant.

2. Comfort for When You've Overdone It

Abuelita insisted on using *hoja de maiz* (cornhusk, *Zea mays*) as opposed to the easier banana leaf for wrapping her *tamales*, but corn was also an important part of her comfort toolbox. Whole corn (organic) was boiled with the husk on. The leftover water was never thrown away but used to drink as a general overindulgence detox or tonic for the kidneys.

The *barba de maiz*, or corn silk, is the silky strands found between the husk and the cob. Some Mexican herbalists make a corn silk wash for skin irritations, taking advantage of its anti-inflammatory properties.

Corn is easier to grow than you think. I have some in container pots on my urban balcony, which draws both smiles and confused looks from passing tourists.

3. Comfort for Aching Ears

Abuelita peeled and cut cloves of *ajo* (garlic, *Allium satvium*) and pressed them gently onto spider bites, mosquito bites, and, yes, scorpion stings. "She also placed a warm clove of garlic in your ear if you had an ear infection, and the pain would slowly disappear," said Elizabeth. *Cebollitas,* or little onions, were also warmed for the same purpose when there wasn't garlic on hand.

Push an unpeeled clove of garlic pointy-side up into loose earth a month or two before the first frost and you may get lovely green shoots stretching skyward before fall.

4. Comfort for Dieters

Parsley (*Petroselinum crispum*) is wasted as a wilting garnish on that crudité platter. Abuelita would occasionally make a morning infusion of *perejeil* and cilantro leaves when anyone wanted help dieting or longed to decrease the swelling in their ankles. Parsley is known for its diuretic properties.

My Californian juice-addict friends feed a bunch of parsley leaves into their giant juicers along with spinach, celery, and a bit of apple when they are detoxing or dieting. Note that large doses of parsley seeds or their essential oil can be toxic, especially for people with kidney inflammation. Avoid during pregnancy.

5. Comfort for Aching Backs

Rosemary (*Rosmarinus officinalis*) is a natural disinfectant. Some Mexicans and Mexican-Americans physically and ritually cleanse their homes with it. Maria Estefana saved it for another purpose.

She always tried to have some *romero* (both the branch and root) soaking in alcohol on a windowsill to serve as rub-on rescue-remedy for backaches and arthritis. Herbalists have been relying on rosemary to help deal with the pain of rheumatism since the days of the first Queen Elizabeth. Avoid during pregnancy.

6. Comfort for Sore Feet and Legs

Did you know basil (*Ocimum basilicum*) was used for centuries as an antimicrobial to fight off the ravages of nasty stuff like dysentery? Rico's abuelita used to cut up *albahaca* leaves and place them into a little pot with alcohol, warm it up a tiny bit, and immediately massage the blend on aching legs. If you had foot pain, Abuelita would make you a special footbath with an added shot of alcohol infused with basil and rue.

Note that basil should not be given to infants, toddlers, or pregnant or nursing women.

7. Comfort for Exhaustion or Burnout

Cilantro (*Coriandrum sativum*) is famous for its tasty, pungent leaves, but the seeds of the plant are highly valued too and go by the name of coriander. Abuelita gave infusions of cilantro, or a combo of cilantro, basil, parsley, and *yerba santa* (discussed shortly) leaves, to those looking for relief from fatigue and exhaustion-related depression.

8. Comfort for Minor Rashes

Abuelita used yerba santa (*Piper auritum*) to make delicious dishes like *amarillo de pollo* and *caldo de pollo* (chicken stew and chicken soup). She placed the heart shaped leaves whole in tamales and added to them to *frijoles* (black beans) to impart them with a heavenly, subtle, smoky licorice flavor. Each velvety yerba santa leaf can grow to be up to eleven inches wide.

Abuelita would boil five yerba santa leaves in water, let it cool, and use the liquid to soak poultices she then applied to calm minor rashes.

Yerba santa is hard to find in the States. Rico grew our yerba santa from a cutting kindly given to us by a Oaxacan neighbor who lives down the block from his sister in our city.

The essential oil of safrole (similar to that in sassafras) found within the yerba santa leaf has been said to be toxic for certain animals. Don't feed it to pets.

9. Comfort for That Time of the Month

Ruda (*Ruta graveolens*) is a small perennial woody shrub that was favored by the Aztecs. The strong-smelling plant has blue-gray-green leaves shaped like little mittens. Rue loves to grow out of old stone walls and bursts with tiny greenish-yellow blooms every spring.

Abuelita used to make a tea of this antispasmodic root for menstrual cramps and stomach troubles. She would also warm her homemade oil of the root to comfort those with earaches.

Be respectful and sparing with rue. It can be toxic in large doses. Pregnant and nursing women need to avoid it altogether because it can provoke menstruation. Some people are allergic to it and break out in rashes. Like bergamot, it can cause photosensitivity.

10. Comfort for Sleepless Nights

The tasty, calming, sweet teas produced from chamomile (*Matricaria chamomilla*) leaves, as well as spearmint and lemongrass, are enjoyed instead of coffee as daily pleasures in much of Mexico.

Abuelita used an infusion of cooled *manzanilla* in gentle eyewash she made for children with eye irritations or an overabundance of "sleepy dust" in eyes.

She administered cups of chamomile tea to family members plagued with insomnia. Abuelita also wisely employed chamomile as a bedtime bath remedy for colicky babies so they could sleep peacefully through the night.

Buying Mexican Herbs

Mexican cuisine is finally enjoying an upsurge of international interest. This means the majority of these herbs, with the exception of rue and yerba santa, can be found in the fruit and vegetable aisle of grocery chains like Whole Foods. Adventurous urbanites among you will be rewarded with a stimulating sensory experience if they forage for dried or fresh herbs in the colorful and cozy aisles of a corner Mexican grocery (*la tiendita* or *la bodega*).

To learn more about the astonishing, unsung history of Mexican herbalism consult the following resources.

Resources

Davidow, Joie. *Infusions of Healing: A Treasury of Mexican-American Herbal Remedies.* New York: Fireside, 1999.

Graber, Karen Hursh. "A Culinary Guide to Mexican Herbs: Las Hierbas de Cocina." Mexconnect.com. Last modified April 1, 1990. http://www.mexconnect.com/articles/2187-a-culinary-guide-to-mexican-herbs-las-hierbas-de-cocina.

Torres, Eliseo, and Timothy L. Sawyer. *Curandero: A Life in Mexican Folk Healing.* Albuquerque: University of New Mexico, 2005.

Herbs That Harm Dogs

by Dallas Jennifer Cobb

Just as we do for a new child, we have to make changes for safety's sake when an animal joins the family. With a new puppy, my friend recently asked my advice, wondering if there were any common houseplants that could make her puppy sick. I've compiled an extensive list of plants that could have disastrous effects on her "chewy" little puppy. The list includes herbs, flowers, shrubs, and trees that are common to North American gardens, parks, fields, and trails and also harmful to dogs.

For simplicity's sake, assume that any plant with the word *poison* in its name is poisonous not just to dogs but to humans as well. As such, know how to identify and avoid poison ivy,

poison oak, poison hemlock, and poison sumac. These and other noxious plants, like giant hogweed and wild parsnip (which have become invasive species in much of North America), should all be carefully removed from any area where humans or dogs play.

Herbs That Harm Dogs

Know how to identify these plants so that you can avoid them while on nature walks, in parks, on trails, or in wilderness settings:

Comfrey (*Symphytum officinale*): all parts

Ephedra, *ma huang* (*Ephedra vulgaris*): all parts

Jimsonweed (*Datura stramonium*): all parts

Lambkill, sheep's laurel (*Kalmia angustifolia*): leaves

Locoweed, milkvetch (*Astragalus*): all parts

Marijuana (*Cannabis sativa*): all parts

Milkweed (*Asclepias*): all parts

Pennyroyal (*Mentha pulegium*): all parts

Rosemary (*Rosmarinus officinalis*): leaves

Sage (*Salvia officinalis*): leaves

Tea tree (*Melaleuca alternifolia*): oil

Tobacco (*Nicotiana*): all parts

White willow (*Salix alba*): bark

Wormwood (*Artemisia absinthium*): all parts

Yucca (*Yucca gigantea*): all parts

Careful with Common Flowers

There are many flowers common to gardens that are also toxic, whole or in part, to dogs. If you have any of the following in your garden, familiarize yourself with them and know their dangers: azelea, bluebonnet, buttercup, daffodil, delphinium, hyacinth, hydrangea, impatiens, ivy, iris, jack-in-the-pulpit, lupine, periwinkle, philodendron, poinsettia, poppy, rhododendron, snapdragon, sweet pea, tulip bulbs, trumpet vine, and Venus flytrap.

Suspect Shrubs and Trees

While surveying your surroundings for hazards that could harm your dog be sure to be able to identify the following trees and shrubs that can be toxic to canines: boxwood, cherry, cherry laurel, dogwood, elderberry, mistletoe, mock orange, oak, wild black cherry, wisteria, and yew.

Forbidden Food

It is wise to note which food plants can harm dogs. Most people already know that chocolate is not good for dogs, so now add these to your list: mushrooms and toadstools, peach seeds, pear seeds, potato sprouts and foliage, rhubarb leaves, and tomato foliage and vines.

Puppy Proofing

I can almost hear you thinking, "That is a huge list. How will I ever get rid of all those plants?" The good news is you don't have to. Adult dogs seem to have an innate sense of what is edible and what isn't and mostly limit their "grazing" to grass to help with digestion. Puppies, however, don't show the same discernment and rely more on us to make sure they are safe.

Keeping a dog from harm takes more than just reading a list of what plants are toxic. The real trick is to create good habits in your pet that will enable them to be safe from poisoning. It requires knowing what is toxic and then teaching your dog not to chew on those toxic things. Puppies instinctively chew lots of things as a natural part of their development. Older dogs don't have as strong a chew instinct as puppies, but chewing is still a normal part of their repertoire. Understanding this will enable you to work with your puppy or dog, teaching them what to avoid when they are chewing.

For these identified plants to be toxic to your dog, the dog has to eat the plant. And for many of these plants it takes a very large volume of consumed plant material to reach toxic levels for dogs. The easiest way to keep your dog safe from the toxic herbs and plants is to simply limit their access to the plants.

Create Helpful Habits

Success comes from repetition and positive reinforcement. Use these techniques with dogs to help them learn to appropriately channel their chewing instincts and create helpful habits.

When puppies are in their "chewy" stage, it makes no sense to try to stop them from chewing, because it is instinctual and in part how they learn. Give them suitable chew toys to enjoy. When their need to chew is directed toward chew toys, they are less likely to chew off-limits items. When you catch them chewing unacceptable stuff, scold them in a stern voice, redirect them to the approved chew toy, and use a praising voice to affirm them. It doesn't take long to establish good habits that teach your dog what is off limits and what is acceptable.

Dogs love to chew, so be wise in deciding what is okay for them to chew. Never let them chew things that resemble other things you don't want destroyed. For example, don't provide a length of hose to chew, because it could easily be confused with your garden hose, and you don't want that shredded. The same can be said for pieces of leather, old boots and shoes, or anything that resembles a common household item.

Choose toys that are specifically for your dog, and only your dog, like a Kong or Chuckit! ball. When you go outdoors, make regular time to engage in a game of throw and retrieve. You can play with your dog for a while, providing fun and exercise, and as the dog tires, allow them to hold on to the toy and chew it. While they're engaged, you can garden knowing your dog is safe. Use a playpen to keep puppies contained and nearby while you garden. Set it up near where you are working in your garden so you can keep an eye on the puppies. They get used to being near the garden but not in it.

When you are going off your private property,
leash your dog. It is a great practice to teach your dog not
to eat anything from the ground while on a leash.

Healing Herbs for Dogs

With some repetition and positive reinforcement, you will create helpful habits in your dog. You can relax and not worry so much about your pet getting into your garden. By planting a canine-friendly garden, you ensure that you have herbal allies on hand when you need them. Even though these herbs might be beneficial, it is important to not let your dog chew or graze in this bed either.

The best plants to grow are those that you will enjoy as a culinary or healing ingredient, and are good for your dog. I grow the following versatile culinary and healing herbs, which I've learned are beneficial for dogs:

Basil (*Ocimum basilicum*)

Cilantro (*Coriander sativum*)

Echinacea, coneflower (*Echinacea pupurea*)

Garlic (*Allium sativum*)

Ginger (*Zingiber officinale*)

Oregano (*Origanum vulgare*)

Parsley (*Petroselinum crispum*)

Peppermint (*Mentha* × *piperita*)

Turmeric (*Curcuma longa*)

Whether you're an herb lover with a dog, a dog lover with herbs, or a gardener with friends who have dogs, I hope you feel empowered to keep yourself and your canine friends safe from herbs that harm dogs.

Selected Resources

"Plants Potentially Poisonous to Pets." Humane Society of Southern Arizona. Accessed September 6, 2016. http://www.humanesociety.org/assets/pdfs/pets/poisonous_plants.pdf.

"Garden Plant Identification." UMass Extension Greenhouse Crops and Floriculture Program. Accessed September 2016. https://extension.umass.edu/floriculture/plant-identification.

"Herbs That Are Good for Dogs." Modern Dog. Accessed October 2, 2016. http://moderndogmagazine.com/gallery/herbs-are-good-dogs?.

An Herbal First Aid Kit

by Elizabeth Barrette

Natural remedies provide an alternative to conventional ones with harsh ingredients. Some people find that mainstream remedies don't work well for them or have nasty side effects. Others just prefer natural remedies. Herbs can treat a wide range of complaints.

Types of Complaints

A first aid kit should cover a range of common problems. One division is between providing complete care for minor issues that don't require professional attention and providing initial damage control for major issues that need a doctor. Another division is between injuries and illnesses. Pay attention to the people you care for and stock materials needed to address

163

their special needs that aren't covered in a generic kit. For example, asthma sufferers often have backup medication to keep in their household first aid kit. On the herbal side, some essential oils are among the few things that soothe severe headaches, so if a migraine sufferer has a preferred blend, add that.

Injuries

Abrasions: These are shallow, bloody scrapes that may contain grit. They should be cleaned gently and covered if large. Stock antiseptic rinse, cream, or ointment; nourishing cream to help the skin heal; and a "wound wand" of herbal balm to clean and soothe broken skin.

Bites and Stings: Insects and other pests can leave painful or itchy marks behind. Antiseptics, astringents, and antihistamines help. Choose from a solid balm stick or roll-on with essential oils or tinctures.

Bruises: Blunt trauma can break blood vessels under the skin. Apply a cold pack to slow bleeding. Herbal treatments include bruise liniments and salves.

Burns: Heat, radiation, chemicals, and electricity can all damage skin. The most common are heat burns and sunburn. Cool the burn first with running water. Minor burns with reddened skin can be treated at home. Aloe vera gel is the go-to herbal remedy, although you can also find burn sprays made with oils such as peppermint or lavender suspended in a carrier fluid. Burn cream is helpful too. Burns that are large or have blisters or charring are more serious and need expert care; cover with a sterile dressing but no medication.

Cuts: Minor cuts may bleed sluggishly or freely. Clean and dress them, applying pressure if necessary to stop the bleeding. Stock antiseptic rinse, cream, or ointment; styptic powder to stop bleeding; and nourishing cream to help the skin heal.

Pain: Injuries hurt, and so do things such as headaches. Include both aspirin (including all willow derivatives) and non-aspirin painkillers. Peppermint, rosemary, and lavender essential oils can soothe headaches. The same ones work for sore muscles, as do black pepper, eucalyptus, and ginger; choose from liniment or massage oil.

Splinters: Tiny foreign objects under the skin cause pain and infection. Wash the area, remove the splinter with tweezers, and then apply antibiotic cream. If you can't get it out, use a drawing salve such as black salve.

Sprains and Strains: Minor damage to muscles and tendons can be treated with a compression bandage, a cold pack, rest, and elevation. Major damage requires professional care. Liniment or other muscle rubs can ease pain and speed healing.

Illnesses

Allergies: When the immune system overreacts to harmless things, it causes sniffles, itchiness, wheezing, and other problems. Astragalus, barberry, horehound, mullein, reishi mushrooms, stinging nettle, and turmeric may help. Stock antihistamines, soothers such as cough candy, skin cream, and skin powder.

Cough: Chest congestion can come from various illnesses or allergies. Stock cough candy and cough syrup, preferably both an expectorant and a suppressant. Elderberry, honey, horehound, hyssop, mullein, peppermint, and yarrow all help. Include a chest rub with menthol, eucalyptus, or both.

Fever: Bacterial infections and some other problems raise the body temperature. Let a low fever do its thing. If it gets uncomfortable, sponge the skin with cool water and peppermint oil. Garlic capsules induce sweating and fight infection.

Feverfew, willow (or aspirin), and yarrow can reduce fever. High fever benefits from expert care.

Gastrointestinal Problems: These include nausea, diarrhea, constipation, and other issues. Many herbal remedies soothe digestion from end to end, while others are more specific. Aloe vera, chamomile, ginger, licorice, marshmallow, peppermint, senna, and spearmint are all helpful.

Nasal Congestion: Allergies and colds cause stuffy nose. Cayenne, eucalyptus, garlic, and menthol are popular choices. These are often included in cough candy, cough syrup, and all-purpose cold remedies.

Skin Problems: Rashes, itches, and other skin issues are typically caused by irritating substances, but can happen for other reasons. As a general rule, if it's dry, make it wet; if it's wet, make it dry. Almond, coconut, olive, and shea make excellent base ingredients; aloe vera, calendula, chamomile, comfrey, rosemary, and sage are active ingredients. Carry antihistamine, antiseptic, astringent, skin powder, and an all-purpose skin cream.

Sore Throat: This can come from an illness or overuse of voice. Lozenges made with chamomile, elderberry, honey, horehound, marshmallow, or licorice are soothing.

Types of Supplies

Herbal remedies come in many forms. Each form is good for certain types of problems and certain active ingredients. A good first aid kit should stock a variety of products.

Lotions, creams, salves, and ointments use a semiliquid carrier to distribute active ingredients over skin. Lotions are thin, creams medium, and salves and ointments thick. Balm is a solid stick. These treat skin complaints. Stock at least an all-purpose healer, such as calendula cream, and an antibiotic one, such as tea tree salve. Anti-itch lotion and herbal sunscreen are useful too.

One category where herbalism excels and conventional first aid doesn't offer much is **medicinal candy**. Stock a cough candy such as horehound or licorice. Honey, slippery elm, and willow are good for sore throats. Chamomile, cinnamon, ginger, honey, marshmallow, and peppermint relieve nausea and other digestive complaints. Adaptogens help the body cope with all manner of challenges; choose from tasty ones like elderberry or licorice. Emergency chocolate squares soothe emotional and spiritual upsets, with physical benefits. Choose clinical-grade chocolate (organic, non-GMO, high cocoa content) like NibMor, not snacking chocolate. If your patients can't stomach dark chocolate, include milk chocolate, although it's less effective. Medicinal candy doubles as an emergency sugar supply for low blood sugar and as treats for patients. Even a minor injury can burn through energy reserves and leave people in need of a pickup or simple comfort.

Another category particular to herbalism is **essential oils**. These treat many different complaints, including emotional and psychological ones that get little support from a conventional kit; stock something uplifting, soothing, mood-balancing, and healing. A useful format is to put several individual oils into a box along with an unscented carrier oil or cream, so you can mix and match. Popular choices include eucalyptus, lavender, lemon, myrrh, peppermint, rosemary, and tea tree. Roll-on bug repellent and blemish reducers are also very popular.

Tinctures preserve herbal ingredients in alcohol. Most are for internal use, and you can buy blends for common complaints like fever, headache, or stomachache. It's nice to include one for bruises too. Like essential oils, it's a good idea to fill a small box with several favorite tinctures for different purposes.

Pharmaceuticals such as painkillers usually come in pill or liquid form. Aspirin (willow) is among the best-known herbal options, but it's not good for everyone, so include alternatives. Immune-system boosters may be pills or chewables. Echinacea, garlic, and vitamin C all work. Use to prevent infection from broken skin or help the body fight off illness. Antihistamines, decongestants, antinausea, antidiarrhea, and laxatives should also be in your pharmacy section. It helps to keep these in their own pouch or box.

Adaptogens come in various forms, and all these herbs help your body cope with whatever challenges come your way. They include American ginseng, ashwagandha, astragalus, elderberry, eleuthero, holy basil, *jiaogulan*, licorice, maca, panax ginseng, reishi mushroom, rhaponticum, rhodiola, schisandra, and sea buckthorn.

Ethnic Considerations

While rarely addressed in basic first aid, ethnic variations are important to consider in a diverse world. Talk with the people you take care of and find out if their needs differ significantly from yours.

Sometimes you need to guess someone's age to help figure out what might be wrong, because some complaints happen more within a certain age range. There is a cultural tendency in America to overestimate the age of African-American people, especially children and teens. Conversely, Asian skin tends to wrinkle less, which can make it easy to underestimate age from middle to senior years.

The darker the skin, the more difficult it is to see bruises. This can lead to underestimating the severity of an injury. Try to feel for heat, swelling, or stiffness of the skin in addition to looking for dark spots. Very pale skin tends to show bruising much more, which can look worse than it really is. Some people also bruise worse than others and may need extra care.

Darker skin is more prone to drying out, when it can take on a chalky or ashy appearance due to the top layer flaking off. Rich, thick oils such as shea butter can help. If they feel too heavy, try a lighter lotion. Avoid tinctures and other alcohol-based products, which dry the skin. Any skin type can become dry, and moderate skin usually responds well to lotion or cream. If that's not enough, try heavier oils. Asian skin is prone to getting oily. Try to avoid using heavy oils or greasy ointments; instead use lighter cream or lotion. Stock an alcohol-based tincture for pimples and other blemishes.

Lighter skin is less prone to scarring than darker skin, although all skin will scar if injured badly enough. African-American skin is the most prone to scarring, especially a type of raised tissue called a keloid scar. Asian skin is more likely to scar than lighter European-type skin, but less prone to keloids than African-type skin. Pay special attention to olive skin because Mediterranean heritage often includes some African ancestry that can raise the risk of keloids. With light brown to dark skin, be extra gentle with cleaning wounds, and take steps to reduce scarring.

With regard to herbalism in particular, understand that the world has several completely different systems of herbal medicine! Europe, Asia, India, and North America are particularly well known for theirs, and while there is some overlap of remedies from widespread plant families, many items are unique to their locale. Some herbalists further theorize that traditional medicines match the complaints of the people who developed them. It is worth exploring the remedies your ancestors would have used to see how those work for you. If you take care of people from a different background, ask about their preferred remedies and stock their favorites too. However, some crossovers have been enthusiastically adopted— many martial arts studios have a Chinese-type herbal first aid kit with all the lovely oil blends for sore muscles, even if neither the students nor the teachers are Asian.

A Sample Kit

A first aid kit needs basic tools and supplies in addition to the medicines. Tools include things like bandage scissors, a blanket (cloth or foil), CPR mask, safety pins or bandage clips, a thermometer, and tweezers. Supplies include bandages, bandage tape or webbing, biohazard garbage bags, butterfly stitches or surgical tape, gloves, instant cold packs and heat packs, splints, and other consumables. It's considerate to match the color range of bandages to the skin tones of people you regularly treat, and children often appreciate cartoons on adhesive bandages. Stickers and a pen are useful for writing the type of injury and time and dose of treatments given; stick these on clothes for the convenience of later caregivers. This is especially useful with herbal remedies as fewer professionals are familiar with them. Also include a first aid manual with local emergency numbers and, if you have a professional herbalist, their number too. A typical first aid kit could include:

Antiseptic ointment with a coconut oil base and essential oils, including frankincense, helichrysum, myrrh, and tea tree.

Antiseptic wash such as a blend of aloe vera juice and witch hazel plus essential oils of lavender, sage, oregano, and thyme. Use this for blemishes on oily skin.

All-purpose healing cream made from beeswax, shea butter, vitamin E oil, calendula, chamomile, comfrey, echinacea, plantain, and yarrow.

For a tight budget, build your herbal first aid kit one item at a time. Start with products that treat a wide range of complaints, such as all-purpose healing cream.

Black salve with a base of beeswax, coconut oil, vitamin E, activated charcoal powder, kaolin clay, lavender essential oil, and olive oil infused with comfrey, calendula, and plantain. Use for drawing out infections, splinters, or venomous bites or stings.

Blemish stick with rosehip seed oil as a carrier plus bay laurel, lavender, palmarosa, peppermint, rosemary, and thyme. It soothes insect bites or stings and dries out pimples.

Bug repellent stick with a solid base made from unrefined shea butter, coconut oil, beeswax, and essential oils of citronella, eucalyptus, lavender, lemongrass, myrrh, peppermint, and tea tree.

Burn gel of aloe vera and menthol. You can also buy this with lidocaine if you want a conventional anesthetic. This can actually "erase" a mild burn if you get it on there fast enough and reapply every time the gel dries out until the burn stops hurting.

Mentholated rub with a base of almond oil and beeswax; menthol crystals; and essential oils of eucalyptus, rosemary, and wintergreen. This works equally well as a chest rub for congestion and a joint rub for arthritis, gout, or rheumatism. For sensitive skin, put the rub on the inside of a folded cloth and lay it in place.

Healing rub with a carrier oil such as jojoba infused with arnica, chamomile, cypress, eucalyptus, ginger, helichrysum, and wintergreen. Good for sore muscles, joints, sprains, strains, and similar structural complaints.

Lip balm made from beeswax, sunflower and coconut oils, vitamin E oil, and lime essential oil.

Sunscreen with a base of aloe vera gel, coconut oil, olive oil infused with calendula, shea butter, vitamin E, and beeswax. Also include zinc oxide to block sunlight and lavender and tea tree essential oils.

Essential oil set: Blue chamomile soothes jangled nerves, overstrain headaches, and other complaints. Clove can draw toxins and relieve constipation; it also has a notable numbing quality for toothaches, headaches, and other pain, but it irritates sensitive skin, so test for acceptability before including it. Frankincense is soothing and purifying and enhances other oils; it lowers inflammation, headaches, and restlessness. Helichrysum reduces bruising, swelling, shock, allergies, viruses, and other infections; don't use on broken skin. Lavender is calming and cooling, good for insomnia, burns, anxiety, bug bites, and bruises. Lemon is cleansing and uplifting, helpful for discouraging pests, colds, digestive issues, fatigue, and sore throats. Myrrh is antiseptic and stimulating, useful in treating cuts, bruises, coughs, and infections. Oregano provides immune support and pain relief; it also discourages bacterial and yeast infections, removes warts, and cleanses the digestive system. Peppermint is cooling and soothing, useful in addressing distraction, nausea, allergies, menstrual issues, muscle aches, and inflammation. Tea tree is astringent and disinfectant, good for bug bites, athlete's foot, scrapes, and skin complaints. Include a container of carrier oil or cream for custom blends, along with blending sticks and tiny jars.

Medicinal candy set of chamomile, ginger, and honey lozenges for sore throats and digestive complaints. Include horehound, licorice, and honey for coughs and sore throats. Candied fennel eases the symptoms of overeating, nausea, indigestion, and flatulence. Fisherman's Friend is an aggressively strong cough drop made with cayenne and menthol that clears up coughs, congestion, and sore throats—if you can stand to keep it in your mouth. Ricola makes broad-spectrum cough candy that treats the same range with a little less strength and a lot better taste, including horehound, lemon, and cherry flavors. You can also buy or make simples such as ginger chews, honey drops, lemon drops, licorice, peppermints, and so on. Chocolate squares (milk or dark) soothe physical and emotional complaints.

Pharmacy set: Aspirin and nonaspirin painkillers. Immune system boosters such as echinacea, garlic, and vitamin C capsules or tablets. Elderberry syrup as an adaptogen, antibacterial, antihistamine, decongestant, and immune booster. Antidiarrheal powder or capsules including astragalus, barberry, carob, and echinacea. Laxative powder or capsules including dandelion, fenugreek, licorice, senna, and slippery elm. Psyllium is an herbal fiber supplement that soothes both diarrhea and constipation by buffering the intestines toward healthy function. Skin powder for bathtime or wet rashes can be made entirely from natural ingredients using arrowroot powder, marshmallow root powder, colloidal oatmeal, and French white clay as a base, plus ground flowers of chamomile and calendula for soothing qualities. Styptic powder to stop bleeding may incorporate astringent herbs such as cayenne, plantain, self-heal, witch hazel, and yarrow.

Tincture set: Alertness tincture including astragalus, ginger, gingko, ginseng, rosemary, and sage. Bruise tincture including arnica, black tea, and witch hazel. Dandelion root to stimulate kidneys and liver, flushing out toxins and relieving bloat. Feverfew for reducing dizziness, fevers, migraines and other severe headaches, muscle tension and pain, menstrual issues, stomach irritation, and kidney complaints. Moon tincture including cramp bark, black cohosh, chamomile, raspberry leaf, and motherwort. Rosemary as an antioxidant, antibiotic, and decongestant. Thyme as an expectorant and relaxant for cough or sore throat as well as a disinfectant.

Selected Resources

Editorial Staff. "What Do I Need in My First Aid Kit?" Familydoctor .org. Last modified 2017. https://familydoctor.org/what-do-i -need-in-my-first-aid-kit/.

"Skin Conditions in Dark Skin." WebMD. Last modified July 15, 2017. http://www.webmd.com/skin-problems-and-treatments/skin -conditions-people-with-dark-skin#1.

"The 10 Most Useful Herbal Tinctures." Pestle Herbs. Accessed January 10, 2018. https://pestleherbs.co.uk/recipe/the-10-most -useful-herbal-tinctures/.

Aromatherapy in Your Kitchen

⤜ by Diana Rajchel ⤛

Aromatherapy is described as the use of essential oils for therapeutic (read: stress) treatment. While still labeled an alternative therapy—code for "superstition"—a growing body of medical research consistently finds that the right essential oils reduce cortisol levels, improve sleep quality, and ease the process of aging. The most researched oils are well known: lavender, rose, black pepper, mint, and jasmine.

While aromatherapy these days refers to oils, initially it meant simply the use of fragrance for healing. If oils are beyond your pay grade, you can use the food and spices in your kitchen. You may unwittingly experience aromatherapy in your day to day already. When cutting a lemon, the citrus scent releases a flood of physical and emotional associations. A bottle of lemon essential oil might do the same thing, but essential oils, because of their chemical concentration, require different handling from the lemon juice you use to flavor your lemon pepper chicken. If you cook, enjoy tea, or garden at all, your home already has the benefits of aromatherapy waiting for you, in forms very different from the usual online recipes.

Home cooks often collect soul-soothing wonders just waiting for aromatherapeutic use. If they don't, one trip to the grocery store will fix that. Starting with your fruit-and-vegetable crisper, you might have lemons or lemon juice and other citrus, strawberries in the right season, and cucumbers. They offer many benefits to go with the great smells.

Citrus

The scent of lemons and oranges, along with having that "clean" scent, combats depression and reduces blood pressure. If you save orange peels and boil them in water on the stove, they release the scent into your home, reducing anxiety and promoting a convivial feeling.

Strawberries

While strawberries keep poorly, their leaves tincture well, accruing a sweet but not cloying scent that blends well in homemade scent sprays. Strawberries offer several medicinal benefits: they can calm the stomach, they can reduce anxiety, and a tea from the leaves makes a wonderful skin toner.

Cucumbers

Cucumbers, popular for reducing eye puffiness, also reduce blood pressure and may regulate diabetes. They make a potent anti-inflammatory. Add them to salads, eat them with a favorite dip, and enjoy the way their scent promotes a sense of calm and relaxation. You can take in the scent as you use slices to cover your eyes.

Beauty Mask

One of the best ways to enjoy the therapeutic benefits of cucumbers and strawberries is with a succulent beauty mask. The astringent in the cucumbers helps tighten pores, while the strawberry's natural salicylic acid can treat blemishes.

    1 cup strawberries, hulled

    1 medium cucumber, sliced but not peeled

    ¼ cup water

In a blender or food processor, mix all ingredients until smooth. Transfer to a bowl. Apply to clean skin, leave on for 20 minutes, and then rinse off.

Vanilla Extract

Any baker knows the worth of high-quality vanilla. It adds depth of flavor to cookies and breads, can reduce the need for more sweeteners, and has a documented aphrodisiac effect. While its medical applications have been mostly forgotten, vanilla's history includes its use for treatment of hysteria and mild fevers. These days it's known for increasing penile blood flow and reminding most people of grandparents who bake cookies. If you want to add a romantic mood in your kitchen, but have enough dishes for a meal, try using this recipe to add a little scent and mood to your space.

Stovetop Potpourri

Here's one aromatherapeutic recipe that can add a little calm to your home:

1 cup water

1 tablespoon lemon juice

Peelings from 1 orange

Peelings from 1 cucumber

1 teaspoon vanilla extract

Pour 1 cup water into a saucepan and add the other ingredients. Stir. Turn on low heat and allow to simmer. The fragrance should fill your kitchen within 20 minutes, and you can transform your kitchen into an aromatherapy engine.

Garlic and Onions

You may not think of these ubiquitous members of the genus *Allium* as aromatherapeutic since their pungent scent doesn't fit with typical aesthetics of scent therapies. They and their distinct fragrances offer medical benefits such as possible cancer prevention and, more immediately, relief from allergies and breathing ailments. Garlic and onions are often the first go-to add-ins for chicken noodle soup when someone has a cold, and for good reason: the anti-inflammatory effects clear sinuses and the throat by thinning excess mucus.

Mint

Mint stimulates our minds while settling our stomachs, and it gives a lovely "clean scent" alternative to lemon. Its stimulating properties do come with an advisory: peppermint can raise blood pressure, which may create stress rather than alleviating it. Other mint-family herbs are popular in cooking and aromatherapy. Sage is well known for its purgative properties and for raising basal body temperature, thyme treats mucus-heavy coughs, and oregano provides an excellent antiseptic.

Keep an eye out for bodegas and smaller grocery stores—many stock fragrant items you might never find in a supermarket!

Cinnamon

Cinnamon oil is volatile, is acidic, and can cause phototoxicity. Working with it still in plant form is safer and easy to do when using kitchen spices. Its warm scent adds a social feel to any home—one reason for its popularity as a fragrance agent in so many holiday candles. It also tastes wonderful when sprinkled in coffee grounds and run through a coffee maker. Along with making people feel a bit happier, it regulates blood flow in women and regulates blood sugar.

Wake Up Tea

> 1 tablespoon mint
>
> 1 teaspoon ground cinnamon
>
> 1 cup water

The mint gives you a lovely wake-up kick, while the cinnamon balances your blood sugar. Heat water to simmering and pour in a mug. Place herbs in a tea strainer, and place strainer in water. Allow to seep for 4 minutes. Add sweetener as preferred.

Experiment with Scent in Your Kitchen

These common kitchen spices, herbs, and fruits are only the beginning of what's possible with your kitchen goodies. It's well worth the time to research your favorite flavoring agents for their uses in both traditional folk medicine and modern aromatherapy. You'll find a host of old tools made new again as you mix and match the possibilities.

Resources

Calderon de la Barca, Pedro. "Cucumber Oil." Avurvedic Oils. September 11, 2017. http://ayurvedicoils.com/tag/5-health-benefits-of-cucumber-oil.

Chang, Ying-Ying, Chao-Ling Lin, and Li-Yin Chang. "The Effects of Aromatherapy Massage on Sleep Quality of Nurses on Monthly Rotating Night Shifts." *Evidence-Based Complementary and Alternative Medicine* 2017 (2017): n.p. doi:10.1155/2017/3861273.

Chen, Pau-Ju, et al. "Effects of Aromatherapy Massage on Pregnant Women's Stress and Immune Function: A Longitudinal, Prospective, Randomized Controlled Trial." *The Journal of Alternative and Complementary Medicine* 23, no. 10 (October 2017): 778–86. https://doi.org/10.1089/acm.2016.0426.

Keville, Kathi. "Aromatherapy: Lemon." How Stuff Works. Accessed January 10, 2018.

Monica. "Medicinal Strawberry—Root, Leaf, and Fruit." *The Herb Nerd* (blog). Accessed January 10, 2018. http://www.theherbnerdpodcast.com/medicinal-strawberry-root-leaf-and-fruit/.

Rose, Jeanne. *The Aromatherapy Book: Applications & Inhalations*. Berkeley, CA: North Atlantic Books, 1992.

Herbal Hair Rinses

↣ by Anna Franklin ↢

I'm a great fan of herbal hair rinses. I first learned about them in the 1980s and have been using them ever since, but they have recently become big news in the blogosphere. If you wait long enough, the world eventually catches up with you!

Why Use a Hair Rinse?

Just as herbs can be valuable for your health, they can offer great benefits for your hair too. Choose the right ones and they can cleanse, moisturize, and nourish your hair: they can restore the pH balance, boost circulation in your scalp to promote hair growth, treat dandruff, smooth the hair shaft, add shine, reduce excess oil, and remove odors. Some herbs will even bring out natural colors and highlights.

Many commercial hair care products claim to use natural herbs and flower essences in their formulation, but read the label and you'll see they are a tiny proportion of the whole, bound up with lots of chemical nasties.

Your hair goes through a lot on a daily basis. It is exposed to pollution, heat, and the harsh chemicals from shampoos, conditioners, dyes, and other treatments. While you trust these chemical products to make your hair glossy and beautiful, they also strip its natural oils, damage it in the long run, and furthermore have been linked to many chronic health conditions. A herbal hair rinse can be used to remove the chemical build up these products leave behind while leaving your hair naturally clean, soft, and silky.

Making a Hair Rinse

Hair rinses are really easy to make and use. If you can make a cup of tea, you can make a hair rinse. In fact, you can use herbal tea bags from the supermarket, dried herbs from your kitchen cupboard, or pick fresh herbs and flowers from your garden.

Simply bring a cup of water to boil in a saucepan, add a tablespoon of herb(s) and turn off the heat. Allow this to cool down at room temperature and infuse overnight (or for several hours at least). Strain, discarding the herbs and retaining the liquid.

Using a Hair Rinse

Wash your hair as usual and rinse well with warm water. Have your hair rinse ready in a jug or, better still, a spray bottle. Spritz it on your hair, and massage it gently through your hair and into your scalp. Leave it on for at least five minutes or for sixty minutes if you want to use the rinse to add subtle color highlights to your hair.

If you have only used herbs, you don't need to rinse this out again and you can go on to style your hair as usual, but if you have added cider vinegar or lemon juice (see page 187), you will need to rinse again with warm water.

Some Useful Hair Herbs

Basil, *Ocimum basilicum*
Basil stimulates hair follicles, increases blood circulation in the scalp, and promotes hair growth, as well as adds shine to dull hair. The magnesium in basil helps protect hair from breakage, the antioxidant properties protect the hair from environmental damage, and its antiseptic and antifungal properties treat dandruff and an itchy scalp.

Calendula, *Calendula officinalis*
The beautiful yellow or orange calendula (pot marigold) petals are antibacterial, antifungal, antioxidant, and anti-inflammatory. They help soothe and heal irritated scalp conditions that may lead to hair thinning. Calendula improves blood supply to the scalp, and its regenerative properties promote the growth of new cells and collagen. Calendula contains antioxidants, which combat the effects of pollution and environmental damage on your hair, as well as saponins (soap-like phytochemicals) to cleanse your hair, and mucilage (slippery phytochemicals) to

smooth and detangle it. Calendula flower rinses can lighten the hair with regular use. Make sure you use *Calendula officinalis*, not *Tagetes* species, which are also called marigold.

Chamomile, *Matricaria recutita*
Antiseptic chamomile helps treat dandruff, soothes an irritated scalp, promotes hair growth, and reduces greasiness. Chamomile is deeply nourishing and helps your hair shine. It contains flavonoids, which can brighten and lighten blonde hair—but don't expect it to have any noticeable lightening results on dark hair.

Comfrey, *Symphytum officinale*
Healing comfrey is full of minerals, vitamins, and antioxidants, as well gamma-linoleic acid, which stimulates hair growth, plus mucilage to soften, detangle, and add shine. It has antifungal, antiviral, and antibacterial properties that can help treat dandruff and an irritated scalp.

Fenugreek, *Trigonella foenum-graecum*
Rich in proteins, mucilage, vitamins, and minerals, fenugreek nourishes your hair and makes it sleek. It strengthens hair from the roots, helping prevent hair loss. It is also said to help hair retain its natural pigments and prevent premature grayness. Grind the seeds into a fine powder and soak in water overnight.

Hibiscus, *Hibiscus sabdariffa*
This is one of my favorite rinses, adding subtle red shades to the hair with regular use as well as smoothing the hair shaft and helping detangle, owing to the high mucilage content of the flowers. Hibiscus is anti-inflammatory and will soothe and detoxify an irritated scalp and treat dandruff. The astringent

properties of the flowers also reduce excessive oiliness in the hair.

Horsetail, *Equisetum arvense*
Rich in minerals, particularly silica, horsetail helps keep hair strong and glossy, encouraging growth. It is great for removing product buildup and excessive oiliness.

Lavender, *Lavandula* spp.
Lavender has a balancing effect on the production of sebum (oil), which makes it beneficial whether you have dry or greasy hair. It has antimicrobial, antibacterial, and anti-inflammatory actions which make it valuable in treating scalp problems and dandruff. It stimulates circulation in the scalp, promoting new hair growth.

Lemongrass, *Cymbopogon citratus*
If you have greasy hair, lemongrass is a wonderful rinse that will reduce oiliness, moisturize, and strengthen the hair follicles and the hair shafts, as well as brighten dull hair.

Licorice Root, *Glycyrrhiza glabra*
If you suffer from scalp problems, licorice root might be the hair rinse for you. It has antioxidant and anti-inflammatory properties that sooth irritation.

Marshmallow Root, *Althaea officinalis*
The high mucilage content of marshmallow root makes it perfect for conditioning the hair as well as making it easier to detangle. It soothes irritation if you suffer from a dry scalp, eczema, or psoriasis.

Mint, *Mentha* spp.

Whether you use garden mint, peppermint, or spearmint, it makes a refreshing and invigorating hair rinse that will increase blood supply to the scalp and stimulate the hair follicles. Mints have antifungal and anti-inflammatory properties that are soothing to irritated scalps. A mint rinse will reduce greasiness and help heal environmental damage to your hair.

Nettle, *Urtica dioica*

Nettle is packed full of vitamins and minerals and provides a nourishing treatment for all hair types, but it especially reduces the production of excess oil in greasy hair. It combats hair loss and promotes stronger growth.

Rosemary, *Rosmarinus officinalis*

Perhaps the most popular herb in natural hair care, rosemary is full of vitamins and has antibacterial and antioxidant properties. It is used to increase shine, prevent hair loss, boost circulation to the scalp and stimulate hair growth, reduce oiliness, and darken the color of hair to disguise any gray.

Sage, *Salvia officinalis*

Sage promotes both the growth and strength of hair. It is oil balancing, so it can be used whether you have dry or greasy hair.

Tea, *Camellia sinensis*

Because tea contains caffeine, it will stimulate hair growth. Using a black tea rinse will slightly darken your hair, so if you don't want this coloring effect, substitute green tea, famous for its antioxidant activity, or use rooibos tea to add reddish highlights in red and brown hair. Make a strong cup of tea using one or two tea bags.

Thyme, *Thymus vulgaris*

Thyme has antiseptic and antifungal properties that treat dandruff and other scalp conditions and clarify clogged hair follicles. It also has nourishing vitamins and minerals, such as magnesium, potassium, and selenium, essential for healthy hair growth and to keep your hair lustrous.

Additions to Herbal Hair Rinses

Cider Vinegar

Cider vinegar is marvelous for removing product buildup from hair. Just add a couple of tablespoons of cider vinegar to a pint of water and use this as a rinse, or add a tablespoon of cider vinegar to your prepared herbal hair rinse. It's great for removing excess oil from greasy hair too and will leave it shiny, soft, and silky.

Lemon Juice

Add a tablespoon of lemon juice to a cup of water or add it to your prepared herbal hair rinse to treat greasy hair and stimulate hair growth. Over time, this will lighten your hair color.

Storing Hair Rinses

Once you have prepared your herbal hair rinse, it will keep in the fridge for five to seven days—after that, it will develop mold. If you wish, you can freeze prepared rinses in ice cube trays. When you want to use one, add a cup of warm water to a couple of cubes to defrost them and proceed to use the rinse as described earlier.

DIY
and
Crafts

Trim and Train:
Espaliering for Beginners

≈ by Natalie Zaman ≈

Nestled in a quiet and scenic corner of Fort Tryon Park in New York City just north of the George Washington Bridge is the Cloisters. The museum is a series of covered walkways that surround and lead to secret gardens. One of the museum's living treasures is tucked between a pair of walls in the Bonnefont Garden that overlooks the Hudson River: an espaliered pear tree.

The Bonnefont pear looks like a living candelabra. Look closely and you'll see how it came to have this extraordinary shape. The tree has a central trunk from which only six branches (three on each side) have been allowed to grow. In the winter when it's bare, the iron rings embedded in the wall used to train it are visible; when the tree was a sapling, its young branches were passed through the rings to bend and direct them upward. The rings remain in place as a retainer, ensuring that the tree keeps its shape. Smaller, fruit-bearing boughs extrude from each branch and are carefully pruned back each spring—for looks and to keep the tree flowering and fruiting, which it's done for over fifty years. Interestingly, the pear had been allowed to overgrow and the museum's horticulturalists are in the process of returning it to a more traditional, sparser tree, a task that requires observation, diligence, and patience—key skills for gardeners who wish to practice espaliering.

Like the other plants at the Cloisters, the Bonnefont pear is carefully tended and always looks perfect. Seeing the tree in its finished glory makes the process seem deceptively easy: you plant, you trim, you train. Inspired, I was determined to give the technique a try as soon as I got the chance.

Beginning with the Basics

The first detailed record of espaliering dates from the sixteenth century, but it's a technique that has its roots in the classical world. The practice is perfect for tiny gardens because it makes for super efficient use of space. Fruit trees were and still are popular choices for espalier because of their practicality: they produce fruit! Multiple trees are needed for this purpose, and being planted in close proximity makes for optimal pollination. Plants are installed against a wall or frame (solid walls provide support and also absorb and distribute heat), and then branches are trimmed, bent, and trained to create shape and form. Trees subjected to this careful cut-and-contort process tend to thrive with great efficiency: delivering nutrients to a minimal number of branches coupled with fewer leaves for the sun to penetrate allows for fruit to develop more abundantly and ripen quickly.

Most espaliered trees you'll encounter are fruit or flower bearing, but really any tree can be espaliered. *Garden Design* magazine suggests that fruit trees—especially apple, pear, pomegranate, and fig—are the easiest to manipulate and control. I've tried both fruiting and flowering trees, and I have to agree with that assessment. I'll add that even if your implementation of the practice doesn't produce something absolutely symmetrical, it has other benefits. While I didn't succeed completely in shaping my grape vines into a perfect fan (a traditional espalier pattern), they produced more fruit and had healthier foliage when I used espaliering techniques to train the vines over a trellis on my deck.

The basics of espaliering are simple—but perhaps not easy if, like me, you tend to be a distracted gardener:

1. Select your trees. Increase your espalier success by using plants that will thrive in your area. Find your hardiness zone (see pages 221–22 or visit http://planthardiness .ars.usda.gov/PHZMWeb/) and then check with local nurseries and garden programs to determine what trees will thrive in your climate and soil conditions.

2. Build a wall. You'll need a wall or a framework against which to plant your trees—for support in training, and, if solid, to distribute and direct heat to your plants.

3. Before planting, decide on the shape you want to create, and then make a plan to achieve it. Native American trail trees are a rarity today, but you'd know one immediately if you stumbled upon it. The tree's trunk grows straight for several feet, forms a hard right angle, and then shoots

upward. These trees were used to give direction as well as mark hunting grounds and sacred space. The method used to shape them is similar to espaliering: a thong is wrapped around the sapling trunk, which is carefully bent and tied down to a stake driven into the ground. The thong is adjusted and the branches trimmed until the tree reaches maturity. Shape is only limited by your imagination. Depending on what you want to create, you may need to install a trellis or, as at the Cloisters, drive metal rings into the wall where your espalier is planted to secure the tree's limbs while it's growing. Horizontal wires strung tightly on metal posts also make sturdy supports.

4. Plant your trees. Trees should be installed about six inches from the wall's base. If you're planting multiple trees, check with your local nursery, garden center, or favorite reference to see how far apart they should be spaced for optimal pollination.

5. Prune judiciously. Depending on your desired shape, cut off any extra branches; only keep those branches that you're going to allow to develop and grow. Check your favorite resource for the best times to prune; some plants need to be established, even for a short time, before pruning.

6. Secure branches to your support system to train them. Carefully secure the branches to your trellis or wires, or slip them through metal rings, being careful not to break them.

7. Check your plants regularly. Trim back any unwanted growth, check for problems, and repair your support system when needed.

8. Wait, watch, and repeat steps 5 through 7.

Adventures in Amateur Espaliering

The basic principles of espalier seemed simple enough to me, but, alas, I had no wall to work with. I did, however, have fences, pillars, beams, and trellises—enough to put espaliering to work, or so I thought . . .

The Blackberry Fence Fail

Plant fences have long been a means of establishing borders in an attractive way. The Belgian fence is a checkerboard pattern created by intersecting diagonal branches. I figured that blackberries would be a good candidate for this method, as the initial plants I got at the nursery were single canes. It started out well enough and might have worked had I not been a neglectful gardener.

I planted the canes one to two feet apart against the chain link fence (which I also intended to use as the support system) that ran along the side of my house. It didn't take long for the blackberries to cover the fence—and then quickly spread everywhere else. If I didn't cut them, the canes, heavy with leaves and fruit, bent earthward and planted themselves. After returning from a two-week trip, I found that I had clumpy bushes instead of single intersecting rows. I ended up letting these go, trimming the now-thick groups of canes down in the autumn when the fruiting season was over.

I'm not sure if blackberries were the best choice for my Belgian fence. Despite having strong stalks, they seem to do better as bushes that get cut down regularly. Keeping them as a Belgian fence would have meant recutting and shaping them every year. I might try this again with a less aggressive plant on another area of fence, and despite *Garden Design's* recommendation, I think I'm going to try it with a camellia—who doesn't love flowers?

The Wisterious Creature

There's a lovely house on Hughes Street in Cape May that I've admired for many years. The porch is lined with wisteria that in the spring rains down a curtain of lavender-colored flowers over the front porch. At the height of summer, the curtain turns a cool, dark green providing much needed shade. I've seen the plant in the winter as well; it's a single trunk planted at one corner of the porch with two "arms" that stretch out and wrap around the edge of the porch's ceiling, creating a kind of frame—a sculpted tree in the spirit of espalier if ever there was one. I was determined to try it, and that plant schooled me.

I planted two wisteria saplings in front of my porch, one at each corner. Once they got growing, I got my first lesson: stick to your plan. I liked the way one of the plants started twisting around the pillars of the porch. I shouldn't have allowed it to do that. One storm "untwisted" the branch, which ended up damaging the porch.

Keep this in mind as you're trimming away:
most of the time it'll grow back.

When it was time to give the wisteria a trim, I got lesson two: prune judiciously. When left to its own devices, wisteria is a wild plant. It shoots out tendrils in all directions from above and below. One day, to save time, we gave it a haircut with the hedge trimmer. It looked neat for about two weeks and then it became a creature of myth: where we cut one branch, five grew back, and it became completely unmanageable. It took forever to trim it back, one bough at a time, to reach the single, central branch I'd originally cultivated, but it was worth it. The next spring, my flowers doubled.

For the Love of Grapes

I grew up in a house that had a grape arbor. Our landlady never pruned it, but year after year it produced fruit, much of which was allowed to fall, which attracted lots of bees—not the best way to manage grapes. Years later I got to see a far more efficient system up close when I toured some wineries up in New York's Finger Lakes region. There, the hillsides are lined with rows and rows of grapevines, trained on horizontal wires, much the same way apple espaliers are trained when they're saplings—save that the grapes were free standing with no wall, the better for the fruit to imbibe the air circulation and moisture off the lakes, which renders a variety of different-flavored wines.

A vine, not a tree, grapes can be easily espaliered, I found. I planted two vines to create a natural covering for my back deck. The plan was to have a central thick vine from which I allowed smaller branches to grow—these would produce shade from the leaves and, hopefully, a fair amount of edible (rather than dropped!) fruit. I allowed one vine to grow thick and woody while selected smaller ones "fanned" out to either side. Every autumn I trimmed it all back to a single branch. The first time my husband saw this he was convinced that I'd killed it—but, of course, it was very much alive.

Further Adventures in Espaliering

The Cloisters chronicles the seasons of their espaliered pear (and the rest of their gardens) at their blog, *The Medieval Garden*

Enclosed (http://blog.metmuseum.org/cloistersgardens/2011/04/15/our-pear/). It's a great place to begin any kind of research on ancient horticultural techniques.

When I first started my adventures in espaliering, I got super simple instructions from *Better Homes and Gardens* (http://www.bhg.com/gardening/trees-shrubs-vines/care/how-to-espalier/) and then more detailed, step-by-step instructions and troubleshooting tips from Peter Thevenot's article "Espalier" in *Fine Gardening*, issue 70 (http://www.finegardening.com/espalier). Further inspiration can be found in the photo gallery that Thevenot maintains on his website, River Road Farms (http://www.espaliertrees.com/espalier-tree-gallery/), and in the YouTube video "The Art of Espalier," in which he shows of many of his trees, including one that is heart-shaped (https://www.youtube.com/watch?v=Gjotnm_iXdI)!

Candlecraft: Light Up Your Own Little Corner of the World

✤ by Susan Pesznecker ✤

People once used pitchy wood for torches and then made more elaborate ones of bundled plant stems, cattails, or rolled papyrus, which were eventually dipped in melted beeswax or animal fats. The process evolved into candles that were shaped, molded, and dipped. Candles were an important resource in societies past: the now-obsolete term "candlepower" was once widely used to indicate a specific level of illumination. Some candles were even "metered" and used to tell time according to how quickly the candle consumed its wax. At some point colors and scents were added, and candles took on an increased variety of uses. Today the aesthetics of candles absolutely transcend their

practicality. These days, candles come in every imaginable shape and size. They may illuminate a romantic dinner, top a birthday cake, provide heat to a chafing dish, drip sealing wax onto a letter, add ambience to a room, or stock an emergency kit. Regardless of their use, what we think of as a candle is a solid waxen object with an embedded wick. The wick is lit, and the candle burns. But is it really that simple? Let's think for a moment about fire.

A fire needs three things to burn: oxygen, heat, and fuel. When a candle is lit, oxygen from the air meets the temporary fuel of the wick, and the lighter flame heats the wick until it ignites. Once the wick begins burning, its heat melts the candle wax around it. The molten wax is then pulled up the dry wick via capillary action. When the melted wax meets the hot, ignited wick, it vaporizes and bursts into flame, creating a burning candle as we know it. The burning wax becomes the new fuel, leaving the wick to be much more slowly consumed by the flame. As long as the heat, oxygen, and fuel are available, the candle will keep burning.

The Substrates: Waxes, Oils, and Fats

The substrate of the candle—the material that surrounds the wick and provides fuel for the flame—may be made of waxes, oils, fats, or a combination of them. Let's explore some of these in more detail.

Petroleum-Based Substrates

Paraffin wax is derived from petroleum—oil. It is soft, colorless, easy to melt, and extremely flammable. Usually sold in blocks, paraffin wax is inexpensive, is easy to work with, and makes a candle that burns steadily and gives a bright light. The drawbacks? It emits a lot of soot and also gives off toxic fumes when burned. Occasional exposure to paraffin fumes is probably not dangerous, but frequent exposure is ill-advised, as is burning paraffin candles in a close, unventilated space.

Mineral oil, another petroleum by-product, is a liquid but may be combined with paraffin, resins, and other waxes to make a firm candle substrate. This may create a option less toxic than burning plain paraffin, although there still will be some issue with fumes. Mineral oil gels—stabilized with chemical polymers—are another form of substrate that is available from many candle suppliers. A plus with gels is that they take color and scent additions quite well. A drawback is that burning the petroleum plus a polymer product may release questionable fumes.

Petroleum jelly, present in many of our bathrooms, is yet another petroleum derivative and one that burns quite readily. It can be stiffened with the addition of waxes and resins. The jelly may also be packed into a small container around a wick and will make a small, serviceable candle.

Animal Substrates

Beeswax is gathered from the comb of honeybee hives; because this process is somewhat complicated, beeswax tends to be expensive. Natural beeswax is very soft; processed versions may be compacted and become much firmer. Soft beeswax sheets are rolled around wicks to create long taper candles, which tend to burn quickly and with a sweet scent. The beeswax itself smells like honey, and the soft forms are also often used for herbal balms and lotions. The wax is also available in processed bricks (for chopping and grating) or granules that can be melted for use in molded candles. Beeswax candles tend to be somewhat sticky and can sag or wilt when exposed to external heat. Their deep gold color may make it harder to add color. They are drip-free and relatively soot-free when burned. (No candles are truly soot-free. Some of the soot comes from substrate, but much also comes from the wick. The longer the wick, the more soot and smoke will be present.)

Any sort of animal fat may be used to make a candle. For example, beef fat (tallow) and rendered beef fat (lard) were historically used for candle making. The drawbacks? The fat quickly becomes rancid if not refrigerated. There's also lots of smokiness when burned, and they give off a strong hint of *eau de hamburger*. While this isn't most people's idea of the ideal candle, animal fats still have a place in candlecraft, even if only historically or just for emergencies.

Vegetable Substrates

Soy wax comes from processed soybean oil and is sold in pellet and granule form. Candles made from soy wax are fairly sturdy and burn cleanly with little soot, and they're known to be especially nontoxic. A drawback is that they sometimes burn with an odd scent; this can be covered with the addition of a scenting agent. Another issue is that soy wax can melt easily in hot weather.

Palm wax comes from palm trees. It makes an ideal candle that's very hard when cooled and burns clean with little soot. However, the ethics of palm harvest have become more widely known: palm groves are being devastated for their ingredients instead of sustainably harvested. This has resulted in horrific environmental effects, and many reliable candle sources no longer carry palm products.

A number of plants, trees, and herbs have waxy plant substrates that can be incorporated in candlecraft. One of the best known is the bayberry, a small berry that is rich in wax. Bayberry wax is extracted through a multistage simmering process and results in a rather brittle substrate that is often mixed and softened with beeswax. Bayberry candles tend to be a light sage-green color and have a distinctive pleasant smell.

The "desert candle" plant (*Euphorbia antisyphilitica*), common rosemary (*Rosmarinus officinalis*), common mullein (*Verbascum thapsus*), wax myrtle (*Myrica cerifera*), and a number of other *Myrica* trees and shrubs can also be used for wax and resin extraction, although none of these plants come close to the abundant waxiness of the bayberry. Mullein stalks can also be used as wicks or burned as simple torches.

Coniferous trees are resinous, and when the bark is damaged or broken, the trees tend to weep pitch. The chunks of hardened pitch can be broken off, simmered in water to melt and release dirt and bits of bark, skimmed, and then rehardened around wicks. For a more primitive candle, put a chunk of pitch on a stone and light it—no wick needed!

Oils can be extracted from a number of plants, as in the wide range of cooking, carrying, and essential oils that we know well. Carrier oils—for example, sunflower, apricot, olive, and others—can be mixed with solid waxes to form a pleasant candle substrate. Some oils, like coconut, are softly solid at room temperature and can be packed into wicked jars to make a quick-burning candle. Partially hydrogenated oils—solid vegetable shortenings—are oils that have been artificially modified and stiffened in the laboratory. Although very toxic in our diet, they can be used in candlecraft.

The Wicks

The wick is the part of the candle that gathers the melted wax or hot oil and pulls it upward, where it can become hot and catch fire, giving both heat and light. The only trick is that the wick has to heat up and burn first, so the wick material must be substantial enough to be able to burn and remain intact while the candle substrate melts and begins to soak the wick. Technically, any substance that can do this can be a wick. Cotton is traditional, but any natural string or fabric can work, as can sturdy plant stems and even very dry pieces of wood. I saw a really wonderful candle once that used a piece of pumice in a saucer of oil. The pumice was soaked in oil in advance. Placed atop the oil, the uppermost part of the pumice was lit and began drawing oil up through the stone, providing something between a candle and a lamp. It was fascinating, and it just goes to show that all ideas are worth a try!

Candle wicks are typically made of cotton and are braided. The braiding was traditionally "roundish," and in times past these wicks—whether used for candles or oil lanterns—had to be trimmed frequently to remove the burned portion. Modern braided wicks use a flat braid; the shape causes the wick to curl over as the melted wax burns, and the wick actually catches on fire and shortens itself.

Some wicks are attached to a piece of metal, as in votive candles. This helps hold a wick in place inside a mold, with a few drops of melted wax affixing the metal piece to the mold's bottom. When you make your own candles, this wick anchor could also be made of a small stone or crystal, a shell, or anything that accomplishes the purpose.

Purchased wicks may be stiffened with wire or stiff paper, allowing them to stand up straight while wax is poured into a mold around them. This is handy, but beware: depending on the wire material, toxic gases and particulates may be related into the air around the candle. Stiffeners used to be made of lead, but legislation from 2003 now prevents lead wicking from being made in the United States or imported.

Wicks purchased in a store have been treated with a mordant—a substance that helps prevent the wick from igniting too rapidly and burning up before it begins capturing melted wax. If making your own wicks at home, a mixture of borax and table salt dissolved in water makes a good mordant: allow the wicks to soak in the mordant for a couple of hours, then remove and dry completely before using. I've had success with a mordant of one tablespoon of salt, two tablespoons of borax, and one-half cup of water. Purchase borax in the laundry section of your supermarket or in your favorite hardware store.

Note that there's a bit of technique needed when working with wicks. A soft wax that burns quickly (e.g., a rolled beeswax candle) will need a short, thinner wick, while a candle of hard wax will need a longer, thicker one. Mastering these proportions may take some trial and error, but experimentation is always fun, right?

The Additives

Candles can be colored with commercial candle dyes or by adding bits of colored wax to the molten substrate. Broken crayons are excellent for this. Your favorite essential oils may be used to scent candles, and alcohol-based extracts—such as vanilla and others used for cooking—also work for scenting.

Candles can be textured in many ways, including by adding "roughage" (crystals, sand, dried herbs, etc.) to the molten wax, by carving the finished candle, or through various candle-crafting techniques. And there are a number of ways to directly incorporate herbs in your candle making: the herbaceous plants themselves may furnish wax or oil; plant-based carrier oils may be mixed with waxes to form a substrate; essential herbal oils may be added to provide scent or healing qualities; and dried aerial parts may be used decoratively within the candles.

The Methods

All candle substrates (especially paraffin) are extremely flammable: always use a double boiler to melt waxes, melt them slowly over low heat, watch them constantly, and never leave melting wax unattended. Some sources suggest melting wax in a microwave; I do not agree with this, for it's very difficult to assess whether or not microwaved wax might be overheating, and it can easily ignite. If your wax should ignite, cover it with a lid. If a small amount of hot wax splatters on your skin, put the affected area under cold running water immediately, and gently peel off the wax as soon as it solidifies. If a large area of skin is covered with wax, put it under cold water, apply a clean rag or gauze bandage wrung out in cold water, and get yourself to urgent care immediately.

Once you're finished with your melted wax, take it off the heat and place it in a location where no one else might accidentally tip it over. It will solidify quickly.

A wide range of candle-making techniques are available to you, and deciding which one to use is half the fun. If using molds, oil them lightly, and remember to place your wicks before you start. Plan on letting your candles cool overnight before disturbing them, and if removing them from molds, wipe the candles clean of oily film and trim the wick.

Molded Candles

Choose a mold, install a wick, and pour in your melted wax. Use commercial molds or try a clean, empty can or waxed carton. Molded candles can be any shape, from short and squat to slender tapers. Small paper cups can be used to make votive candles. Pouring different colored waxes one at a time and cooling in between creates a layered candle.

Dipped Tapers

Cut a length of wicking the length you want your candle to be plus about four inches. Tie a loop in one end. Holding the loop, dip the wicking into the hot wax and lift it out. Allow it to cool and solidify briefly. Then repeat. Repeat as many times as needed until the taper is as thick as you want. Thread a chopstick or dowel through the loop and suspend the chopstick between two tall objects, allowing the new candle to hang freely and cool. Use the same process to make your own tiny pillar candles for birthday or special occasion cakes.

Rolled Tapers

Roll a sheet of beeswax or soft wax around a full-length wick, with one to two inches of wick protruding from one end.

Sand Candles

Dig a hole in dry sand, install a wick, and pour in your melted wax. Alternatively, prepare a mold as for a molded candle, and before adding the wax, toss dry sand into the mold, allowing sand to stick to the oiled surfaces.

Ice Candles

Place a wick in an oiled mold and fill with large ice cubes or chunks. Pour in hot wax. Once this cools, the candle will be filled with irregular holes from the melted ice—a very pretty effect.

Jarred Candles

Weight one end of a wick so it will stay put in the bottom of a clear glass jar. Pour in wax, insuring that the unweighted end of the wick stays above the candle's surface. Another method is to install a wick in the jar and then pour in commercial granular candle wax. The granules—which are often colored and scented—will gradually melt when the candle is lit. Give it your own spin by stirring a few drops of essential oil into the granules before pouring them into the mold.

Crayon-Based Candles

Fill an oiled mold with staggered pieces of broken crayons. Fill the mold with colorless wax. This makes a brilliant, color-varied candle. For another version, fill the mold alternately with crayon bits and ice cubes, then add hot wax. Did you know that crayons themselves will burn like candles, even without a wick? Bundle several together around a wick for a fun effect.

Wine Bottle Drip Candles

You'll need a wine (or other narrow-necked) bottle and a large taper candle that drips wax. Install the candle in the bottle neck, light it, and allow wax to drip down the sides of the bottle. For a better effect, change the candle or color periodically. Don't leave this (or any) candle unattended while burning!

Floating Candles

Make small molded candles that are rather wide on top, shallow in depth, and much smaller on bottom. When cool, their shape allows them to float on water, making for a lovely special effect.

Carved Candles

Use a sharp stick, large safety pin, scissor or knife tip, or other sharp object to carve designs into a finished candle. You can then use fine-tipped permanent markers to fill in the carved areas if desired, providing a nice contrast with the candle surface.

Store your candles in a cool, dark place. Candles may become tacky over time, and keeping them in an airtight box or zipped plastic bag will keep them dry, dust-free, and ready to use.

Miniature Gardens

⫷ by Autumn Damiana ⫸

If you have been to a home improvement, craft, or book store recently, you have probably heard about fairy gardens. Right now there are books, online tutorials, and even whole websites dedicated to making fairy gardens, and many stores stock ready-made accessories and even complete landscapes. Fairy gardens are a recent trend in an otherwise older tradition of miniature garden making. Some people believe that fairies, gnomes, pixies, and other "wee folk" are attracted to or inhabit these gardens, and some simply put them together because it is an enjoyable hobby or because they take up little space. Whatever your reason, if you want to make your own miniature garden, you have a plethora of options.

Miniature Garden Varieties

The Aforementioned Fairy Garden

This kind of garden has specific features. Usually there is a "fairy door," which is a tiny, detailed door or hatch of some sort, glued or otherwise set into the side of a tree, building, or large plant container. The idea is that fairies will pass through the door and into the surrounding garden, which may also have fairy houses or furniture for the fairies to use.

Terrariums

These are miniature gardens that are usually decorative in nature, planted inside clear glass containers. The inside of a closed terrarium is usually its own ecosystem, as light passes through and water vapor is recycled inside the container. An open terrarium is optimal for plants that need little water or soil—usually succulents or air plants.

Zen Gardens

Just like their larger cousins, mini Zen gardens are focal points of meditation and are designed to still the mind, reduce stress, and create feelings of peace and contentment. These gardens typically feature large areas of sand or fine gravel, with larger rocks and plants used sparingly.

Holiday Arrangements

With so many Christmas village and Halloween haunted house collectables and miniatures, it makes sense to design an entire holiday garden around these centerpieces to show them off and add to the ambiance. Miniature trees and ground cover are perfect for this type of setup.

Dollhouse Yards

If your child likes to play with dolls, then you might consider making a garden for them. This can be as simple as a patch of grass with basic accessories, or can be a full-blown scale dollhouse garden with scale miniatures. Another type of garden for children to play with can be constructed for the size of their favorite action figures, with big stones and fortress-type structures amid larger plants and bushes for their figures to hide in and explore.

Birthday Party Gardens

Crafts are a recent trend in children's birthday party activities, so making inexpensive mini fairy gardens has become one way for children to have fun at a party while taking home something meaningful that they have made themselves. Of course, this idea doesn't have to be limited to children. Anyone with a fondness for miniatures and gardening can take advantage of this idea. Consider making miniature gardens at your next adult gathering—a birthday, a tea party, craft night, during the holiday season, and so on.

Miniature Garden Gifts

Perfect for anyone who "has it all." A mini garden that you have made from scratch makes a thoughtful gift, since it will be completely unique and you can tailor the garden to reflect the recipient's personality. Just make sure that this person can and will want to take care of a miniature garden—plants are living things, and, as such, they will require ongoing care and attention.

Locations and Containers

Any corner of your yard—in part of a flower bed, under a fountain, on an old stump, or even nestled in between the roots of a tree—can be the perfect spot to house your miniature garden. Or, to make things easier, you can plant one in some kind of container that is placed in the yard. These can include terra-cotta pots, bird baths, planter boxes, wagons or wheelbarrows, metal washtubs, and so on.

Container gardening is popular because it gives you more choices, especially if you would like to make your miniature garden an indoor one. Vessels made from glazed ceramic, wood, metal, concrete, and even plastic are all acceptable. Glass makes for an interesting visual because you can see the roots, soil, and moisture in your garden in addition to the plants themselves. Naturally, you can purchase a container, but first look around and see if you have anything on hand that you can use so you can save your money for the plants and accessories you will want to buy. Some more unusual container ideas include baskets, chipped crockery, abalone shells, or even a suitcase or an old shoe.

Your choice of location or container should take into account the climate that you live in and its seasonal weather patterns. In areas with harsh winters you have to be prepared to replant your garden if it freezes or gets drowned out by rain. On the other hand, if you live in a hotter environment, then you may have to worry more about drought or the intensity of the summer sun. A small container garden can be moved or brought indoors if weather is a concern. Indoor gardens may also have seasons or cycles, depending on what kind of plants you include. Knowing about these variables can help you choose how and where to plan your garden and determine what you would like to do with it year-round.

Picking out locations, containers, and appropriate plants is a chicken-and-egg type of conundrum: Which should you do first? Since there are so many plant choices out there, I recommend that you begin by deciding on a spot for your miniature garden and see what kind of environment it can provide. Different plants may have widely different needs in terms of sun, moisture, drainage, and space. And if you get stuck or are at a loss, you can turn to books, the internet, or free professional help from your local nursery. I also highly recommend gathering information from local garden clubs and native plant experts, and don't forget about your gardening relatives, neighbors, and friends!

Live and Dried Plants and Cuttings

Arranging your landscape is the same with a miniature garden as it is with a full-sized one. You always want to plant your taller varieties in the back, midsize ones in the middle, and shorter ones up front. Scale is an important determination: Do you want to grow plants that are all miniature and that complement each other in size (a true mini garden), or are you willing to work with regular-size plants?

For a mini garden made to scale, try plants with tiny blooms, such as wood anemone, violet, dwarf sea thrift, miniature daisy, creeping bluestar, heron's bill, blue moneywart, and even wood sorrel.

For a true miniature garden, there are mini evergreens and conifers, bonsai (which are any small or dwarf variety of tree), tiny-leafed herbs, creeping/stonecrop sedum, and miniature ground cover, which includes varieties of ivy, fern, grass, and moss. Some creeping vines and flowering plants are also perfect for a miniature garden, but a lot of these need to have their growth checked by frequent pruning or training for them to retain their diminutive stature. Look for plants that are actually labeled as miniature or dwarf or have words such as *little*, *tiny*, *fairy*, *elfin*, and so on in their names or descriptions.

A miniature garden that is not restricted by scale or size can include just about anything. Inexpensive herbs or flowering annuals are easy starter plants, many of which can be grown from seed. Or you can design a desert landscape made entirely of succulents, which also require very little maintenance. A simple tray full of grass seed or a low-growing sedum is a good place to start for a dollhouse yard. Some fairy gardens also include plants that attract hummingbirds or butterflies. Unfortunately, there aren't many choices for a strictly indoor garden besides houseplants, but this is where dried plants come in.

Dried plants and plant cuttings might be the perfect solutions for a hassle-free or temporary indoor garden or to fill in the spaces between live plants. Fill-in plants include dried moss or pinecones, whereas dried flowers, acorns, seed pods, and even fall leaves can make attractive focal points. These are often the best choices for those who desire a miniature garden but can't or don't want to take care of a live one. For a temporary display, consider also adding plant cuttings or cut flowers.

Store-Bought, Handmade, and Found Accessories

There are endless ways you can decorate your miniature garden. When choosing how to accessorize, here are four ideas you should keep in mind:

1. What kind of aesthetic effect do I want to create?

2. How much money am I willing to spend?

3. Do I want to make my own accessories?

4. Is what I want to add compatible with my garden?

Let's take a brief look at each of these questions and explore the possibilities, some dos and don'ts, and some practical advice.

1. Aesthetics

Depending on how you have created your garden and what it is for, this may be an easy question to answer. Zen or meditation gardens typically have lots of sand or pebbles, a statue of Buddha or a pagoda, and a mini rake to move the sand around and to make patterns with. A dollhouse garden or yard will likely have some tiny furniture, such as a bench, fountain, or birdbath. The trick is to decide if you want to use completely natural accessories made of wood, stone, metal, or glass, or if you are okay with plastic, resin, and whatnot. Most commercially available miniature garden accessories are made of these substances, especially fairy doors and other fairy garden furniture. However, if you know of a dollhouse miniatures retailer, you can pick up amazingly detailed and well-crafted accessories made from authentic materials: real wood or metal benches, actual terra-cotta mini pots, wire or wicker baskets, and lots more.

2. Cost

With so many choices out there, spending on accessories can quickly become quite expensive. If you want to get the most out of your budget, I suggest getting one, two, or at most three very prominent pieces for your garden and then supplementing with inexpensive materials, such as mosaic tiles, round and flat glass marbles, shells, interesting-looking stones, or any of the earlier dried plant suggestions, such as acorns and pinecones. The best part about decorating this way is that you can use what you find around the house or during your outdoor adventures—children love to pick up rocks and shells, and their little treasures added to your garden make cute mementos. As an alternative, you can use your miniature garden as a way to display objects, like glass art or a crystal collection.

3. DIY Accessories

Even if you feel that you are not crafty, you should be able to make some of your miniature garden decorations quite easily. Online resources are a big help here, and read the directions beginning on the next page. Also check out these books: *Miniature Gardens* by Katie Elzer-Peters and, for children, *Super Simple Fairy Gardens* by Alex Kuskowski. Both of these books have some easy-to-follow directions on how to landscape your miniature garden with glass, pebbles, and shells as well as a few craft projects you can try your hand at.

4. Compatibility

Unfortunately, you can't always make every accessory that you would like to add to your miniature garden work well with the garden setup. You can't, for example, put little paper cocktail umbrellas in an outdoor garden, because they will deteriorate almost immediately. It's also difficult to use solar-powered lights indoors, because these may not be able to charge correctly. Knowing in your planning stage what kind of aesthetic you are looking for can help resolve these problems before they occur. Naturally, you will also have to choose decorations that will not interfere with the continued growth and health of your plants. Fine, colored sand, for example, is usually a no-no for plants that require lots of water because the sand won't hold moisture—and frequent waterings will cause the sand to seep further into the soil and will also ruin the decorative effect of the sand in the process.

Making Your Own Accessories

If you know how to sculpt and you have access to a kiln, custom ceramics can be a wonderful addition to your miniature garden. Glazed or unglazed, after being fired these pieces will withstand the elements and will give your garden a unique quality that only handmade accessories can give. Another idea is to find a ceramics studio where you can paint a piece of pottery that the studio will then fire for you. These places typically have a large assortment of containers, plaques, and statues of animals, fairies, gnomes, dragons, and so on.

Polymer "clay," although artificial, is another option if you choose to make furniture or other items for your miniature garden. It is available in many colors and in small amounts for just a few dollars. You can easily fashion birdbaths, benches, fairy doors, stepping stones, mini containers, and more. Simply choose the clay colors you would like, sculpt something, and then bake them in your oven according to the package directions. The resulting pieces can be filed or sanded to remove imperfections and can even be painted, drilled, or have other items (like rhinestones or pebbles) glued to them. Keep in mind that modifications to the baked clay may not hold up over time against sun, water, and extreme temperatures.

There are also a number of accessories that you can make out of natural materials. Turn over a terra-cotta pot and glue a saucer to the top to make a birdbath, or stack these pot-and-saucer combinations in descending order by size to make a fountain. Balance stones on each other and then glue them in place for an impressive Zen garden piece. Find branches of different diameters and cut them into thin slices to make stepping stones or thick slices to make stools and tables. Use toothpicks or popsicle sticks (depending on the size you are looking for) and glue them together to make picket fences, doors, and bridges. Painted rocks are another fun and inexpensive addition to your garden—they can be decorated like bees or ladybugs, mushrooms, or small woodland critters or with inspirational words and inscriptions. Again, there are many, many more ideas online; YouTube and Pinterest are especially helpful if you are looking for tutorials.

In Conclusion

The world of miniature gardens is the same as the world of regular gardens around us, just much, much smaller. I, for one, am very happy to see the popularity of fairy and other miniature gardens growing (no pun intended) because it gives people a chance to connect with gardening in a way that they may not previously have. Even if you have next to nothing in the way of space, money, or time, or if you feel that you're lacking a "green thumb," there's no reason that you can't enjoy gardening—in miniature.

Plant
Profiles

Plant Profiles

This section features spotlights on individual herbs, high-lighting their cultivation, history, and culinary, crafting, and medicinal uses. Refer to the key below for each plant's sun and water needs, listed in a helpful at-a-glance table.

Key to Plant Needs	
Sun	
Shade	—
Partial shade	☀
Partial sun	☀ ☀
Full sun	☀ ☀ ☀
Water	
Water sparingly	◊
	◊ ◊
Water frequently	◊ ◊ ◊

USDA Hardiness Zones

The United States is organized into zones according to the average lowest annual winter temperature, indicating a threshold for cold tolerance in the area. This USDA Plant Hardiness Zone Map uses the latest available data. For best results, plant herbs that can withstand the climate of their hardiness zone(s) and bring less hardy plants indoors during colder weather. Seek additional resources for high summer temperatures, as these can vary within zones.

It is helpful to keep track of temperatures and frost dates in your neighborhood or check with a local gardening center or University Extension for the most up-to-date record. Climate change and local topography will also affect your growing space, so compensate accordingly.

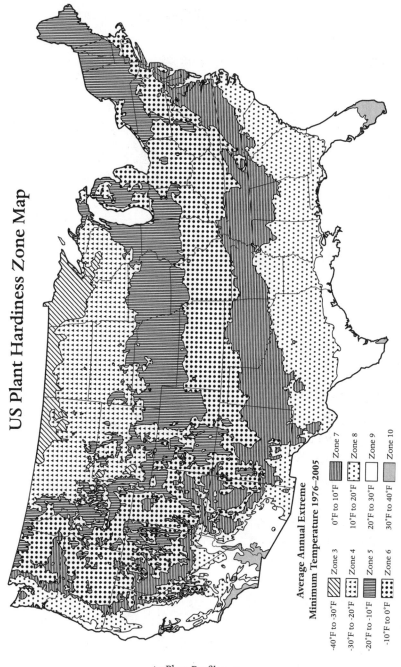

US Plant Hardiness Zone Map

Average Annual Extreme
Minimum Temperature 1976–2005

Zone 3 -40°F to -30°F
Zone 4 -30°F to -20°F
Zone 5 -20°F to -10°F
Zone 6 -10°F to 0°F
Zone 7 0°F to 10°F
Zone 8 10°F to 20°F
Zone 9 20°F to 30°F
Zone 10 30°F to 40°F

US Plant Hardiness Zone Map (Cont.)

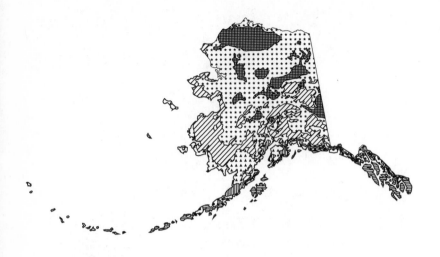

**Average Annual Extreme
Minimum Temperature 1976–2005**

-60°F to -50°F	Zone 1	10°F to 20°F	Zone 8
-50°F to -40°F	Zone 2	20°F to 30°F	Zone 9
-40°F to -30°F	Zone 3	30°F to 40°F	Zone 10
-30°F to -20°F	Zone 4	40°F to 50°F	Zone 11
-20°F to -10°F	Zone 5	50°F to 60°F	Zone 12
-10°F to 0°F	Zone 6	60°F to 70°F	Zone 13
0°F to 10°F	Zone 7		

Chives: Invite Them to Your Table All Summer Long

✺ by Anne Sala ✺

D id you plant chives in your gar-den and then completely forget to use them? Chives are such a hum-ble herb whose usefulness can be drowned out by the urgent needs of other short-lived herbs, like cilantro (which always bolts on me) or basil (and its massive amount of leaves). But look over there, in the corner of your garden—your chives are wait-ing to be used. Every year, the plant sends up its delicate onion-flavored greens and darling purple pom-pom flowers, trying to get your attention. I hope this article will help you come up with ways to enjoy this easy-to-grow perennial all season long.

Allium schoenoprasum is the small-est and mildest-flavored member of

Chives	
Species	*Allium schoenoprasum*
Zone	3–10
Needs	☀☀☀☀ 💧💧
Soil pH	6.0–7.0
Size	6–12 in., out & up

the onion family, which also includes garlic, scallions, and leeks. It grows from edible bulbs with a fine, papery skin, similar to the white or yellow onion, but it does not grow nearly as large. Thin, hollow, tubular leaves, or scapes, rise up from the bulbs in a grasslike clump to a height between six and twelve inches. In late spring or early summer, pink or lavender-colored flowers bloom at the top of stems that rise dramatically above the leaves. These blossoms form a pert-looking ball and are also edible.

Garlic chives, *Allium tuberosum*, look similar to onion chives, except they have flat, solid leaves that grow to about sixteen inches and have white, star-shaped flowers. Also, as the name attests, they have a distinct garlic flavor.

Chives are the only member of the onion family to grow wild in North America, Europe, Asia, and Australia. While Europeans do not appear to have formally cultivated chives until five hundred years ago, documentation of the plant's culinary and medicinal uses in China go back three thousand years.

Like many of the greens that are the first to appear in spring, chives are rich in vitamins A and C. They have mild antiseptic qualities and were once used to stop bleeding and as an antidote for poison. Hung in the corners of a room, they were thought to keep evil and disease away.

Chives are also thought to lower blood pressure and, like garlic, might help prevent cancer. Farmers appreciate them as a companion plant, claiming they keep carrots free of greenflies and prevent scab on apple trees and black spot from rose bushes.

Chives are hardy and rarely need much tending other than an occasional dose of liquid fertilizer. The plant prefers a well-draining, rich soil and a good deal of sun. However, it can tolerate partial shade and poor soil without much complaint. This easygoing nature makes it a perfect container plant. Just make sure to water it often.

If growing to use the leaves, remove the flower buds when they appear, for the leaves will turn tough after they bloom.

To ensure your chives live for
many years, allow some of the flowers
to bloom and drop their seed.

When winter arrives, the plant will die back down to the ground. I find it nice to put a blanket of leaves over it for the winter, but it's probably not necessary.

To harvest chives, use kitchen shears to snip the greens singly or all of them in one remarkably satisfying cut. The plant can tolerate several full haircuts during the summer as long as you allow it to recover before cold weather arrives. Also, it is nice to enjoy at least one harvest of blossoms, so let a few bloom.

Recipes

Chives have such a long culinary history, it is difficult to improve on the food pairings our ancestors discovered so long ago. The herb is great with eggs, butter, creamy cheeses, potatoes, tomatoes, chicken, and fish and in salad dressings and mayonnaise-based salads. If used in a hot food, such as soup, it is best to add them at the end. They lose their flavor if cooked too long. They also lose their flavor if dried by conventional methods. Dried chives that you get at the store have been freeze-dried and retain their oniony-ness.

When spring finally returns to my corner of Minnesota, I immediately have to start guarding my chives, or else my children will eat each shoot as it appears. If I can keep the kids away from at least two sprouts, I have enough to begin using them in the kitchen.

Creamy Omelette with Chives and Tomatoes

Some say less is more. When it comes to creamy eggs, though, I say more is more, hence the double dose of dairy. When your chives have only recently awakened from their winter slumber, make this recipe with the eagerly awaited shoots. I suggest draining the tomatoes so the omelette's filling will be melty instead of runny.

> 4 large eggs
>
> 1 tablespoon sour cream
>
> Salt and pepper to taste
>
> 1 tablespoon butter or olive oil
>
> 5–6 onion chives 4 inches in length, snipped fine
>
> 2 ounces cream cheese, softened and cut into small pieces
>
> 4–6 cherry tomatoes, chopped and drained

In a medium-size bowl, whisk together the eggs, sour cream, salt, pepper, and a splash of water.

Heat the oil or butter in a medium-size skillet over medium heat. When hot enough to sizzle, add the eggs. Allow them to cook through on the bottom. Use a flat-tipped spatula to pull back the edges of the cooked eggs to allow the runny eggs to make contact with the pan. Reduce the heat to medium low.

When the eggs on the top of the omelette begin to solidify, scatter the chives, cream cheese pieces, and tomatoes on half the eggs. Fold over the other half and continue to cook until the cheese is melted. Serve immediately. Serves 2.

Fish Cakes with Chives

This fish cake recipe is inspired by the one created by the Herb Queen herself, Jekka McVicar. I love the way she cooks the fish in milk because it makes everything so tender. It is a great recipe for when your chives plant is perking up and starting to fill out.

  1 pound russet potatoes, peeled and diced

  Salt and pepper to taste

  1 pound cod or salmon fillets

  2–3 cups milk

  1 small bay leaf

  1 tablespoon onion chives, minced fine

  ½ cup all-purpose flour

  Butter and oil, such as canola or grapeseed, for pan-
    frying

Preheat the oven to 350°F. Place the potatoes in a large saucepan. Add enough cold water to cover and place over high heat. Bring the water to a boil and then simmer until tender, about 10–12 minutes. Drain the potatoes, add salt and pepper to taste, and then mash until mostly smooth.

While the potatoes are boiling, lay the fish in a casserole dish or baking pan that can hold it all in a single layer. Pour in the milk until the fish is almost completely covered. Add the bay leaf and cook until the fish is firm and flakes easily, about 12–15 minutes, depending on the thickness of the fillets and type of fish.

Remove the fish from the milk and then separate the flesh from the bones and skin. Use a fork to break the fish into large flakes. Discard the milk.

Gently mix the fish in with the potatoes and 1 tablespoon chives.

Using your hands, form the mixture into small balls. Flatten slightly, then coat the patties in flour.

Fry the cakes in the oil over medium-high heat. Leave them undisturbed until they just start to crisp and brown. Flip and cook until browned on the other side. Serve immediately with lemon wedges, vinegar, or tartar sauce. Serves 4.

Avocado and Chive Soup with Shrimp

When the days are heating up and you think your chives plant can handle its first haircut, try this simple soup, which is tasty warm or cold.

2 ripe avocados

2–3 cups chicken or vegetable broth

½ cup heavy cream

½ cup plain yogurt (not Greek)

2 tablespoons onion chives, snipped into ¼-inch pieces, plus more for garnish

2–6 fresh shrimp, peeled and deveined

2 tablespoons butter or olive oil

Salt and pepper to taste

Place the avocados, 1 cup of broth, cream, and yogurt in a blender. Process until smooth. You may splash in additional broth if it is too lumpy.

Pour the mixture into a saucepan with at least 1 more cup of broth and the 2 tablespoons of chives. Heat until just warmed through and the chives are fragrant. If you plan to serve it chilled, place the soup in a heat-safe container and cool in the refrigerator.

Heat the oil or melt the butter in a medium skillet. Add the shrimp. Cook until pink and opaque, about 2–3 minutes per side.

Ladle the soup into bowls. Top with the shrimp and chives garnish. Serves 4.

Egg Salad with Chive Blossoms

When I was just out of college, I would throw "Soup and Sandwich" parties for my birthday. My roommate and I would make a ton of different sandwiches and a huge pot of soup. My birthday is in January, so offering soup was a surefire way to get people to leave their warm homes. I love this sandwich, and if I ever do another Soup and Sandwich party, this sandwich will be the centerpiece.

You will want to use chives blossoms that recently opened and haven't yet formed seeds. If you would prefer to make this sandwich in a way that is not so "fancy," go ahead and mix the chives blossoms into the egg salad and omit the butter. Please feel free to cook the eggs with your preferred method.

6 large eggs

2 tablespoons salt and more to taste

2 tablespoons mayonnaise, or to taste, plus more for edging

1 stalk celery, minced

12 slices white bread

4 tablespoons unsalted butter, softened

4 fresh onion chives blossoms, rinsed, dried

Black pepper to taste

Place the whole eggs in a saucepan large enough to hold them in a single layer. Add cold water and tablespoon of salt, and set to boil over high heat. Once the eggs have reached the boiling point, remove the pan from the heat. Allow the eggs to sit in the hot water for 15–20 minutes. Drain the eggs and then immediately refill the pan with cold water. Keep adding new cold water until the eggs are cool enough to handle.

Crack and peel each egg under cold running water. Place all the shelled eggs in a large bowl. Mash them with a fork until the eggs are almost smooth in consistency. Add the mayonnaise, celery, salt, and pepper to taste. Set aside.

Carefully tug apart each chive blossom into its individual flowers. Scatter them evenly on a plate and set aside.

Gently butter one side of each bread slice. Spread a layer of egg salad on 6 slices. Top with the remaining slices. Use a serrated knife to slice the crusts off each sandwich. Then, depending on the size of the bread you are using, cut the sandwiches into thirds or triangles.

Carefully spread mayonnaise along the edge of one side of each sandwich, and dip that side onto the plate of chives blossoms.

Arrange the completed sandwiches on a serving platter. Cover with plastic wrap and store in the refrigerator until ready to serve. Serves 6–8.

Homestyle Bo Ssam

If you ever think your chives plant needs a serious haircut, make this dish. *Bo ssam* is Korean pulled pork. I first heard about it when the hip New York City restaurant Momofuko shared its recipe with the *New York Times*. It is a habit-forming way to eat pork and is a great food for a crowd. Unlike the party-ready egg salad sandwiches I just told you about, I'm going to show you how to make bo ssam into a simple affair. The taste, however, is still worth celebrating. This recipe serves 2–4.

Grocery stores in North America are starting to offer more Korean food staples, like kimchi. However, you might need to visit an Asian or specialty grocery to find *ssamjang* and *gochujang* (also spelled *kojuchang*)—important ingredients in the dressing. You can also order them online or even make them yourself. I've always had good luck following the recipes on Maangchi.com.

For the pork:

    1 tablespoon soy sauce

    1 tablespoon brown sugar

    1½ teaspoons mirin

    ½ teaspoon gochujang paste

    1½ teaspoon rice vinegar

    1½ pounds pork butt or shoulder, cooked and shredded, fat removed

Preheat oven to 450°F. Stir together all the ingredients, except the pork, in a medium bowl. Add the pork and mix until the meat is evenly coated.

Scatter and separate the pork mixture on a sheet pan lined with foil. Place the sheet pan in the oven and cook until shreds of pork begin to crisp and brown. Remove from the oven, cover with foil, and keep warm until ready to serve.

For the sauce:

    ½ cup (or all that your plant can give—up to ¾ cup) minced onion chives

¼ cup scallions (or less if your chives had a lot of leaves), thinly sliced

¼ cup ginger, peeled and minced

2 tablespoons ssamjang

1 teaspoon gochujang, or more to taste

1½ teaspoons soy sauce

½ cup rice wine vinegar

¼ cup peanut or grapeseed oil

Mix all the ingredients together. Chill until ready to use. It can be made a day ahead too.

For the meal:

Here is where you can decide to go party mode or homestyle mode. Place everything in a separate serving dish and set in the center of the table so each person can customize their meal.

1–2 heads bibb or Boston lettuce, leaves separated, washed and dried

3–4 cups cooked white rice

1 small English cucumber, peeled and sliced into ¼-inch matchsticks 2 inches long

1–2 cups kimchi, or to taste

For the party method, take a leaf of lettuce and top it with a little rice, pork, cucumber, kimchi, and sauce. Carefully fold up the sides and pop the whole packet in your mouth. Repeat.

For the homestyle method, scoop a portion of rice into each person's bowl. Tear a few leaves of lettuce on top, then add pork, kimchi, cucumbers, and a generous amount of sauce. Stir together and enjoy.

*In the language of flowers,
chives mean "usefulness."*

Bouquet Garni for Fish

Chives have a unique shape that makes them useful as a tool as well as a food. When the greens are long enough, they can be used to tie together bouqets garnis, especially ones for fish soups, which don't require long cooking times.

- 2–4 onion chive stems or stems with unopened flower buds, 12 inches long
- 2 sprigs Italian parsley
- 2 fronds of dill, 6 inches long
- 2 sprigs lemon balm

Lay the chives stems horizontally across a clean, dry work surface. Lay the rest of the herbs perpendicular across the chives. Carefully wind the chives around the other herbs and tie the ends in a double knot. Use immediately in the fish soup recipe of your choice.

Resources

"Chives: Planting Growing and Harvesting Chives." *The Old Farmer's Almanac.* Accessed September 10, 2017. https://www.almanac.com/plant/chives.

Cutler, Karan Davis, and Kathleen Fisher. *Herb Gardening for Dummies.* Foster City, CA: IDG Books Worldwide, 2000.

Divock, Rosemary. *Growing and Using Herbs in the Midwest.* Amherst, WI: Amherst Press, 1996.

Grieve, Maude. "Chives." In *A Modern Herbal*. New York: Dover, 1971. Electronic reproduction by Ed Greenwood at Botanical.com, 1995. Accessed September 10, 2017. http://www.botanical.com/botanical/mgmh/c/chives65.html.

Hollis, Sarah. *The Country Diary Herbal*. New York: Henry Holt and Company, 1990.

McVicar, Jekka. *The Complete Herb Book*. Buffalo, NY: Firefly Books, 2008.

———. *Jekka's Herb Cookbook*. Buffalo, NY: Firefly Books, 2011.

Schlosser, Katherine K. *The Herb Society of America's Essential Guide to Growing and Cooking with Herbs*. Baton Rouge: Louisiana State University Press, 2007.

Sifton, Sam. "The Bo Ssam Miracle." *New York Times Magazine*, January 12, 2012. http://www.nytimes.com/2012/01/15/magazine/the-bo-ssam-miracle.html.

Spungen, Susan. "Tea Sandwiches." Oprah.com. Accessed September 15, 2017. http://www.oprah.com/food/tea-sandwiches.

Kale: A Decorative and Delicious Superfood

⁂ by Doreen Shababy ⁂

I first met kale in the mideighties when learning how to decorate a salad bar. I'd never even heard of it before then. I'm not sure when I became fascinated with kale, but once I learned how to cook it and eat it, I then learned how to grow it. And growing it is easy and fun, because not only are there several "types" of kale for the kitchen garden, there are many ornamental hybrids that look almost like peonies or even roses.

Kale in the Garden

Kale, *Brassica oleracea*, is a primitive cabbage and is nonheading, a member of the acephala group. All the main forms of kale we know today have been grown for at least two thousand

Kale	
Species	*Brassica oleracea*
Zone	3–10
Needs	☀—☀☀☀ 💧💧💧
Soil pH	5.8–7.0
Size	up to 2 ft.

years, especially among the ancient Romans, who grew a wide variety, including tall and short, curly and plain, blue-green, yellow-green, and red kales.

There is also a plant called sea kale, *Crambe maritima*, the leaves of which greatly resemble cabbage kale, but it is not at all related; sea kale is a wild, salt-loving plant of coastal Europe. That being said, kale is sometimes used to take up soil salinity in coastal regions and as a rotation crop to prevent overmineralization.

Brassica napus, or Siberian kale, is typically milder in taste and of a more tender leaf. 'Ragged Jack' is one cultivar, and 'Red Russian' is a popular variety that can be enjoyed raw when still young. They are very winter hardy, down to 10 degrees Fahrenheit according to some folks, if well mulched. This makes them an early sprouting crop in the spring.

In Old Europe the cabbage or kale root was sometimes dried and then smoked; the word calumet, *a ceremonial pipe, comes from the same root word as kale.*

Growing kale is not difficult, although starting your seed indoors (or buying starts) and planting out later gives you sturdier plants than direct seeding. When setting out seedlings, follow the recommended spacing as written on the seed pack, since the plants you set out now will surely fill the space in a month or so. Planting too close causes two problems: first, it can stunt the growth of the plant and you will end up with the same amount of veggie from two plants crowded together as you would from one specimen; second, it can invite aphids in late summer. Plant your kale where it can be well mulched in the fall to carry you into winter. Frost doesn't hurt the leaves; some say they taste better after a frost. In the spring, the old stalk should sprout, giving you early greens to toss into soup.

A few historical types of kale include the following:

- Flanders kale, a subvariety of tree-cabbage, is the probable ancestor of brussels sprouts and can grow up to six feet tall.

- Cow cabbage is a forage kale that grows from six to twelve feet in height.

- Thousand-headed kale is similar to the Flanders kale, growing up to five feet tall. It can overwinter in mild climates and live for years.

Kitchen Lore

Cooking kale can be a learning experience, and eating it might be considered an acquired taste. Its flavor can be somewhat assertive, but the sturdy leaf can be prepared in many savory ways, including oven-baked "chips."

The popular dish colcannon is of Irish origin. Its name comes from Irish Gaelic *cál ceannann*, meaning "white-speckled cabbage," though *cannon* may also come from *cainnenn*, meaning onion, garlic, or leek, writes food historian Alan Davidson. The first written mention of preparing colcannon with potatoes comes from an Englishman's travel journal in 1735. In the United States the recipe appears as simply "Cabbage and Potatoes" in an 1847 *Mrs. Crowen's American Lady's Cookery Book*.

With an Irish fondness for cream and butter, the following recipe ought to pluck at your heartstrings with visions of rolling green pastures and cows grazing contentedly.

Colcannon

This quintessential dish is often served on Halloween. According to Davidson, colcannon was sometimes used as a marriage divination tool. Yes, kale and leeks can predict your future mate! Before serving, special charms were hidden in each diner's bowl, and if unmarried young women were lucky enough to find, say, a ring, it was a portent of marriage. This game also made one careful to not eat too fast. Another method used to find one's future mate instructed the seeker to fill a stocking with a few spoonfuls of colcannon and hang it from the front doorknob, and the first man through the door would become the hopeful maid's husband. I think a man who goes past a stocking full of kale on the door has the courage of Cúchulainn and deserves recognition.

- 2 pounds red boiling potatoes, peeled and cut into quarters
- 3 teaspoons salt, divided
- 4 cups thinly sliced kale, tough ribs removed
- 1 cup thinly sliced leeks, washed well
- ½ cup milk
- ½ cup (1 stick) butter, divided
- ¼ teaspoon pepper, or to taste

Place potatoes in a medium saucepan, cover with water, add 1 teaspoon salt, and then bring to a boil. Reduce heat to simmer, cover, and let cook until fork tender, about 15–20 minutes. Drain and then keep at low heat, shaking pan to dry the potatoes.

While the potatoes are cooking, place the kale in another saucepan with water to cover and ½ teaspoon salt, and then bring to a boil. Reduce heat and cook approximately 5–10 minutes until tender as desired—do not overcook. Drain into a colander.

In the same saucepan used for the kale, melt 2 tablespoons butter at medium heat and sauté the leeks until soft, about 10 minutes. Add the milk and ½ teaspoon salt and bring to a boil. Reduce to a simmer and cook uncovered for about 10 minutes.

Mash the potatoes in their saucepan with 4 tablespoons butter, 1 teaspoon salt, and the pepper. With a wooden spoon, beat in the leek-infused milk with the potatoes until well blended. Stir in the cooked kale and heat on low for about 5 minutes.

Transfer the mixture into a serving bowl, creating a well in the center for the remaining 2 tablespoons butter. Please feel free to reduce the amount of butter used, but all the traditional recipes call for a big gob melting on top. Serves 8 as a side dish.

Kale with Bacon and Pecans

While colcannon may arguably be an Irish national dish, Italian cooks turn out inspired versions as well. Braising the leafy greens is a common method of cooking, and the following recipe is my version of a dish found in *Lidia's Italian-American Kitchen* by Lidia Bastianich.

    2 tablespoons olive oil
    1 pound kale, sliced and ribs removed
    4 whole garlic cloves, peeled
    4 slices bacon, cut into small pieces
    ¼ cup toasted pecans, chopped
    Salt and crushed red pepper to taste

Heat oil in a wide heavy skillet over medium heat. Stir in the bacon. Press down on the garlic cloves with the side of a knife to release the flavor and aroma, leaving them whole. Toss them into the skillet. Cook until all begins to turn golden, 3–4 minutes.

Take a handful of kale and stir into the skillet with the bacon, stirring and adding more kale as it wilts. When all the kale is in the pan, add salt and red pepper.

Cover the skillet, turn heat to low, and simmer about 10 minutes, stirring occasionally. Add a little water if the kale starts to stick.

Taste for seasoning, toss in the pecans, and serve immediately. Adding a chopped hard-boiled egg turns this into a small meal. Serves 6.

Kale for Health and Beauty

Kale is the darling of the superfoods, and it is no exaggeration to say that it is a nutritional powerhouse. It is rich in beta-carotene and vitamins A, C, and K as well as the minerals iron, calcium, manganese, and potassium. It provides a good balance of omega-3 and omega-6 fatty acids and contains carotenoid compounds called lutein and zeaxanthin, which may play an important role in preventing macular degeneration. Healthy food makes for beauty from within—kale and pineapple juice smoothies all around!

But what about using kale externally? All the antioxidant vitamins, along with chlorophyll and omega fatty acids, make kale a cool, refreshing, anti-inflammatory face mask, an especially good choice for acne flare-ups.

Kale Face Mask

    3–4 kale leaves, ribs removed

    1 tablespoon yogurt

    1 tablespoon honey

Using a food processor or a blender, process the kale leaves, yogurt, and honey until smooth. You can adjust viscosity by adding another leaf if too thin or more yogurt if too thick.

To use, apply the mask to face and neck. Relax for about 10 minutes and then rinse in warm water. Pat dry.

Make Friends with Kale

I hope the information I have provided here will inspire you to experiment with eating kale, not only for its healthful benefits, but also because it tastes good. It is an attractive plant in the garden and is sort of like growing a little piece of history. It will be probably the only fresh vegetable you'll be able to pick for your new Halloween colcannon tradition, and that really is something.

Resources

Bastianich, Lidia. *Lidia's Italian-American Kitchen*. New York: Knopf, 2002.

"Colcannon." Merriam-Webster.com. Accessed January 24, 2018. https://www.merriam-webster.com/dictionary/colcannon.

Davidson, Alan. *The Oxford Companion to Food*. 3rd ed. Edited by Tom Jaine. Oxford, UK: Oxford University Press, 2014.

Asafoedita: Enriching Soil with Companion Planting

⤜ by Estha K. V. McNevin ⤛

There is a narrow band of ethereal growing zones in the world well above 2,000 feet, places where warm high-altitude wind generates the arid conditions and the extreme temperature fluxuations needed to produce micronutrient rich morning and evening fog, on which the fascinating plant asafoetida thrives. Only a wry imp of a plant could survive a parched plateau environment, and devil's dung, as it is also known, has its own brand of satanic funk keeping it alive despite all those odds in detail. In its raw form, the plant emits a pungent sulfuric aroma from its milky latex gum, the compound responsible for asafoetida's near-miraculous tolerance to drought. A foul perfume

Asafoedita	
Species	*Ferula assa-foetida*
Zone	8–10
Needs	☀☀☀ 💧
Soil pH	5.5–8.0
Size	3.3–12 ft.

protectively pervades the fresh plant, making it smell strongly reminiscent of a tossed fart salad, lavishly featuring the aroma of freshly sliced rotten eggs with diced onion skins gone rancid as its garnish. This herbal plant smells truly putrid.

This olfactory deterrent makes asafoetida unappealing to most herbivores chancing a trek through the high-elevation deserts of the world, but as it happens, it's not quite uninviting enough to deter humans. When cooked, the plant will release its heady volatile oils and oleoresin flavors, which most humans actually find very tasty. These flavors stimulate the salivary glands, causing a mouthwatering umami sensation while encouraging the appetite. One whiff causes the anticipation of something delicious, drawing the family to the kitchen like moths to a flame. Believe me when I say, dear reader, that simply by inhaling this ironically inviting aroma, a mouthwatering hunger is evoked. Those who have cooked with asafoetida surely know why they call *asant* (Latin) the "food of the gods." If you have ever eaten a truly authentically prepared traditional curry, then you will recognize this smell as quintessentially ubiquitous to Central Asian, Iranian, and Hindustani (Indian) cuisines. These motherlands of curry are the leading producers and consumers of asafoetida, and the things they can do with a few chips of resin never cease to amaze me.

Adopted from the Mesopotamian homeland of Zoroastrianism, *azaz* (Farsi) was favored by Persians as a water purifier and antimicrobial. Persia is known to be the land of the first monotheistic sun god, and the West Asian highlands were also the botanical birthplace of *Ferula foetida* and many other Apiaceae species. Throughout the Mediterranean, images of the plant feature on silver coins from the period and survive as evidence of the importance of the plant in global trade during

As early as the fifth century BCE, Ferula foetida *was cultivated commercially to compete with a more potent and now
extinct species of giant fennel,* Ferula commonus, *known
commonly in classical Egypt, Greece, and Rome as silphium.*

the third century BCE. By the time that the Greek physician Pedanius Dioscorides wrote about *silphium*, its overuse as a food additive and its popularity as animal fodder made it all but extinct. It was then that asafoetida as it has come to be known it began to take its place.

Commonly featured in motif art, its seeds bore the shape of a heart, symbolically indicative of its Venusian applications with regards to family planning. In fact, modern asafoetida is an antispasmodic and an anticoagulant also known to reduce menstrual cramps by inducing bleeding; the same plant will, however, induce labor in pregnant women even from a single bite of curry in some cases. (It is particularly known to act as an abortifacient if taken internally in concentrated quantity.) Many of the medicines in the parsley family have a pronounced effect on the female reproductive tissues, stimulating expulsion of toxins and tissue repair or regeneration. Wild carrot, or Queen Anne's lace, is similar. By contrast, when used topically as an anti-inflammatory, *hing* (Hindi) improves circulation by warming the blood to ease pain, reduce swelling, and break fevers. This is one of the many reasons why authentic curry dishes are regarded as medicinal.

The Crusades increased the European demand for asafoetida as a medicine as both Jewish and Islamic manuscripts touted the herb for its curative, antiaging, and revitalizing properties. Classical herbal texts like *De Materia Medica*, penned by Dioscorides in the first century CE, made a popular return during the Renaissance. Asafoetida was among those antibiotics employed to combat the plague. When science began in earnest to translate the libraries of antiquity, many lost and forgotten treasures like asafoetida were plucked from colonial folk herbal medicine and given real commercial viability through colonial trade. By the 1600s, the Portuguese, Dutch, French, and British colonies all were exporting hing back to Europe with the intention of using the resin for everything from hair loss tonics and skin lightening creams to the medicinal and culinary applications inherent in a good curry. We have consistently cultivated *Ferula assa-foetida* since antiquity, making it one of the most long-standing and lucrative herbal crops in the world.

The Devil May Deceive, but His Dung Can Heal

Growing your own *merde du diable* (French) is no easy task. The seeds are difficult to come by in the United States, and cultivating your own supply of the mastic involves harvesting and aging the milky latex into a solid resin. From seed to table takes three to five years of care. Yes, dear reader, years! Seeds are often passed among families from chef to chef. Many cooks have success acquiring seeds from medicinal herbal seed suppliers because *hinga* (Marathi) is famously used to treat a wide range of gastrointestinal disorders.

Since the Middle Ages, *hënjâna* (Pashto) has featured strongly in Western herbal medicine, although *Ferula assa-foetida* was revered in Vedic as well as Chinese natural medicine since the dawn of antiquity. With careful patience and the right conditions, growing your own "stink gum" plant can be a healthful and rewarding long-term gardening goal—although this aromatic plant is not a bloom to host anywhere in the vicinity of your next garden party.

Perun-kayam (Tamil) is an herbal medicine that can "improve the propriety of your poops and farts," as I teach my students. This cheeky, malodorous beast will clean your gastrointestinal clock in a matter of hours, helping to fight pollutants—quite ironic for such a stinky herb—and helps reduces gas, bloating, and flatulence. In fact, India produces inexpensive herbal tablets called *hingoli* for this very purpose. Asafoetida can be a real blessing to those with whom we share confined spaces, greatly improving our outlook on interpersonal longevity.

As a gum, the raw resin of *inguva* (Telgu) is first disbursed into warm water or oil prior to internal use. This releases the alkaloid salts and minerals that detoxify the body's lymphatic system. As it warms the system to sweat toxins, it enhances our immune system and acts as an antioxidant. Used topically as a poultice, asafoetida is an Ayurvedic medicine with antiseptic and anti-inflammatory properties and is useful in treating colic, asthma, bronchitis, and shock. It is well known as a diaphonic useful in flushing fevers. Internally, hing is taken as an antidiabetic that slows the body's uptake of sugar and is useful as an antibiotic blood thinner. A pinch a day will keep the cardiovascular surgeon away.

The Pollen-Bound Pleasures of a Self-Sustainable Hermaphrodite

Ferula assa-foetida is a perennial herb from the Apiaceae (or Umbelliferae) family. It grows from 3.3 to 12 feet tall and prefers the 5.5 to 8.0 pH of a sandy and well-drained medium loam above clay-and-stone-pack drainage. Like its delicious cousin fennel, asafoetida likes fibrous mulch that will help gather dew and moisture around the base of the plant. *Ferula assafoetida* will not bloom if shaded, and it quite prefers relatively harsh conditions, high elevation, and full sunlight. This means that mountainous zones 8 through 10 are the natural habitat for the herb and demonstrate seasonal cycles reliant on monsoonal weather systems to irrigate deep taproots.

One of the hardest things about growing this special herb is in maintaining its soil conditions. As a relative to carrot and parsnip, it loves to dig deep and will rely on a cavernous claypack of sand and gravel to hold in nutrients and moisture in the sweet spot, a nutrient-rich sponge layer, which is a furtive spot where clay and soil meet and retain nutrients such as nitrogen, proteins, and sugars for later use. These spots are a cache of life hidden safely beneath the soil.

In zones 8 through 10 asafoetida thrives easily when germinated in a well-prepared tropical desert with layered sandy loam in a sunny location. The best results are yielded by digging down the bed at least four feet and filling it with a layer of gravel for drainage, then adding a stratum of clay, sand, medium loam, and more sand before finally topping with black garden fabric and a final layer of both sand and coconut husk. When you are ready to plant, soak the seeds overnight and insert into the bed by poking small holes into the garden fabric and inserting the seeds one inch below the soil's surface.

Plant seeds out in spring and sow in their permanent location for the best results. Seedlings do not take well to transplanting and prefer a little pampering while germinating. I soak my seeds overnight in milk, and clutch them for the first two months in greenhouse conditions, in order to ensure hearty stem development. As they will not survive our Montana winters, I either bring the containers indoors or winter them in a warm, dry greenhouse that gets full sun. When planting seeds, keep them four to six feet apart and maintain mulch as needed. Try planting near helpful nitrogen-rich companions, such as peas, leaf lettuce, chives, leeks, onions, rosemary, sage, or vine tomatoes, for best flavor and improved growth. Misting water in the early mornings with a soak-hose for thirty minutes is enough for even the hottest of days. Let the soil dry completely between watering. Do not overwater the plant, as root rot and soil bacteria are always a concern when cultivating sand-loving Apiaceae plants. This desert native prefers a soft pumice rock and coconut husk ground cover between plants to help the roots pull heat and moisture from the soil's surface.

In mid-to-late July the massive stalk thickens and begins to climb for want of flowering. As it does, side sleeves emerge and unfurl long aromatic leaves that can be steamed, grilled, or boiled for consumption. The fresh sprouts and young stalks are especially favored in traditional Indian salads and pickles. A sweet and starchy flavor is imparted to the stalk when it is slow-stewed with date juice. Once the stalk reaches its limit, large greenish-yellow flowers bloom in an explosive burst of surreal color as they open in a bulbous mass at the top of the stalk. When roots are given the right conditions, side stalks will even bloom.

From the moment asafoetida begins germinating, an odd smell too begins to take a form and life all of its own. Among all the varieties, it is the *Ferula assa-foetida*, true devil's dung, that is perhaps the most fragrant. By the time the plant is a foot or more in height, insects of all renown will buzz for miles just to get a whiff. Once the hermaphroditic flowers are established, the frenzy of pollen swapping begins. The heady aroma of deliciously ripe asafoetida in full bouquet draws butterflies, bumblebees, and every type of fly known to Beelzebub. This self-fertile beauty is an extraordinary perfumed wand of attraction or repulsion, but even the allure of its quizzical scent is palled by the healing properties of the liquid gold held within.

Milking Medicinal Ambrosia

The oleoresin latex milk is a capsicum white suspension solution of volatile oils, proteins, minerals, sugars, alkaloid salts, and gum starch, all floating in a plasma of essential and fatty oils. It takes three to five years for a plant to mature to its full potential, and many will not flower until they have developed enough latex. Overcrowded asafoetida plants will produce a long spindle stem with a single umbel at the top because without room for the roots to stretch down and out, this asterid will bonsai itself to survive.

Once the plant has lived for more than two years, a woody core will develop and allow the umbel to reach higher from year to year. It can be a stunning display of color, and a real whiff of curiosity surrounds it, drawing other gardeners and passersby to ask, "What is that faint stench of the bowels of hell?! Can you smell it? What is its providence?" This is one of those perennials worthy of a Victorian copperplate sign for the number of times *Ferula assa-foetida* will draw inquiring noses toward your garden.

Every year the plant must be harvested or covered with insulation and snuggled in for the dry season. Like all monsoon crops, it should only be watered occasionally from January to

March because overly moist conditions will prevent the rhizome from putting out new shoots. *Ferula assa-foetida* is not frost hardy and will not tolerate temperatures below 40 degrees Fahrenheit. However, it can be mounded with black sand and lava rock or can be nested with straw and wrapped in burlap or black gardening fabric. It will then withstand near-freezing temperatures. These weathering ideas may be ideal because growing such a unique plant indoors can sometimes lead to domestic revolt if a constant hint of sulfur and massive amounts of yellow pollen floating through your home aren't your thing.

As the woody stalk matures and the wet season comes to an end, the rich latex within will turn a thick milky white and can yield high-quality hing after three years of age. Young asafoetida is used in skin-lightening soaps and antibacterial lotions and is a common fodder for goats. The leaves and any new shoots can also be harvested as a vegetable and are popular in Indian curries and stuffed breads because they have a savory green flavor very similar to fennel. The aromatic quality they lend to a dish is earthy and herbaceous with an aftertaste similar to sweet leeks.

When the plant is ready to harvest, begin by removing all the leaves and flowers. Letting the flowers go to seed is important if you are trying to germinate an area of the garden for these perennials to take over. They most love a dry, sunny fence corner and can appear like a real alien landscape when many plants are blooming together in a single location. Begin by brushing away all the mulch and sandy loam. Dig down two inches or so. Cut a hole in the bottom center of a one-gallon zip-top bag and slip it over the bare stalk. Slide the bag down into the hole around the rhizome base. Cut the stalk in a clean, even keel, making a fluid arch. Rest the removed stock inside the bag and let the milk drain completely from the stalk. The root too will begin beading latex in an effort to heal. Let the plant leach as much milk as possible. To process the stalk, remove the skin and add to boiling soups or stew stock to tenderize meats and enrich broth with antitoxic and antiviral properties. In Persia hing is processed into balms and lotions that are used topically to remove viral skin conditions. Throughout India, the core of the stalk is sliced wafer-thin and candied in sugar syrup for a healthful, sweet teatime treat.

Allow the latex to rest for twenty-four hours. Overnight it will turn from a milky white to a solid amber tone. As the resin hardens, it begins to create a cake of asafoetida gum. If you collect your resin in the heat of the midday, it will become soft and malleable for shaping into a ball or working into a square mold. Wrap in wax paper and store in an airtight double-walled spice jar. Improper storage will result in a loss of flavor complexity and can lead to mold contamination or rot. Hing will share its smell and flavor with everything that happens to be within a six-foot radius. To limit this contamination, the kitchen tools and herbal boards used for preparing asafoetida should be designated and made requisite to that purpose alone.

To use the raw resin, crack off a small chip and grind it into a powder. As you do so, add a small amount of wheat or rice flour and turmeric powder to help prevent the gum from sticking. This compound asafoetida mix can be added to oil just before stir-frying meats and vegetables in order to improve the flavor. It is also common in bean and lentil dishes, where hing counteracts the enzymes that can create bloating and flatulence. For a more floral tone, a chip of resin can be affixed into the top center of a hot pan lid and later placed in the dish when steaming fresh or adding fragile vegetables. The flavor penetrates the vapors inside the pot, highlighting the floral and fragrantly earthy tones of zucchini, *methi* (fenugreek) greens, okra, sweet peas, chickpeas, beans, steamed potatoes, mushrooms, and sweet peppers.

Store-bought asafoetida is pressed into small bricks that can be broken with a small hammer or finely grated into *ghee* (clarified butter), oils, or soup stocks. The raw resin is common in Central Asian and Middle Eastern cuisine, in which it is placed in the water used to steam vegetables and is also commonly found in meat rubs and marinades. It is manufactured using all sorts of additives, such as guar gum and gum arabic, to name a few. Usually this is done to improve shelf life and prevent the resin from caking in humid climates.

The styles of brand-name hing range from white or yellow to amber and even black; each type is used in a different regional style of Middle Eastern, Central Asian, or Indian cuisine. Amber hing is the raw resin and is the most common form while the rare Kali Hingu is religiously used as a Hindu ceremonial and ritual offering to ward off the "evil eye." Admittedly, I am a fan of the brands Laxmi and Vandevi because they are reputable, free of unwanted additives, and have always been consistent and potent products. Laxmi brand is a white asafoetida and is wonderful for tofu and vegetable dishes, while Vandevi hing uses turmeric and other spices to flavor and tenderize meat as well as neutralize lactose acids, while thickening and improving the flavor of savory dairy dishes.

Experimenting in the garden or kitchen with asafoetida will challenge your sense of raw herbs and help improve your quality of life with its celebrated medicinal properties. When combined with warm ghee, asafoetida is an ideal garnish for breads and steamed vegetables—a genuine comfort food. In our household it is the go-to herbal remedy for nearly any kind of aching belly. Although the smell might fool you, this herbal lifesaver is a vital part of any herbal first aid kit. *Ferula assa-foetida* won't disappoint as an exotic gardening challenge if you take care to pamper this ancient and zone-specific herbal medicine, a golden gift from the sun.

Resources

Bladholm, Linda. *The Indian Grocery Store Demystified*. Los Angeles, CA: Renaissance Books, 2000.

Burnie, Geoffrey, ed. *The Practical Gardener's Encyclopedia*. San Francisco, CA: Fog City Press, 2000.

Buttrey, T. V. "The Coins and the Cult." In "Gifts to the Goddesses—Cyrene's Sanctuary of Demeter and Persephone," special issue, *Expedition* 34, no. 1–2 (2012): 59–66.

Damrosch, Barbara. *The Garden Primer*. New York: Workman Publishing, 2008.

Devi, Yamuna. *The Art of Indian Vegetarian Cooking*. Old Westbury, NY: BALA Books, 1987.

Elpel, Thomas J. *Botany in A Day: The Patterns Method of Plant Identification*. 6th ed. Pony, MT: HOPS Press, 2013.

Favorito, E. N., and K. Baty. "The Silphium Connection." *Celator* 9, no. 2 (February 1995): 6–8.

"Ferula foetida." Plants for a Future. Accessed September 2017. http://pfaf.org/User/Plant.aspx?LatinName=Ferula+foetida.

Perrin, Sandra. *Organic Gardening in Cold Climates*. Missoula, MT: Mountain Press Publishing, 2002.

Robuchon, Joël, and Prosper Montagné. *Larousse Gastronomique*. New York: Clarkson Potter, 2001.

Seymour, John. *The New Self-Sufficient Gardener*. New York: DK Press, 2008.

Cardamom: For Flavor and Health

⤚ by Magenta Griffith ⤙

Do you like chai? Are you fond of Thai curries? Scandinavian pastries? Cardamom is an important ingredient in these and many other tasty treats. It comes in small pods and has a strong, uniquely spicy-sweet flavor. There are two different types of cardamom: one with smaller green pods, sometimes called true cardamom, and a variety with larger black or brown pods. Keep the pods whole until use; you'll get the most intense flavor if you break open the whole pods to release the tiny black seeds, which can be ground using a mortar and pestle or a spice mill. A little goes a long way: each cardamom pod contains around twenty seeds. Ten pods will yield about one and

True Cardamom	
Species	*Elettaria cardamomum*
Zone	9–11
Needs	☀ 💧💧💧
Soil pH	6.1 to 6.6
Size	6–10 ft.

a half teaspoons when ground. The flavor is intense, so not much is needed.

Cardamom is native to southeastern Asia, from India south to Sri Lanka and east to Malaysia and western Indonesia, where it grows on the shady jungle floor of tropical rainforests. The Greeks imported it from India, possibly as early as the third century BCE, though records that old are unreliable. The first reference to trade from Sri Lanka may be as long ago as the twelfth century. Botanically, true (green) cardamom is *Elettaria cardamomum*, in the family Zingiberaceae, which means it is related to ginger, galangal, and turmeric. Black or brown cardamom is *Amomum subulatum* and the flavor is somewhat different; it is not used much in baking and sweet dishes.

Growing Cardamom

Cardamom grows in hot, humid or very humid subtropical or tropical forests in a thick clump of up to twenty leafy shoots. A perennial plant with rigid and erect aromatic leaves, it usually reaches a height of between six and ten feet. It is usually planted under the canopy of much higher trees in a location with partial shade or filtered sunlight. The leaves are long, dark green, and sword-shaped. The underside is paler and may have a covering of tiny hairs. The flowers form along a stalk that can grow to more than three feet long. Cardamom flowers are small and usually white in color with a yellow, red, or violet stripe.

Because it is a tropical plant, it should only be grown outdoors in USDA zones 9 through 11; Hawaii is the only place in the United States that would have both the heat and humidity necessary. Otherwise, it can be grown with care indoors or in a greenhouse. Cardamom can reach heights of ten feet or more by the third year; it prefers a rich, loamy, slightly acidic soil with a pH of approximately 6.1 to 6.6. The small seeds should be planted in a light but rich soil approximately one-eighth inch beneath the surface of the soil. It cannot tolerate drought. If growing in a greenhouse, it should be kept humid; it should be kept in a location with many hours of partial or indirect sunlight.

Cardamom requires approximately three years of growth to produce pods. Once the pods are collected and dried, they are easy to break open. Usually, the pods are kept intact until the seeds are needed. If you have whole pods, place them in a bowl and apply light pressure to break the dried seed pod; you can then extract the tiny black seeds for use. If you don't use the seeds right away, store them in a sealed container in a dry, cool location out of direct sunlight. If you get the seeds or ground cardamom, keep them in an airtight container until you use them.

Health and Medicine

Nutritionally, cardamom is rich in vitamins and minerals: a single tablespoon contains 80 percent of the recommended daily dose of manganese. Cardamom also contains iron, vitamin C, calcium, magnesium, potassium, vitamin B_6, riboflavin (B_2), thiamine (B_1), vitamin A, and zinc.

In folk medicine cardamom is used, like cinnamon, as a general remedy for all digestive complaints, especially gas. Chewing cardamom seeds freshens the breath. In India cardamom is considered a remedy against urinary tract problems. Researchers are currently investigating the antiviral properties of cardamom.

In India cardamom is boiled and the steam of the hot water inhaled to treat headaches. Ayurvedic medicine describes a drink to treat impotence or depression made by boiling cardamom seeds in milk sweetened with honey. A tea to promote digestion can be made of one teaspoon freshly crushed cardamom seeds infused for ten to fifteen minutes in a cup of boiling water. Cardamom entered European medicine during the Renaissance as an ingredient in one formula for the elixir of life. Because of its strong flavor, it was commonly used for masking bitter botanical medicines in nineteenth-century United States.

Herbalists consider cardamom an effective tonic for helping the liver, the appetite, the stomach, and the intestines. In Germany, cardamom is approved for use against the common cold, to relieve coughs, to counter bronchitis, to lower fevers, to ease inflammation of the mouth and pharynx, to resolve liver and gallbladder complaints, to counter loss of appetite, and to improve the ability of the immune system to counter infection.

Cardamom is the world's third most expensive spice by weight, following saffron and vanilla.

Valued for its aphrodisiac properties, it is the most frequently mentioned spice in the stories of the *Arabian Nights*. Because this herb is considered an aphrodisiac, the famous herbalist Culpeper assigned it to Venus.

Cooking with Cardamom

In Asia both types of cardamom are widely used in both sweet and savory dishes, particularly in the south. They are frequent components in spice mixes, such as types of Indian and Nepalese *masala* (spice mixture) and Thai curry pastes. Green cardamom is often used in traditional Indian sweets, and in *masala chai*, the spiced tea we often just call chai. Both types of cardamom are often used as garnishes in basmati rice and other dishes. Individual seeds are sometimes chewed in the same way as we use chewing gum, as a breath freshener. In India and the Middle East the pods or ground seeds are added to coffee as it is brewed to neutralize the acidity. It is also one of the spices added to Turkish coffee, which is sometimes served with an elaborate ritual.

Kheer

Kheer (Indian rice pudding) is almost always flavored with cardamom, and is very different from the typical English rice pudding. It contains no eggs and has a much creamier texture.

    1 cup cooked white rice

    2 cups milk

    ¼ cup sugar

    ½ teaspoon ground cardamom

    2 tablespoons slivered blanched almonds

    2 tablespoons raisins

    2 tablespoons shredded coconut

    ½ teaspoon rose water (optional)

Combine the ingredients and simmer on low fire for about an hour. Stir frequently, scraping the sides and bottom to keep from sticking. Serve warm or cooled. This is a great way to use up leftover rice. If you use a rice cooker to cook your rice, you can add the ingredients and turn it back on, checking occasionally. Serves 3–4. This recipe can be doubled.

Julekake

Cardamom was so prized in Scandinavia that following the opening of trade routes to India and Ceylon, it quickly came to define the flavor of many traditional Nordic breads and sweets, including custards. At least partially because of its high price, it is seen as a "festive" spice. Cardamom is also used to flavor *aquavit*, the quintessential Scandinavian alcohol; it is also used in some Russian liqueurs. You can add it to apple pie and many other sweet desserts in addition to, or instead of, cinnamon. Other uses are in pickles, especially pickled herring; in punches and mulled wines; and with meat, poultry, and shellfish.

There are many variations of Christmas breads using cardamom. This *Julekake* (Norwegian Christmas bread) recipe is relatively simple.

¾ cup whole milk

½ cup sugar

¼ cup salted butter, cut into small pieces

1½ teaspoons salt

5½ teaspoons active dry yeast

½ cup warm water (75–80°F)

2 eggs, beaten, plus 1 more for brushing

5 cups sifted flour

2 teaspoons freshly ground cardamom

1½ cup raisins

½ cup candied citron or candied mixed fruit

Warm the milk in a small saucepan over medium heat. When bubbles begin to form around the edge, remove from heat and stir in sugar, butter, and salt, stirring to melt the butter. Set aside to cool to lukewarm.

In a large mixing bowl, sprinkle the yeast over the water and stir until dissolved. Add the lukewarm milk mixture and then stir in 2 beaten eggs. Add 2 cups of the flour and the cardamom and beat with a wooden spoon until the mixture is smooth. Stir in raisins and citron. Stir in remaining flour, ½ cup at a time, until a soft dough forms. Let the dough rest, covered with a towel, for about 10 minutes.

Knead the dough on a lightly floured surface until smooth and elastic, about 8 minutes, and then transfer to a large buttered bowl. Turn the dough so that the butter coats the entire ball. Cover with a towel and set in a warm place (a gas oven with a pilot light works well), about 85°F, to rise until it's doubled in bulk, about 1–1½ hours.

Punch down the dough and divide in half, forming the dough into 2 balls. Cover them for 10 minutes, and butter baking sheets. Place each round loaf onto a baking sheet and let them rise again in a warm spot, covered with towels, until they've doubled in bulk, another 1½–2 hours.

Toward the end of the second rise, preheat the oven to 350°F. When ready to bake, gently brush the remaining beaten egg over each loaf, taking care not to press down on the dough too much. Bake for about 45 minutes, until the bread is a deep golden brown. Immediately transfer to wire racks and cool. Makes 2 round loaves.

Selected Resources

"Cardamom #2 Green Pods." Penzeys Spices. Accessed January 26, 2018. https://www.penzeys.com/online-catalog/cardamom-3-black-pods/c-24/p-1230/pd-s.

Chris. "The Spice Series: Cardamom." *The Homestead Garden* (blog). Accessed March 14, 2018. https://www.thehomesteadgarden.com/the-spice-series-cardamom/.

Lust, John. *The Herb Book*. New York: Bantam Books, 1974.

Rose, Jeanne. *Herbs & Things*. New York: Grosset & Dunlap, 1972.

Strong, Dayona. "Julekake (Norwegian Christmas Bread)." *Outside Oslo* (blog), Devember 20, 2013. http://www.outside-oslo.com/2013/12/20/julekake-norwegian-christmas-bread/.

Weaver, William Woys. "The Spice Is Right: Discover Cardamom," *Mother Earth Living*, December/January 2009. http://www.motherearthliving.com/Cooking-Methods/spice-right-discover-cardamom.

Lavender: Purple Reign

⁂ by Mireille Blacke ⁂

Lavender	
Species	*Lavendula angustifolia*
Zone	5–9
Needs	☼–☀☀☀ 💧
Soil pH	6.7–7.3
Size	2–4 ft. × 2–2.5 ft.

Several years ago in my career as a registered dietitian, I was working with a patient who described using lavender in her salad. "You mean in a sachet?" I asked, thinking I misheard her last word.

"No, in my *salad!*" she insisted.

While I was well aware of the fragrant flower's use in candles, hair color, hand soap, room spray, lotion, massage oil, potpourri, and, of course, bouquets and ornamental landscapes, despite my profession, I was not savvy about culinary uses for lavender at the time. Luckily, that day my patient was also patient with me and introduced me to a new concept for lavender. An ample number of years, patients, and salads later, I am well-versed in the multiple uses of lavender, and you might be surprised at all this perennial herb has to offer.

Members of the mint family, Lamiaceae, the three main species of lavender are English, French, and Spanish. The beautiful purple-pink French lavender and Spanish lavender are not cold hardy and prefer Mediterranean climates, but they will impress as potted plants.

The English lavender cultivar 'Hidcote' is the deepest purple of all lavenders, boasting needle-like silvery-green foliage and delicate flower spikes in late summer, each part intensely fragrant. This cultivar withstands more cold than other types. Try 'Hidcote' in a sunny, sheltered spot in regions colder than zone 5. Due to its stunning color, beloved fragrance, and increasing culinary appeal, I will focus on English lavender (*Lavandula angustifolia*) in this article.

This resilient shrubby evergreen thrives in northern Africa, mountainous Mediterranean regions, southern Europe, and parts of Australia. Lavender also thrives across the United States, in climates from Connecticut to Arizona. This hardy plant spreads on its own and works well planted in a rock garden or as ground cover in a sunny orchard. It sprawls across pathways and complements many types of roses.

As versatile as it is fragrant, lavender has a tremendous range of applications beyond traditional bouquets and flower arrangements. From food and fragrance to cosmetics and herbal remedies, lavender is currently one of the highest trending plants in crafts and culinary trends. As an herb and essential oil, lavender is believed to purify and uplift the body and mind, primarily through one of the most unique and beloved scents in the world.

Cultivation

Lavender is an appealing choice for your yard because it's attractive, it's fragrant, and herbs in general are among the least demanding plants to grow. It will also attract hummingbirds, butterflies, and pollinator bees to the yard.

Because it can grow and spread quickly, lavender is considered a weed in some parts of the world. As shown by the herb's lengthy presence in diverse parts of the world, lavender thrives in poor soil conditions that other plants might find challenging. However, in general, lavender grows best in sandy, well-drained soil with at least six hours of full sunlight each day. 'Hidcote' will typically reach a height of one and a half feet with purple-blue flowers, in tight, narrow clusters. The blooming period is usually early summer, sometimes repeating in August.

To grow lavender from seeds, refrigerate the seeds four to six weeks before sowing (usually in early spring). Place the seeds in flats on top of your refrigerator. Lavender grows from seed very slowly, so the warmth from the refrigerator will speed the growing process. Thin the seedlings to two inches apart. After the last frost, select an area outdoors with well-drained soil and full sun (direct sun for at least six hours per day).

When planting, dig a hole twice as large as the root ball of the seedling. Add two handfuls of sand. In heavy or clay soil use gravel instead of sand. Plant the lavender at a slightly higher level than it grew in its container. Add more soil and sand to the hole to raise the plant if necessary. Fill in around the plant with more sandy soil so the plant seems to be growing out of a slight mound, about one inch higher than ground level. Adding peat moss around the first lavender plant is essential, as is giving it enough water during the first season. Once the lavender is established, it will be resilient enough to handle drought conditions. In subsequent seasons, do not add peat moss, as lavender prefers thin, gritty soil. Water the plant thoroughly and mulch with gravel to block weeds. Water thoroughly every ten days unless you have a soaking rain. Continue watering this way for a few weeks until roots are growing well.

Increase your crop of lavender by cutting off a five-inch piece of stem. Take off the cutting's flowers and lower leaves and plant it in a pot of damp sand. If the cutting is not well rooted before fall, do not plant it outdoors. Bring it indoors for winter and then plant it outside in late spring.

Not into growing lavender from seeds? No problem. Lavender does well in containers because it needs little maintenance. Set out container-grown plants in early spring, late summer, or early fall. For planting, dig to a depth twice the height of the container for adequate drainage. Place the plants fifteen to thirty inches apart and water well.

For established plants, when new growth appears on old stems in spring, prune one to two inches from the branch tips and remove old flowering stems. Every two to three years shear the bush back to about six to eight inches to encourage fresh new growth and to promote blooming. Do not cut lavender to the ground, as you do perennials, and do not prune it after late August or in winter.

Companion Planting

English lavender is often planted in ornamental and herb gardens. It is useful as an edging plant or in configuring knot gardens. For borders, combine lavender with other plants that hate "wet feet" and require a well-drained area, such as yarrows and sundrops.

English lavender is also a fine bushy companion for climbing roses, as this pairing allows lavender to hide the "bare legs" of its partner. Similarly, English lavender will help disguise the "legginess" in a bed of hybrid tea roses.

To create a soothing color scheme, consider combining blue cornflowers, dianthus, and magenta, blush pink, or white yarrow with lavender. The ornamental grass blue fescue (*Festuca glauca*) also grows well with lavender.

Harvest and Storage

At midsummer (June), harvest the fragrant stems of your lavender plants to encourage more blooming. Usually, this is when the color just begins to show and the buds begin to open. Cut off as much stem as possible to foster another set of blooms. Lavender often reblooms in late summer (August) if the first set of flowering stems has been harvested.

Tie the stems in loose bunches and hang them upside down to air dry. Strip off the buds and store them in a sealed container or use them to scent linens and pillows. Scented flower spikes in pockets of clothes will deter moths.

You have several storage options. For culinary use, select brightly colored and tightly closed buds. These buds will retain flavor and scent for up to six months if kept in a tightly sealed container away from sources of heat and moisture.

Another option is to hang or dry bundles of lavender in your kitchen as a natural air freshener or in your bedroom as a soothing fragrance to help you sleep.

Cooking

Lavender is a versatile herb. Its leaves and dried or fresh flower buds are edible, making this herb widely adaptable for culinary use. Lavender's flavor is floral and mildly sweet with a slightly bitter aftertaste. Select fresh buds for desserts, as they provide a sweet and stronger flavor. Choose dried flowers for more savory dishes as they tend to lean toward the herbal side.

Dried and fresh lavender buds add a sweet mint-anise-rosemary flavor to herbes de Provence, honey, butters, dressings and condiments, savory sauces and marinades, cheeses, grilled fish and steaks, and stews and soups. Lavender will add a refreshing, colorful twist to your favorite salads, dishes, sorbets, jellies, and desserts. It can be candied to make edible decorations or combined with chocolate and baked goods. Lavender can also flavor beverages; hot lavender is currently a popular blended tea. For a refreshing alternative to iced tea on a hot day, try chilled lavender-infused water.

Remember: a little goes a long way. The longer lavender has dried, the stronger the scent; you probably don't want your food to smell like perfume. Small amounts complement grilled salmon with fresh lemon. Add a hint of lavender to crumbled bleu cheese to put a spin on your sweet potato.

Lavender Tea

Drinking lavender tea releases soothing, stress-reducing fragrances that reduce anxiety and increase ability to sleep more restfully.

Add 2 teaspoons of dried lavender flowers to an 8-ounce cup of boiling water. Sweeten with 1 teaspoon organic honey.

Alternatively, place 4 teaspoons of fresh lavender buds into a tea ball after you have boiled 8 ounces of water. Add the tea ball to the water, and steep for 10 minutes.

Lavender Dijon Dressing

This recipe is featured in *The Lavender Cookbook* by Sharon Shipley.

½ cup extra-virgin olive oil

2 tablespoons red wine vinegar

2 tablespoons dijon mustard

2 teaspoons dried culinary lavender, ground

¾ teaspoons salt

½ teaspoon minced garlic

¼ teaspoon freshly ground black pepper

Combine all ingredients in a jar with a tight-fitting lid. Shake well until combined. Mix the dressing further with a blender of your choice for best emulsion.

Chocolate Lavender Brownies

This brownie recipe is from *The Lavender Cookbook* with modifications by Lavender Hill Farm, a family-owned farm in Michigan that offers farm-made lavender honey and a variety of natural products.

2 teaspoons dried culinary English lavender

3 cups sugar

1¾ cups all-purpose flour

¾ cup plus 2 tablespoons unsweetened Dutch-process cocoa

½ teaspoon salt

¼ teaspoon instant espresso powder or instant coffee powder

¾ pound (3 sticks) unsalted butter

4 large eggs

2 teaspoons vanilla extract

1 cup chopped walnuts or pecans (optional)

Preheat the oven to 325°F. Butter a 13 × 9-inch baking dish. Place the lavender in a spice grinder or mortar and pestle with 1 tablespoon of the sugar. Pulse until the lavender is finely ground. Transfer to a large bowl. Add the cocoa, salt, espresso or coffee powder, and the remaining sugar. Mix well.

Place the butter in a medium-size microwave-safe bowl and microwave on high for 1 minute at a time until melted. Let cool for a few minutes. Whisk in the eggs and vanilla.

Make a well in the center of the dry ingredients and pour in the butter mixture. Using a wooden spoon, mix until just combined. If you're using nuts, stir them in. Pour the mixture into the pan and smooth the top. Bake for 35 to 45 minutes, until a toothpick inserted in the center comes out mostly clean.

Nutrition and Other Health Benefits

In addition to its scent, flavor, and culinary versatility, lavender offers nutrition and health benefits. Lavender is low in calories and fat; a 100-gram serving of lavender has only forty-nine calories and one gram of fat. (You must consider the calories, fat, and sugar included in whatever foods the lavender is served with, of course.) In addition, lavender is a source of several vitamins and minerals, including vitamin A, calcium, and iron. Vitamin A contributes to eye health, including the prevention of cataracts, macular degeneration, night blindness, dry eyes, and eye infections. Vitamin A is also necessary to keep your skin and mucous membranes healthy. Calcium is essential for bone strength, prevention of osteoporosis, blood clotting, neural messaging, and heart, muscle, and nerve functioning.

Health benefits of iron include blood oxygenation, muscle health, regulation of body temperature, and increased brain function. Iron deficiency may lead to anemia, a condition involving fatigue and shortness of breath.

Lavender also contains over 100 known compounds, including phytochemicals, polyphenols, and antioxidants reported to have anxiety-relieving and anticarcinogenic properties. Specifically, limonene and caffeic acid in lavender have been shown to have tumor-shrinking properties and inhibit cancer growth. Coumarins, compounds contributing to lavender's fragrance, also may inhibit HIV, tumor growth, hypertension, and osteoporosis.

Medicinal Uses

The medicinal applications of lavender have been popular through the ages. Perhaps we associate purple with nobility and royalty due to lavender's long association with queens through history. Lavender lore indicates that Queen Elizabeth I sipped lavender tea daily for migraine relief, while Queen Victoria commanded her staff to use lavender to cleanse her belongings and residence. Egyptian Queen Cleopatra's secret weapon of seduction was a lavender-infused perfume that worked well on Julius Caesar and Mark Antony. This lavender connection extends beyond these queens to the dearly departed Prince, a member of rock royalty, as famous for his iconic use of the color purple (and all its relatives) as for his incredible songwriting and performances.

Due in large part to its calming and relaxing effects, lavender is reported to have a beneficial impact on various ailments. Reported health benefits of lavender include its ability to improve sleep (insomnia, restless sleep patterns), reduce anxiety and stress, improve concentration, relieve headaches, promote pain relief, strengthen the respiratory system, treat skin problems, prevent infections, reduce inflammation, improve hair and scalp conditions, and soothe stomach bloating. That's some pressure to place on this purple plant!

Studies do show that lavender has antibacterial, anti-inflammatory, and antiseptic qualities; however, I suggest taking your lavender with a grain of salt. If you look closely at many of the ailments, you will see that many if not all of them are linked with anxiety and stress. The soothing and relaxing properties for which lavender is known may be helping to alleviate other ailments by relieving stress, which can lead to depression, skin problems, headaches, impaired concentration, and so on. For example, lavender's calming scent has been shown to temporarily improve concentration, test taking, and mental performance.

There are a number of ways to enjoy the relaxing and soothing effects of lavender. Steep lavender as a tea, add fresh blossoms to your bathwater, or use essential oil in the form of aromatherapy, as a massage oil or lotion, or combined with meditation.

Side Effects and Words of Warning

Though lavender may be safe for most people, women who are pregnant or breastfeeding should avoid using lavender oil or ingesting the plant. Consuming lavender oil is not recommended for anyone, as doing so will cause vomiting, diarrhea, or other complications.

If mint affects you negatively, you may also experience negative side effects from the lavender plant as well. Such reactions include headaches, constipation, and increased appetite; the topical application can cause irritation and redness.

Lavender may cause drowsiness if combined with other sedative supplements. Consider avoiding lavender in cooking if you take medication for anxiety or pain management. Due to lavender's relaxant properties, it may enhance the effect of depressant medications.

Despite the copious claims that lavender will soothe injuries, nix headaches, calm anxiety, ditch dandruff, freshen fabrics, tone skin, relieve nausea, and fight free radicals, I need more longitudinal research from reputable scientific sources before I accept all the unsupported reports I've read.

Crafts and Miscellaneous Uses

Most people seem extremely familiar with lavender-scented potpourri, drawer sachets, lotions, oils, room sprays, candles, hand soap, laundry detergent, massage oil, and shampoo, as well as the popular hair color, nail polish, and so on.

Feeling crafty? Lavender's color and fragrance can help you there too. I am not suggesting that you go out and purchase or create thirty lavender aromatherapy candles or fifteen room sprays (like one of my coworkers, who is completely obsessed with all things lavender). There are endless online resources to direct you on how to create lavender crafts, from the simple to the extravagant. Then again, if you need a quick gift for a lavender addict, there's always an aromatherapy candle, potpourri, or some scented soap available for purchase at your local supermarket or drug store!

Though lavender is often used in a variety of crafts and household items, I expect fewer people to implement lavender as an effective natural insect, rodent, and deer repellent. Unlike humans, insects loathe the smell of lavender. Soak cotton balls with lavender oil and place these repellent balls strategically around, in, and under your kitchen cabinets, or tuck them into closets and drawers to repel moths, roaches, earwigs, silverfish, and other pests. Replace or recharge monthly. Sprinkled lavender leaves or sachets are effective mouse repellants, and lavender sachets placed in woolen clothing will repel moths. Lavender leaves scattered under woolen carpets are similarly helpful.

While I'm not as obsessed with lavender as some people, I have certainly increased my knowledge about and appreciation for this versatile edible herb. These days I use lavender in healthy cooking demos for patients who want to lose weight or learn how to plan healthier meals on a budget. Often this involves being creative at the supermarket and experimenting with new foods. Sometimes I experience déjà vu. Recently, one young patient looked at the ingredient list for the dish I was preparing and exclaimed, "Wait a minute! Lavender? In a *salad?*"

I paused, inhaled deeply, and smiled.

Resources

"Chocolate-Lavender Brownies." Lavender Hills Farm. Accessed January 26, 2018. http://www.thelavenderhill.com/recipe/chocolate-lavender-brownies.

"Dietary Supplements: What You Need to Know." National Institutes of Health. Last modified June 17, 2011. https://ods.od.nih.gov/HealthInformation/DS_WhatYouNeedToKnow.aspx.

"Growing Lavender." Bonnie Plants. Accessed February 7, 2018. https://bonnieplants.com/growing/growing-lavender/.

"Lavender." National Institutes of Health. September 2016. https://nccih.nih.gov/health/lavender/ataglance.htm.

"Lavender Crafts." Everything Lavender. Accessed January 26, 2018. http://everything-lavender.com/lavender-crafts.html.

Riotte, Louise. *Carrots Love Tomatoes: Secrets of Companion Planting for Successful Gardening.* Pownal, VA: Storey Publishing, 1998.

Shipley, Sharon. *The Lavender Cookbook.* Philadelphia, PA: Running Press, 2004.

Gardening
Resources

Companion Planting Guide

Group together plants that complement each other by deterring certain pests, absorbing different amounts of nutrients from the soil, shading their neighbors, and enhancing friends' flavors. This table of herbs and common garden vegetables offers suggestions for plants to pair together and plants to keep separated.

Plant	Good Pairing	Poor Pairing
Anise	Coriander	Carrot, basil, rue
Asparagus	Tomato, parsley, basil, lovage, Asteraceae spp.	
Basil	Tomato, peppers, oregano, asparagus	Rue, sage, anise
Beans	Tomato, carrot, cucumber, cabbage, corn, cauliflower, potato	Gladiola, fennel, *Allium* spp.
Borage	Tomato, squash, strawberry	
Bee balm	Tomato, echinacea, yarrow, catnip	
Beet	Onions, cabbage, lettuce, mint, catnip, kohlrabi, lovage	Pole bean, field mustard
Bell pepper	Tomato, eggplant, coriander, basil	Kohlrabi
Broccoli	Aromatics, beans, celery, potato, onion, oregano, pennyroyal, dill, sage, beet	Tomato, pole bean, strawberry, peppers
Cabbage	Mint, sage, thyme, tomato, chamomile, hyssop, pennyroyal, dill, rosemary, sage	Strawberry, grape, tomato,
Carrot	Peas, lettuce, chive, radish, leek, onion, sage, rosemary, tomato	Dill, anise, chamomile

Plant	Good Pairing	Poor Pairing
Catnip	Bee balm, cucumber, chamomile, mint	
Celery	Leek, tomato, bush bean, cabbage, cauliflower, carrot, garlic	Lovage
Chamomile	Peppermint, beans, peas, onion, cabbage, cucumber, catnip, dill tomato, pumpkin, squash	
Chervil	Radish, lettuce, broccoli	
Chive	Carrot, *Brassica* spp., tomato, parsley	Bush bean, potato, peas, soybean
Coriander/ cilantro	*Plant anywhere*	Fennel
Corn	Potato, beans, peas, melon, squash, pumpkin, sunflower, soybean, cucumber	Quack grass, wheat, straw, tomato
Cucumber	Beans, cabbage, radish, sunflower, lettuce, broccoli, squash, corn, peas, leek, nasturtium, onion	Aromatic herbs, sage, potato, rue
Dill	Cabbage, lettuce, onion, cucumber	Carrot, caraway, tomato
Echinacea	Bee balm	
Eggplant	Catnip, green beans, lettuce, kale, redroot pigweed	
Fennel	*Isolate; disliked by all garden plants*	
Garlic	Tomato, rose	Beans, peas
Hyssop	*Most plants*	Radish
Kohlrabi	Green bean, onion, beet, cucumber	Tomato, strawberry, pole bean
Lavender	*Plant anywhere*	

Plant	Good Pairing	Poor Pairing
Leek	Onion, celery, carrot, celeriac	Bush bean, soy bean, pole bean, pea
Lemon balm	*All vegetables*, particularly squash, pumpkin	
Lettuce	Strawberry, cucumber, carrot, radish, dill	Pole bean, tomato
Lovage	*Most plants*, especially cucumber, beans, beet, *Brassica* spp., onion, leek, potato, tomato	Celery
Marjoram	*Plant anywhere*	
Mint	Cabbage, tomato, nettle	Parsley, rue
Melon	Corn, peas, morning glory	Potato, gourd
Nasturtium	Cabbage, cucumber, potato, pumpkin, radish	
Onion	Beets, chamomile, carrot, lettuce, strawberry, tomato, kohlrabi, summer savory	Peas, beans, sage
Oregano	*Most plants*	
Parsley	Tomato, asparagus, carrot, onion, rose	Mint, *Allium* spp.
Parsnip	Peas	
Peas	Radish, carrot, corn, cucumbers, bean, tomato, spinach, turnip, aromatic herbs	*Allium* spp., gladiola
Potato	Beans, corn, peas, cabbage, eggplant, catnip, horseradish, watermelon, nasturtium, flax	Pumpkin, raspberry, sunflower, tomato, orach, black walnut, cucumber, squash
Pumpkin	Corn, lemon balm	Potato

Plant	Good Pairing	Poor Pairing
Radish	Peas, lettuce, nasturtium, chervil, cucumber	Hyssop
Rose	Rue, tomato, garlic, parsley, tansy	*Any plant within 1 ft. radius*
Rosemary	Rue, sage	
Sage	Rosemary	Rue, onion
Spinach	Strawberry, garlic	
Squash	Nasturtium, corn, mint, catnip, radish, borage, lemon balm	Potato
Strawberry	Borage, bush bean, spinach, rue, lettuce	*Brassica* spp., garlic, kohlrabi
Tarragon	*Plant anywhere*	
Tomato	Asparagus, parsley, chive, onion, carrot, marigold, nasturtium, bee balm, nettle, garlic, nettle, celery, borage	Black walnut, dill, fennel, potato, *Brassica* spp., corn
Thyme	*Plant anywhere*	
Turnip	Peas, beans, brussels sprout, leek	Potato, tomato
Yarrow	*Plant anywhere*, especially with medicinal herbs	

For more information on companion planting, you may wish to consult the following resources:

Mayer, Dale. *The Complete Guide to Companion Planting: Everything You Need to Know to Make Your Garden Successful.* Ocala, FL: Atlantic Publishing, 2010.

Philbrick, Helen. *Companion Plants and How to Use Them.* Edinburgh, UK: Floris Books, 2016.

Riotte, Louise. *Carrots Love Tomatoes: Secrets of Companion Planting for Successful Gardening.* Pownal, VT: Storey Books, 1988.

Cooking with Herbs and Spices

Elevate your cooking with herbs and spices. Remember, a little goes a long way!

Herb	Flavor Pairings	Health Benefits
Anise	Salads, slaws, roasted vegetables	Reduces nausea, gas, and bloating. May relieve infant colic. May help menstrual pain. Loosens sputum in respiratory illnesses.
Basil	Pesto and other pasta sauces, salads	Eases stomach cramps, nausea, indigestion, and colic. Mild sedative action.
Borage	Soups	Soothes respiratory congestion. Eases sore, inflamed skin. Mild diuretic properties.
Cayenne	Adds a spicy heat to soups, sauces, and main courses	Stimulates blood flow. Relieves joint and muscle pain. Treats gas and diarrhea.
Chamo-mile	Desserts, teas	Used for nausea, indigestion, gas pains, bloating, and colic. Relaxes tense muscles. Eases menstrual cramps. Promotes relaxation and sleep.
Chervil	Soups, salads, and sauces	Settles and supports digestion. Mild diuretic properties. Useful in treating minor skin irritations.
Chive	Salads, potato dishes, sauces	Rich in antioxidants. May benefit insomnia. Contributes to strong bones.
Coriander/cilantro	Soups, picante sauces, salsas	Treats mild digestive disorders. Counters nervous tensions. Sweetens breath.

Herb	Flavor Pairings	Health Benefits
Dill	Cold salads and fish dishes	Treats all types of digestive disorders, including colic. Sweetens breath. Mild diuretic.
Echinacea	Teas	Supports immune function. May treat or prevent infection.
Fennel	Salads, stir-fry, vegetable dishes	Settles stomach pain, relieves bloating, and stimulates appetite. May help treat kidney stones and bladder infections. Mild expectorant. Eye wash treats conjunctivitis.
Garlic	All types of meat and vegetable dishes as well as soup stocks and bone broths	Antiseptic: aids in wound healing. Treats and may prevent infections. Benefits the heart and circulatory system.
Ginger	Chicken, pork, stir-fry, gingerbread and ginger cookies	Treats all types of digestive disorders. Stimulates circulations. Soothes colds and flu.
Hyssop	Chicken, pasta sauces, light soups	Useful in treating respiratory problems and bronchitis. Expectorant. Soothes the digestive tract.
Jasmine	Chicken dishes, fruit desserts	Relieves tension and provides mild sedation. May be helpful in depression. Soothes dry or sensitive skin.
Lavender	Chicken, fruit dishes, ice cream	Soothes and calms the nerves. Relieves indigestion, gas, and colic. May relax airways in asthma.

Herb	Flavor Pairings	Health Benefits
Lemon balm	Soups, sauces, seafood dishes	Soothes and calms the nerves. Treats mild anxiety and depression. Helps heal wounds.
Lemon-grass	Marinades, stir-fries, curries, spice rubs	Treats all types of digestive disorders. Reduces fever. May reduce pain.
Lemon verbena	Beverages, any recipe asking for lemon zest	Calms digestive problems and treats stomach pain. Gently sedative.
Lovage	Soups, lovage pesto, lentils	Acts as a digestive and respiratory tonic. Has diuretic and antimicrobial actions. Boosts circulation. Helps menstrual pain.
Marigold	Soups, salads, rice dishes	Effective treatment of minor wounds, insect bites, sunburn, acne, and other skin irritations. Benefits menstrual pain and excessive bleeding.
Marjoram	Vegetables, soups, tomato dishes, sausages	Calms the digestive system. Stimulates appetite.
Nasturtium	Nasturtium pesto, salad dressings, salads	Strong antibiotic properties. Treats wounds and respiratory infections.
Oregano	Chicken, tomato sauces and dishes	Strong antiseptic properties. Stimulates bile production. Eases flatulence.
Parsley	Soups, stocks, bone broths	Highly nutritious. Strong diuretic action and may help treat cystitis. Benefits gout rheumatism and arthritis.
Peppermint	Desserts, teas	Treats all types of digestive disorders. May help headaches.

Herb	Flavor Pairings	Health Benefits
Purslane	Salads	Treats digestive and bladder ailments. Mild antibiotic effects.
Rosemary	Roasted red meats, potato dishes, grilled foods	Stimulates circulation. May stimulate the adrenal glands. Elevates mood and may benefit depression.
Sage	Chicken, duck, and pork	Relieves pain in sore throats. May help treat menstrual and menopausal disorders.
Spinach	Sauteed, soups, salads, spinach pesto, stuffed in chicken, ravioli	Iron-rich; supports healthy blood and iron stores.
Summer savory	Mushrooms, vegetables, quiche	Treats digestive and respiratory issues.
Tarragon	Chicken, fish, vegetables, sauces—"classic French cooking"	Stimulates digestion. Promotes sleep—mildly sedative. Induces menstruation.
Thyme	Soups, stews, tomato-based sauces	May treat infections. Soothes sore throats and hay fever. Can help expel parasites. Relieves minor skin irritations.
Yarrow	Salad dressings, infused oils	Helps heal minor wounds. Eases menstrual pain and heavy flow. Tonic properties.
Winter-green	Ice cream, candies, desserts	Strong anti-inflammatory and antiseptic properties. Treats arthritis and rheumatism. Relieves flatulence.
Winter savory	Beans, meats, vegetables	Treats digestive and respiratory issues. Antibacterial properties.

Gardening Techniques

Gardeners are creative people who are always on the lookout for the most efficient, interesting, and beautiful ways to grow their favorite plants. Whether you need to save money, reduce your workload, or keep plants indoors, the following gardening techniques are just a sampling of the many ways to grow your very own bountiful garden.

Barrel

Lidless plastic food-grade barrels or drums are set on raised supports. Before being filled with soil, slits are cut into the sides of the barrel and shaped into pockets. A PVC pipe is perforated with holes and set into the center and out of the bottom of the barrel as a delivery tool for watering, draining, fertilizing, and feeding the optional worm farm.

Strengths
Initial cost is moderate. Retains moisture, warms quickly, drains well, takes up little space, maximizes growing area and repels burrowing rodents. Little weeding or back-bending required.

Weaknesses
Not always attractive, initially labor intensive, requires special tools to modify. Not generally suited for crops that are deep-rooted, large vining, or traditionally grown in rows, such as corn.

Hügelkultur

These permanent raised beds utilize decomposing logs and woody brush that have been stacked into a pyramidal form on top of the soil's surface or in shallow trenches and then packed and covered with eight to ten inches of soil, compost, and well-rotted manure. The rotting wood encourages soil biota while holding and releasing moisture to plants, much like a sponge. English pronunciation: "hoogle-culture."

Strengths

Vertical form warms quickly, drains well, reduces watering needs, increases overall planting surface, and reduces bending chores. In time the rotting wood breaks down into humus-rich soil.

Weaknesses

Labor-intensive construction and mulch tends to slide down sides. Requires two to three years of nitrogen supplementation, repeated soaking, and filling sunken voids with soil. Voids can also be attractive to rodents and snakes in the first few years.

Hydroponic

Hydroponics is based on a closed (greenhouse) system relying on carefully timed circulation of nutrient-enriched water flowing through a soilless growing medium in which plants grow. Aerial parts are supported above the water by rafts and, at times, vertical supports. With the addition of fish tanks to the system, hydroponics becomes aquaponics.

Strengths

Customizable to any size. Versatile, efficient, productive, and weedless. Produce stays clean.

Weaknesses

Large systems are expensive and complicated to set up and maintain; require multiple inputs of heat, light, and nutrients; and are limited to certain crop types.

Lasagna

Based on sheet composting, lasagna gardens are built up in layers, starting with paper or cardboard that is placed on top of turf-covered or tilled ground to smother weeds and feed ground worm activity. This is then covered in repeating layers of peat moss, compost, leaves, wood chips, manure, and yard waste (green, brown, green), which eventually break down into rich, humusy soil.

Strengths

Excellent natural method to enrich poor soils, utilizes organic waste, supports soil biota, and improves drainage while reducing the need for fertilizers and excessive watering.

Weaknesses

Initially labor intensive and the proper breakdown of bed materials takes months, so is not suited to "quick" gardening. Requires ready and abundant sources of clean, unsprayed, organic materials.

Ruth Stout

This "no work" garden is based on deep, permanent layers of progressively rotting straw mulch, which simultaneously builds soil, feeds plants, blocks weeds, and reduces watering. Seeds and plants are placed into the lower decomposed layers. Fresh straw is added as plants grow and kept at a depth of eight or more inches.

Strengths

No tilling, few weeds, reduced watering and fertilizing. Warms quickly in the spring and prevents winter heaving. An excellent method for rocky, sandy, or clay soils.

Weaknesses

Requires an abundance of straw each season, which can be expensive and difficult to transport, move, and store. Deep mulch may encourage burrowing rodents and provide shelter for slugs, insect pests, and diseases.

Soil Bag

This simple method utilizes one or more twenty- to forty-pound bags of commercial potting soil or topsoil simply laid out flat on turf, mulch, or wood pallets. A rectangular hole is cut into the top and drainage holes are punched through the bottom. A light dusting of fertilizer is mixed in and plants and seeds are sown.

Strengths

Super easy, weed-free, no-till garden and a great way to start an in-ground garden. Fun for kids and those without a yard.

Weaknesses

Limited to shallow-rooted crops, needs consistent watering and fertilizing, and may flood in heavy rains. Cats may find this an attractive litter box.

Straw Bale

One or more square, string-bound straw bales are placed cut side up either directly on the ground or on top of a weed barrier and soaked with water for several days or even months and treated with nitrogen to help speed the decomposition of the straw. Alternatively, bales can be overwintered in place before using. Once ready, bales are parted down the center, filled with soil and compost, and planted with seeds or starts.

Strengths
Good on poor soils, even concrete. No tilling required, few weeds, handicap accessible, versatile, easy to configure, and renter-friendly. Spent bales make excellent mulch.

Weaknesses
Straw bales can be expensive, heavy, and difficult to transport. These gardens can initially be labor intensive, require frequent watering and fertilizing, and must be replaced every one or two seasons. Nitrogen from treated bales can leach into the local environment and affect the watershed.

Square Foot
This modern take on French Intensive gardening utilizes raised beds filled with a special soilless blend enclosed in a box frame that is further divided into twelve-by-twelve-inch squares, or one square foot. Each square is planted or seeded based on the correct spacing requirements of each plant. Large crops, like tomatoes, are planted one to a square, while small crops like radishes are planted sixteen to a square.

Strengths
Proper plant spacing utilizes space, increases yields, and reduces weeds. Adding trellises increases growing capacity. Raised beds drain well, warm quickly, hold mulch, look tidy, and are easy to mow around.

Weaknesses

Initial construction is expensive, labor intensive, and often impermanent. Requires frequent watering in dry spells and not all crops are suitable. Grids can be tedious to use and do not remove the gardener's need to learn proper plant spacing.

Vertical

Vertical gardens make use of nontraditional gardening space in two ways. The first is by training vining and climbing plants onto trellises, arbors, or fences and growing in raised beds, pots, urns, or tubs. The second is by firmly securing containers, troughs, rain gutters, or vertical garden felt pockets onto permanent frames supported by fences, walls, or other sturdy vertical structures. These gardens are typically irrigated by automatic drip or hydroponic systems. Soilless options are available.

Strengths

Attractive and weed-free indoor-outdoor garden perfect for small yards, renters, and disabled persons. Helps hide ugly structures and views and defines outdoor spaces.

Weaknesses

Construction of large systems and very sturdy structures can be initially expensive or labor intensive. Not conducive to all garden crops and requires frequent and consistent applications of moisture and fertilizer.

2019 Themed Garden Plans

Salad Tub

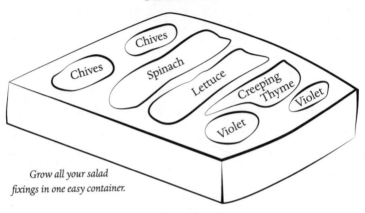

Chives

Chives

Spinach

Lettuce

Creeping Thyme

Violet

Violet

Violet

Grow all your salad fixings in one easy container.

Edible Flower Garden

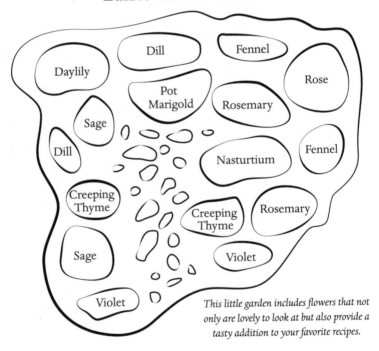

Dill

Fennel

Daylily

Rose

Pot Marigold

Rosemary

Sage

Dill

Fennel

Nasturtium

Creeping Thyme

Creeping Thyme

Rosemary

Sage

Violet

Violet

This little garden includes flowers that not only are lovely to look at but also provide a tasty addition to your favorite recipes.

Easy-Care Part Shade Garden

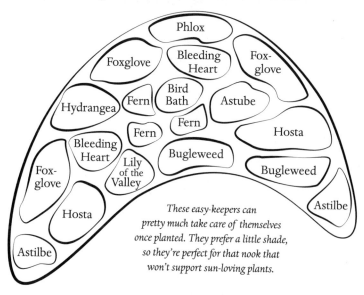

Phlox

Foxglove

Bleeding Heart

Fox-glove

Hydrangea

Fern

Bird Bath

Astube

Fern

Fern

Hosta

Bleeding Heart

Lily of the Valley

Bugleweed

Fox-glove

Bugleweed

Hosta

Astilbe

Astilbe

These easy-keepers can pretty much take care of themselves once planted. They prefer a little shade, so they're perfect for that nook that won't support sun-loving plants.

Lunar Garden

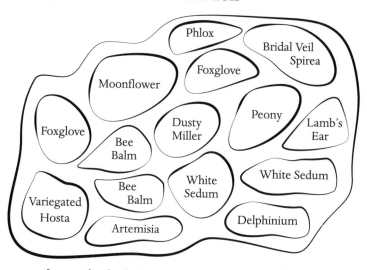

Phlox

Bridal Veil Spirea

Foxglove

Moonflower

Peony

Lamb's Ear

Foxglove

Dusty Miller

Bee Balm

White Sedum

White Sedum

Variegated Hosta

Bee Balm

White Sedum

Delphinium

Artemisia

Lunar gardens feature plants with white flowers or gray, silvery, or variegated leaves that are visible after the sun sets and absolutely glow under moonlight.

Planning Your 2019 Garden

Prepare your soil by tilling and fertilizing. Use the grid on the right, enlarging on a photocopier if needed, to sketch your growing space and identify sunny and shady areas.

Plot Shade and Sun

Watch your yard or growing space for a day, checking at regular intervals (such as once an hour), and note the areas that receive sun and shade. This will shift over the course of your growing season. Plant accordingly.

Diagram Your Space

Consider each plant's spacing needs before planting. Vining plants, such as cucumbers, will sprawl out and require trellising or a greater growing area than root crops like carrots. Be sure to avoid pairing plants that naturally compete or harm each other (see the Companion Planting Guide on page 276).

Also consider if your annual plants need to be rotated. Some herbs will reseed, some can be planted in the same place year after year, and some may need to be moved after depleting the soil of certain nutrients during the previous growing season.

Determine Your Last Spring Frost Date

Using data from the previous year, estimate the last spring frost date for your area and note what you'll need to plant before or after this date. Refer to seed packets, plant tags, and experts at your local garden center or University Extension for the ideal planting time for each plant. For information on planting by the moon, see *Llewellyn's 2019 Moon Sign Book*.

My 2019 last spring frost date: _____

Growing Space Grid

☐ = _____ feet

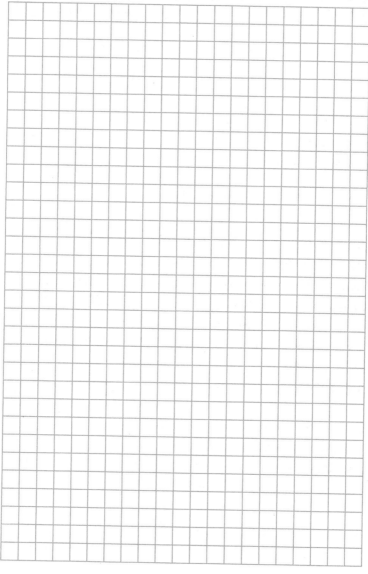

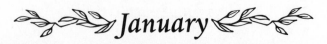

January

To Do	Plants	Dates

Notes:

_____

_____

_____

_____

_____

_____

_____

_____

JANUARY

		1	2	3	4	●
6	7	8	9	10	11	12
13	◗	15	16	17	18	19
20	○	22	23	24	25	26
◖	28	29	30	31		

Deter Deer with Pungent Herbs

Put mint and other pungent herbs in areas where you want to deter deer. The strong smell will confuse their olfactory receptors, and—with a bit of luck—keep them away from your more prized plants!

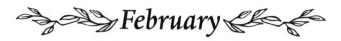

February

To Do	Plants	Dates

Notes:

_____

_____

_____

_____

_____

_____

_____

Vegetable Water Fertilizer

Save the water when you cook your veggies.
Cool it and use it to water your plants. They'll
appreciate the extra vitamins and minerals!

FEBRUARY

					1	2
3	●	5	6	7	8	9
10	11	◐	13	14	15	16
17	18	○	20	21	22	23
24	25	◑	27	28		

March

To Do	Plants	Dates

Notes:

_____

_____

_____

_____

_____

_____

_____

MARCH

					1	2
3	4	5	●	7	8	9
10	11	12	13	◑	15	16
17	18	19	○	21	22	23
24	25	26	27	◐	29	30
31						

Decomposable Seedling Tube

Toilet roll tubes can be used for seedlings. Cut four slits around the bottom of the tube and fold in the flaps, tucking in the last one to seal the bottom. Fill this with potting soil. When you're ready to plant, unfold the bottom and let nature decompose the rest of the tubing.

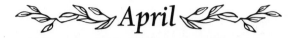

April

To Do	Plants	Dates

Notes:

_____

_____

_____

_____

_____

_____

_____

Freshen with Essential Oil

Make your own "toilet spray" with distilled water, rubbing alcohol, and a few drops of essential oil. Mix a tablespoon of alcohol and 10 drops of essential oil, then top up with distilled water in a two-ounce spray bottle. Shake and spray into the toilet before you sit.

APRIL

1	2	3	4	●	6
7	8	9	10	11	◑ 13
14	15	16	17	18	○ 20
21	22	23	24	25	◐ 27
28	29	30			

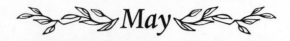

May

To Do	Plants	Dates

Notes:

_____

_____

_____

_____

_____

_____

MAY

			1	2	3	●
5	6	7	8	9	10	◑
12	13	14	15	16	17	○
19	20	21	22	23	24	25
◑	27	28	29	30	31	

Eggshell Powder Nutrient Boost

Don't throw away your eggshells! Ground up, they make a wonderful addition to your garden soil, adding calcium and other nutrients.

June

To Do	Plants	Dates

Notes:

_____

_____

_____

_____

_____

_____

_____

Decorate with Painted River Rocks

Get artistic in your garden with painted river rocks. Not only are they attractive, but they help you to remember what's planted there when it's dormant. Paint the name or a picture of the variety that's growing. Kids love to get involved with this one!

JUNE

						1
2	●	4	5	6	7	8
9	◐	11	12	13	14	15
16	○	18	19	20	21	22
23	24	◑	26	27	28	29
30	31					

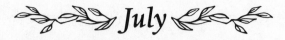# July

To Do	Plants	Dates

Notes:

_____

_____

_____

_____

_____

_____

_____

JULY

	1	●	3	4	5	6
7	8	◐	10	11	12	13
14	15	○	17	18	19	20
21	22	23	◑	25	26	27
28	29	30	●			

Plastic Bottle Waterer

Don't throw away plastic pop bottles or milk jugs. Poke several pencil-sized holes in the sides and bottom, and plant up to the neck among your flowers and veggies. Fill the containers when you water, and they'll steadily leach moisture into the soil, saving you time and effort.

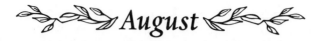

August

To Do	Plants	Dates

Notes:

_____

_____

_____

_____

_____

_____

_____

Sweeten Tomatoes with Baking Soda

Add a bit of baking soda to the soil around your tomatoes for a more flavorful fruit. The alkalinity of the soda neutralizes the acidity of the plants. The result? A much sweeter tomato harvest!

AUGUST

				1	2	3
4	5	6	◑ 7	8	9	10
11	12	13	14	○ 15	16	17
18	19	20	21	22	◐ 23	24
25	26	27	28	29	● 30	31

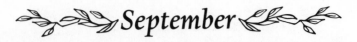

September

To Do	Plants	Dates

Notes:

_____

_____

_____

_____

_____

_____

_____

SEPTEMBER

1 2 3 4 ◑ 6 7

8 9 2 11 12 13 ○

15 16 17 18 19 20 ◐

22 23 24 25 26 27 ●

29 30

Wine Cork Plant Marker

Need an attractive plant marker quickly? Grab an old wine cork, a small dowel, and a marker. Write the name of the plant on the side of the cork. Insert one end of the dowel in the cork and the other end in the soil. Presto! Your plant is labeled!

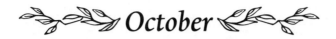

October

To Do	Plants	Dates

Notes:

_____

_____

_____

_____

_____

_____

_____

Temporary Greenhouses

Don't get rid of that clear plastic storage bin just because the lid is broken. These tubs make amazing temporary greenhouses to get your plants started—so do disused fish tanks, for that matter! Put your starter pots in them, and use them to harden off the seedlings.

OCTOBER

		1	2	3	4	◑
6	7	8	9	10	11	12
○	14	15	16	17	18	19
20	◐	22	23	24	25	26
●	28	29	30	31		

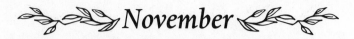

November

To Do	Plants	Dates

Notes:

_____

_____

_____

_____

_____

_____

_____

NOVEMBER

					1	2
3	◑	5	6	7	8	9
10	11	○	13	14	15	16
17	18	◐	20	21	22	23
24	25	●	27	28	29	30

Test Old Seeds

Check to see whether an outdated packet of seeds is still viable by using a moist paper towel. Put a few seeds on the towel and place them in a dark and warm place. Keep the towel damp.
If any of these seeds sprouts, chances are others in the package will too.

December

To Do	Plants	Dates

Notes:

_____

_____

_____

_____

_____

_____

_____

Old Wheel Planter

Old wheels make a good base for fun planters. Paint them, pebble them, tile them, yarn bomb them—do whatever takes your fancy. The holes in the wheel make this discarded item the perfect plant pot for a patio or pagoda. Let your imagination run riot!

DECEMBER

1	2	3	◑	5	6	7
8	9	2	11	○	13	14
15	16	17	◐	19	20	21
22	23	24	25	●	27	28
29	30	31				

Notes

Contributors

Anna Franklin is an herbalist, a third-degree witch, and the high priestess of the Hearth of Arianrhod. She's the author of thirty books, including *The Hearth Witch's Compendium,* The Sacred Circle Tarot, and The Fairy Ring Oracle. She lives in the UK and can be found online at www.AnnaFranklin.co.uk.

Anne Sala is a freelance journalist based in Minnesota. Last year, she and her family moved from a third-story apartment to a single-family home. Anne has never had to deal with animals eating her plants before and has since discovered the rabbits in her neighborhood are quite fond of the herbs she keeps in low-sided pots.

Autumn Damiana is an author, artist, crafter, amateur photographer, and regular contributor to Llewellyn's annuals. Along with writing and making art, Autumn has a degree in early childhood education. She lives with her husband and doggy familiar in the beautiful San Francisco Bay Area. Visit her online at www.autumndamiana.com.

Charlie Rainbow Wolf is happiest when she is creating something, especially if it can be made from items that others have cast aside. She is an advocate of organic gardening and cooking and lives in the Midwest with her husband and special-needs Great Danes. Visit www.charlierainbow.com.

Corina Sahlin homesteads on five acres at the edge of the wilderness near the Cascade Mountains, where she grows a lot of organic food. Together with her husband Steve, she raises goats, pigs, ducks, chickens, an adorable puppy, and a gaggle of three children, whom they homeschool. She teaches wilderness and homesteading skills to children and adults. Visit www.marble mounthomestead.com.

Dallas Jennifer Cobb lives in paradise with her daughter in a waterfront village in rural Ontario, where she regularly swims, runs, and snowshoes. A Reclaiming Witch from way back, Jennifer is part of an eclectic pan-Pagan circle that organizes empowered and beautiful community rituals. Contact her at jennifer.cobb@live.com.

Dawn Ritchie is an organic gardener, cook, passionate beekeeper, and fledgling potter who writes about design, cuisine, gardening, travel, entertainment, and living well. She's a regular contributor to numerous publications in the US and Canada. She's the author of *The Emotional House* (New Harbinger Publications), a home design/healing workbook, and is currently penning a new tome on beekeeping.

Deborah Castellano is a writer, crafter, and glamour girl who serves as a frequent contributor to occult and Pagan sources such as Witchvox, PaganSquare, and *Witches & Pagans*. Her shop, the Mermaid and the Crow, specializes in handmade goods. She resides in New Jersey with her husband, Jow, and their cat.

Diana Rajchel has practiced magic since childhood. She lives in San Francisco, where she runs the Emperor Norton Pagan Social and handles the oft-squirrelly city spirit. She is the author of the Mabon and Samhain books in the Llewellyn Sabbat Essentials Series and of the Diagram Prize–nominee *Divorcing a Real Witch*.

Diana Stoll shares her gardens with her grandchildren in the hopes they will each grow their own green thumbs. As a horticulturist and a garden writer, Diana writes a weekly garden column in the *Chicago Daily Herald* and shares her passion for all things gardening on her blog, *Garden with Diana*, at www .gardenwithdiana.com.

Doreen Shababy is the author of *The Wild & Weedy Apothecary*, and she and her husband run an herb business by the same name. Doreen has been writing and working with food and herbs for over forty years. Please visit www.wildnweedy.com and www.doreenshababy.com to learn more about her work.

Elizabeth Barrette lives in central Illinois and enjoys magical crafts, historic religions, and gardening for wildlife. She has written columns on beginning and intermediate Pagan practice, speculative fiction, gender studies, and social and environmental issues. Her book *Composing Magic* explains how to combine writing and spirituality. Visit her blog at https:// ysabetwordsmith.dreamwidth.org.

Emily Towne is a homesteader, gardener, and student of nature who enjoys digging in the dirt and curating an ever-growing seed bank on her multispecies Missouri homestead, Full Plate Farm, which she shares with her husband and son. She grows heirloom garlic, herbs, flowers, vegetables, honeybees, ducks, chickens, eggs, pigs, and cattle, using regenerative stewardship to provide healthy, clean food for her family and others.

Estha K. V. McNevin (Missoula, Montana) is a priestess and ceremonial oracle of Opus Aima Obscuræ, a nonprofit Pagan Temple Haus. She has served the Pagan community since 2003 as an Eastern Hellenistic officiate, lecturer, freelance author, artist, and poet. To learn more, please explore www .opusaimaobscurae.org.

Holly Bellebuono (Massachusetts) is an international speaker, author, and medical herbalist whose books and lectures feature natural health, herbal medicine, and women's empowerment. She directs the Bellebuono School of Herbal Medicine. Visit her online at www.HollyBellebuono.com.

James Kambos raises a large variety of herbs and flowers in his Ohio garden. He's a writer and an artist. He has a degree in history and geography.

JD Hortwort resides in North Carolina. She is an avid student of herbology and gardening. She has written a weekly garden column since 1991. She is a professional, award-winning author, journalist, and magazine editor, as well as a frequent contributor to the Llewellyn annuals. Recently retired from journalism, she continues to write on topics as diverse as gardening and NASCAR.

Jill Henderson is a backwoods herbalist, author, artist, and world traveler with a penchant for wild edible and medicinal plants, culinary herbs, and nature ecology. She is a longtime contributor to *Llewellyn's Herbal Almanac* and *Acres USA* magazine and is the author of *The Healing Power of Kitchen Herbs*, *A Journey of Seasons*, and *The Garden Seed Saving Guide*. Visit Jill's blog at ShowMeOz.wordpress.com.

Kathy Martin is a Master Gardener and longtime author of the blog *Skippy's Vegetable Garden*, a journal of her vegetable gardens. The blog has won awards including *Horticulture Magazine*'s Best Gardening Blog. Kathy has written four gardening apps and manages the Belmont Victory Gardens' 137 plots. She lives near Boston with her husband, son, and Portuguese water dogs.

Kathy Vilim is a Midwestern girl transplanted to Southern California who writes about the importance of creating outdoor living space using native plants and attracting pollinators. Kathy is a naturalist and photojournalist and finds herself in demand as a garden design consultant. She can be reached at kathy.vilim@yahoo.com. Visit canativegardener.blogspot.com.

Magenta Griffith is a founding member of Prodea, which has been celebrating rituals since 1980, and was a founding member of the Northern Dawn Council of the Covenant of the Goddess. Magenta, along with her coven brother Steven Posch, is the author of *The Prodea Cookbook: Good Food and Traditions from Paganistan's Oldest Coven*. She presents classes and workshops at a variety of events around the Midwest.

Mireille Blacke, MA, is a licensed alcohol and drug counselor, registered dietitian, certified dietitian-nutritionist, and addiction specialist residing in Connecticut. She worked in rock radio for over two decades and has been published in a variety of Llewellyn's annuals as well as *Today's Dietitian* and *OKRA Magazine*. Mireille is an adjunct professor at the University of Saint Joseph and a bariatric program coordinator at Saint Francis Hospital in Hartford, CT.

Monica Crosson is a Master Gardener who lives in the Pacific Northwest, happily digging in the dirt and tending her raspberries with her husband, three kids, many goats, chickens, and Rosetta, the donkey. She has been a practicing witch and educator for over twenty years and is a member of Blue Moon Coven. Monica is the author of *The Magickal Family* and *Summer Sage*. Visit her website at www.monicacrosson.com.

Natalie Zaman is the author of *Color and Conjure* and *Magical Destinations of the Northeast*. A regular contributor to various Llewellyn annual publications, she also writes the recurring feature Wandering Witch for *Witches & Pagans* magazine. When not on the road, she's busy tending her magical back garden. Visit Natalie online at nataliezaman.blogspot.com.

Susan Pesznecker is a mother, writer, nurse, college English teacher, and Baden-Powell Service Association scout living in the Pacific Northwest with her poodles. Her previous books include *Crafting Magick with Pen and Ink, The Magickal Retreat,* and *Yule.* She is also a regular contributor to the Llewellyn annuals. Follow her at www.facebook.com/SusanMoonwriter Pesznecker.

Suzanne Ress runs a small farm in the Alpine foothills of Italy, where she lives with her husband. She has been a practicing Pagan for as long as she can remember and was recently featured in the exhibit "Worldwide Witches" at the Hexenmuseum of Switzerland. She is the author of *The Trial of Goody Gilbert.*

Thea Fiore-Bloom, PhD, is an arts and culture journalist with a doctorate in mythology. Artists and writers of all levels looking for audacious inspiration, information, and encouragement are warmly welcomed at her new blog www.thecharmedstudio .com.

Gardening Resources

Cooking with Herbs and Spices compiled by **Susan Pesznecker**
Gardening Techniques written by **Jill Henderson**
2019 Themed Garden Plans designed by **Monica Crosson**
2019 Gardening Log tips written by **Charlie Rainbow Wolf**